MW01012979

CELEBRACIÓN

Recipes and Traditions

Celebrating Latino Family Life

REGINA CORDOVA
WITH
EMMA CARRASCO

FOR

THE NATIONAL COUNCIL OF LA RAZA

AN ELLEN ROLFES BOOK

MAIN
STREET
BOOKS

MAIN STREET BOOKS/DOUBLEDAY

NEW YORK   LONDON   TORONTO   SYDNEY   AUCKLAND

@@@@@@@@@@@@@@@@@@@@@@@@@@@@@

NATIONAL COUNCIL OF LA RAZA

The National Council of La Raza (NCLR) was founded over 25 years ago to serve the Latino community through the strengthening of Hispanic community-based organizations. NCLR was built on a network of affiliate organizations which represents the wide diversity of nationalities that comprise the Hispanic community. The services they provide range from housing and community economic development to education to health services. NCLR has grown into the premier Hispanic constituency-based organization in the United States, recognized not only for its work with affiliate organizations but also for leadership in policy and advocacy. Additionally, the NCLR Annual Conference is unequaled in the Hispanic community in size and quality.

A MAIN STREET BOOK
PUBLISHED BY DOUBLEDAY
a division of Bantam Doubleday Dell Publishing Group, Inc.
1540 Broadway, New York, New York 10036

MAIN STREET BOOKS, DOUBLEDAY, and the portrayal of a building with a tree are trademarks of Doubleday, a division of Bantam Doubleday Dell Publishing Group, Inc.

Library of Congress Cataloging-in-Publication Data
Cordova, Regina.
   Celebracion : recipes, traditions, and meal memories celebrating Latino Family life / by Regina Cordova & Emma Carrasco. —1st Main Street books ed.
       p.   cm.
   "Main Street books"—T.p. verso.
   Includes index.
   ISBN 0-385-47732-5
   1. Cookery, Latin American.   2. Latin American—Social life and customs.   I. Carrasco, Emma.   II.Title.
TX716.A1C68   1996
641.598—dc20   96-18040
                                                                                              CIP

@@@@@@@@@@@@@@@@@@@@@@@@@@@

CONTENTS

INTRODUCTION: THE LATIN TABLE AND CELEBRATIONS OF THE AMERICAS

It's almost as if it happened overnight: American's fascination with the Hispanic influence in everything from music to dance, theater and movies, art and architecture, business and government, fashion and food is sweeping the country. The undeniable fact is that salsa has replaced ketchup as American's favorite condiment, while tortillas are appearing in more and more bread baskets. The Latinization of American culture and palates is occurring rapidly and without prejudice.

The answer to Americans' growing interest in things Hispanic lies, perhaps, in the completeness of the Hispanic culture. Food, for example, represents much more to Hispanic families than a way to nourish or quiet one's hunger. In fact, food plays an unparalleled role in the preservation of tradition and heritage. And in today's hectic world, this cultural preservation is more important than at any other time in history.

Consider that to a Hispanic family, gathering at a meal represents the opportunity to pass along language, folklore, and cultural legacies to a new generation. In many regards, food provides the bridge between six Hispanic core values:

Strong Belief in Family

The family unit among Hispanics is intact, particularly among first- and second-generation Hispanics. It is the focal point that dismisses distances, daily pressures, or hectic lifestyles. The Hispanic family is larger than most, owing to a deep love of children and the common presence of extended family members. To Hispanics, there is nothing more important than family, and most will go to great lengths to preserve traditions and celebrations that bring them together.

High Level of Respect for Elders

Grandparents and elders hold a special place in the families and hearts of Hispanics. Sentiments that range from respect and reverence to care and loving are expressed over generations of younger Hispanics toward their extended family of abuelos (grandparents) and tíos (aunts and uncles). Hispanics who are able to grow up with their elders in the same household consider themselves the most fortunate of all.

Importance of Relatedness to Neighbors

There is no greater sense of satisfaction than when Hispanics contribute to the betterment of their community, which many consider an extension of their family. Children are often taught early the lessons of kindness, consideration, and respect for neighbors as well the value of community involvement and the responsibility to repay good fortune along the way.

Strength in Spiritual Convictions

Much of Hispanics' fortitude is firmly grounded in unshakable religious and spiritual convictions. It is what has allowed generations of Hispanics to weather myriad social and political challenges with great dignity and resilience. It is also what serves as the foundation of so many celebrations which bring and keep families together.

Intense Work Ethic

Hispanics are fiercely proud of the many contributions they make to society in general and their communities in particular. This pride stems from the value Hispanics place in working hard as a means of not only providing for their family, but an insistence on being productive members of society.

The Spanish Language

There is nothing like a common language to bring people from many different cultures together, to bridge generations, to provide a link to one's heritage. For Hispanics, the Spanish language is much more than a second language; it is, in fact, the cultural backbone which Hispanics often use to stand tall and proud. Whether fluent or sprinkled, the Spanish language touches Hispanics' hearts and souls in very profound ways.

Celebración is a community cookbook which captures these core values through unique meal memories. A compilation of recipes from approximately sixteen Hispanic countries, this book also pays tribute to the preparation of meals, which in many instances is a ritual in and of itself. Consider the young girl who anxiously waits turning a year older so that her grandmother will assign her a task in the intricate preparation of calamares rellenos (stuffed squid), the young man who finally breaks the code on his mother's pozole (hominy soup), or the parrillero's (grill master's) cardinal rules for a successful asado (barbecue).

These are just a few examples of how *Celebración* reflects the roots and customs of Hispanics throughout the Americas. Whether they are well-known personalities, such as Spanish-language television network news anchor Maria Elena Salinas, community activists such as Alicia Bonilla, or corporate executives such as Victor Franco, the two hundred or so cooks who contributed recipes each showed great generosity in sharing a piece of their family history. For many, these recipes document a personal journey, a search for Hispanic identity, a way to recapture childhood. It is for this reason that the shared memories in this book read more like letters to the past and bring life to beloved people and places.

There is no doubt that Latinos' favorite gathering spot is the family meal. It is here that, despite hurried lifestyles and daily pressures, a familia comes alive. Immigrant Latinos use the time at the table to preserve an important part of their earlier lives. The U.S.–born children and grandchildren of these immigrants regard meals as instrumental in promoting and protecting their heritage. In all instances, it is what keeps Hispanic families alive.

The spirit with which Hispanics and Latin Americans embrace life is reflected in the quality and quantity of celebrations that bring family and friends together. These unique holidays are often grounded in religion, and many have been adapted to reflect modern society; others are celebrated with the traditional reverence from which they originate. In each case, Latin American holidays provide the impetus for special meals that are remembered as much for the gastronomic delight they bring as they are for the cultural values they reinforce.

La Boda (The Wedding)

The union of two people who have come together for richer or poorer, "till death us do part," is cause for the preparation of secretly held family recipes that will now be passed along to a new generation. Folklore has it that the special ingredient in wedding foods is the love with which they are made.

La Muerte (Death)

As evidenced by the famous Día de los Muertos (Day of the Dead), this holiday is a celebration of the life-affirming qualities associated with death. For those in mourning, death becomes a celebration of a loved one's life and contributions. Family and friends gather to remember the deceased with the music and food enjoyed while they were still alive.

Pascua (Easter)

The Catholic celebration that commemorates the resurrection of Jesus Christ, Easter Sunday takes on particular importance in the Hispanic culture. The Lenten season begins by giving up something that is meaningful or precious for forty days; often it is a particular food, beverage, or sweet. Easter observances begin on Good Friday, when only fish or seafood can be consumed. When Easter Sunday arrives, however, parishioners fill church pews in brand-new outfits, reaffirm their baptismal vows, and then gather with family and friends for an Easter Sunday feast. Whether this celebration takes place in a park, a reception hall, or the home, one can be assured of a meal unique to the holiday.

Feliz Navidad, Prospero Año Nuevo, Fiesta de los Tres Reyes (Christmas Holidays)

Holiday foods are remembered with particular fondness by cultures around the world. In the Hispanic world, however, the feast begins on Christmas

Eve and ends on January 6, the Day of the Three Kings, which celebrates the biblical tale of the three kings' visit to the Baby Jesus.

El Bautizo (Christening)

The birth of a child is always cause for celebration, but in the Hispanic family it represents a new branch in a family tree of cultural pride, heritage, and tradition. In fact, it is a birth that triggers one of the most important Hispanic traditions: the christening of a new family member. Godparents, or padrinos, are chosen with the highest criteria in mind; these are not ceremonial roles. Godparents are people who will take over the upbringing and religious guidance of the child in the event that the parents cannot. As such, el bautizo, the christening ceremony and party, becomes an affirmation of the value of a human life and the attendant responsibilities.

Santos, Feliz Cumpleaños (Happy Birthday, Saint's Day)

In Hispanic families, children are generally named after a Catholic saint, each of which has a designated date on the calendar. This day is known as el día de tu santo (your saint's day) and is often celebrated with greater fervor than an actual birthday. But no matter if it is a saint's day or a birthday, the most important gift one can receive is the preparation of a favorite meal. Family and friends gather to celebrate another year of life over a meal which has been prepared by the loving hands of mothers, grandmothers, aunts, or sisters. Old family pictures are often brought out as part of the birthday celebration to remember days gone past.

La Quinceñera (The 15th Birthday)

While the debutante ceremony is generally reserved for the coming out of daughters of established community families, the quinceñera is celebrated by 15-year-old girls of every social class. Grounded in a religious ceremony, the quinceñera begins with a Catholic mass, witnessed by the godparents and 15 attendant couples. This is followed by a lavish lunch or dinner reception, during which everyone partakes of music, dancing, and a true gastronomic feast.

La Reunión (Family Get-Togethers)

A backyard barbecue and a Saturday-night dinner are just a couple of the reasons Hispanic families gather to be together, share good times, and wax nostalgic. These are occasions for comfort food, during which familiar smells and tastes transport family members to another time in history, reminding them of a loving grandparent or a special family event.

Celebración invites you, now, to take a seat at the Hispanic table and experience the spirit of family and community one can get only here.

Recipe Testing

All the recipes in this book have been tested at least once, and every attempt has been made to create as close a replica of the original recipe as orally described in interviews. Those recipes that provided loose measurements (e.g., a handful of this, a pinch of that) were converted to standardized forms.

Because each recipe represents a family and a food tradition, greater emphasis was placed on providing accurate instructions and traditional cooking techniques than on drastically reducing the fat, sugar, or salt of many of the recipes, lean cooking tips are provided.

These recipes also represent celebrations when more than one family gathers around the tables. As such, the quantities serve anywhere from eight to fifty. No attempt was made to standardize these recipes to suit a modern-day family of four to eight.

Thanks

The authors wish to thank the many wonderful cooks who kindly shared their families' recipes. We were especially heartened by those of you who made extraordinary efforts to recapture a family's lost recipe or tradition. We hope that you are all as proud of this collection of Latino culture as we are. Warm thanks also go to our partner, Alan Stess, for his vision and passion for things Latino.

CHAPTER ONE

APERITIVOS Y ENTRADAS

APPETIZERS AND

FIRST COURSES

I*n the Latin world there is no single word defining the category of food known as appetizers. Rather, each country has its own term for the little dishes that celebrate the beginnings of a festivity.*

Their names are as colorful and amusing, charming and elegant, or beguiling and enticing as the celebration. . . . botanas, special little dishes meant to quiet the appetite; pasantes, flavorful tray-passed, bite-sized morsels; picadas, bits of food that can be "picked" with toothpicks; antojitos, foods that invite your attention; boquillas, morsels to stop or quiet the mouth; fritangas, fried snacks of little meats, bocaditos, little mouthfuls; frituras or coquetas, savory fried foods; salgadinhos frios o quentes, cold or hot appetizers; and canapés, open-faced cocktail food. Regardless of their origins, aperitivos create that essential unhurried and comfortable Latin ambience fostering a feeling of camaraderie that leads to good conversation mixed in with Latin joie de vivre and a healthy dose of laughter.

EMPANADAS CRIOLLAS
CHRISTMAS / VENEZUELA

VENEZUELAN TURNOVERS

I grew up in Villa de Cura, Venezuela, a small town in the interior. Although both my parents were originally from Spain, our caretaker, Mercedes, would prepare authentic food from la cocina criolla (the Venezuelan kitchen) all year-round. I was particularly fond of her empanadas, especially during the Christmas holidays, when they were offered as "una delicia de la mesa familiar" (a family specialty).

LOLA CANTELI-HESS

MEAT FILLING

1 tablespoon olive oil
1 pound lean ground beef
3 cloves garlic, minced
½ cup chopped green onion
1 teaspoon salt
½ teaspoon ground black pepper
½ cup diced potatoes
⅓ cup diced carrots
¾ cup fresh diced tomatoes or canned diced tomatoes, drained
10 pimiento-stuffed green olives, sliced
15 capers

MASA (CORN DOUGH)

2 cups harina Pan (precooked white cornmeal) (see below)

1 teaspoon salt

3 tablespoons papelón (Venezuelan raw sugar), grated, or 3 table-spoons light brown sugar and 1½ teaspoons molasses

Oil for deep frying

1. *Meat filling:* In a heavy skillet, warm the oil over medium heat. Add the beef, garlic, onion, salt, and pepper; cook, stirring frequently, until the meat is seared. Add the potatoes and carrots and continue cooking uncovered, stirring occasionally, until the beef has completely browned. Stir in the diced tomatoes, olives, and capers. Cover and continue cooking until the potatoes are tender, about 15 to 20 minutes. Taste and adjust seasoning. Makes 3 cups.

2. *Preparing dough:* Combine the cornmeal and salt in a medium bowl. Heat 1½ cups of water in a small saucepan over medium heat. When tepid add the sugar, stirring until dissolved. Remove from the heat and let cool. Add the sweetened water to the flour ¼ cup at a time, mixing to form a dough. Let rest for 5 minutes.

3. *To form empanadas:* Divide the dough into 14 equal-sized balls. Flatten each piece into a disk. Roll out on a lightly floured surface, forming a 3-inch circle ⅜ inch thick. Place 1 heaping tablespoon of meat filling on each circle. Lightly moisten edges of the dough with cold water; fold the dough over the filling, pressing out as much air as possible, and seal.

4. *Frying:* In a small skillet or deep fryer, heat 1 inch of oil to 380°F. Fry empanadas, no more than 3 at a time, for 2 minutes, or until golden brown, turning once. Remove with a slotted spoon and drain on absorbent towels. Serve immediately or keep warm on a baking sheet, uncovered, in a 200°F oven until ready to serve.

HARINA PAN is a brand of finely ground precooked white cornmeal, used in the preparation of Venezuelan and Colombian arepas, hallacas, and bollos. It should not be confused with masa harina, a corn flour used in the preparation of corn tortillas and tamales. Harina Pan can be found in markets specializing in South American ingredients.

MAKES 14 SERVINGS (PORTION SIZE: ONE 3-INCH TURNOVER)

EMPANADILLAS DE MASA DE YUCA
FAMILY CELEBRATION / VENEZUELA

CHEESE-FILLED YUCCA TURNOVERS

I often recall the music, laughter, and food that filled our patio during family celebrations—baptisms, birthdays, or national holidays—back home in Venezuela. Today those memories come alive when I think of these savory, bite-sized empanadillas. Although the yucca dough requires a little more attention in the kitchen, it is very much enjoyed and appreciated by your guests.

LOLA CANTELI-HESS

CHEESE FILLING
2 tablespoons olive oil
¾ cup finely chopped onion
1 lemon slice
1 tablespoon pimentón rojo (ground sweet red pepper) or paprika
4 canned whole red pimientos, chopped (about ¾ cup)

1 cup farmer, Gouda, or Muenster cheese, crumbled or grated
4 hard-cooked eggs, coarsely chopped
Salt and ground black pepper

YUCCA DOUGH
1 pound yuca (cassava or yucca) (see Note)
4 egg yolks
4 tablespoons (½ stick) butter, softened

Pinch of salt
Oil for frying

1. *Cheese filling:* In a skillet, warm the olive oil over medium heat. Add the onion and lemon slice. Sprinkle paprika onto the lemon slice and sauté the mixture until the onion and lemon are soft, about 3 minutes. Stir in the pimientos and continue cooking until the pimiento juices begin to evaporate, about 5 minutes; discard the lemon slice. Remove the skillet from the heat and stir in the cheese and eggs. Season to taste with salt and pepper. Set aside.

2. *Cooking yucca:* With a sharp knife, slice off the ends of each piece of yucca; slice into 3-inch sections and slice again lengthwise. Carefully remove the skin with a paring knife. To prevent discoloration, place the peeled yucca in water to cover until ready to cook. In a pot, combine the

yucca with enough salted cold water to cover by 2 inches. Bring to a boil, lower the heat, and simmer uncovered about 20 minutes, or until tender when pierced with a fork. Check yucca often, as each piece will cook at a different rate. Drain in a colander. When cool enough to handle, remove and discard any fibrous cores.

3. *Preparing yucca dough:* Mash the yucca in the workbowl of a food processor until the consistency of thick mashed potatoes. With the machine running, add the egg yolks, butter, and salt. Process until a soft tacky dough forms, about 25 seconds. Turn the dough out onto a moistened kitchen towel and knead until soft and pliable. Cover with a moist towel until ready to use.

4. *Forming the empanadas:* Divide the dough into 16 even pieces. Flatten each piece, using the palms of your hands, into a 3-inch circle ³/₈ inch thick. Place about 1 tablespoon of cheese filling on each circle. Lightly moisten edges of the dough with cold water; fold the dough over the filling, expelling as much air as possible, and seal, forming a crescent-shaped turnover.

5. *Frying empanadas:* In a small skillet, heat 1 inch of oil to 375°F. Fry the empanadas, not more than 3 at a time, for 2 minutes, turning once, until golden brown. Remove with a slotted spoon and drain on absorbent towels. Serve immediately or place on a baking sheet, uncovered, in 200°F oven until ready to serve.

N O T E : Cassava or yucca is a long, thick tuberous root vegetable which grows anywhere from 8 to 20 inches in length. Inside the brown, bark-like skin, the fibrous white pulp is similar to a potato but much drier. In Venezuela, yucca is a popular vegetable prepared boiled, baked, or fried in place of potatoes. Boiled and mashed, yucca creates a dough that is soft, easy to work with, and flavorful, perfect for savory turnovers or sweet fritters.

MAKES 16 (3-INCH) OR 24 (2¹/₂-INCH) EMPANADAS

Throughout Latin America, turnovers have many names, (e.g., empanadas, empanaditas, empanadillas, pastelitos) depending on the size, type of pastry, and filling, which varies from country to country.

BACALAÍTOS FRITOS

STREET FOOD / PUERTO RICO

COD FRITTERS

Fritters or fritangas (fried snacks) were a part of our daily life while living on the island. Mom could conjure up a batch of fritter dough in minutes, fry them up in her special fritter pot, and we'd have a meal fit for a king.

EVA JUDITH LOZANO

1 pound salt cod, cut into 2-inch pieces (about 3 cups) (see Note)
1½ cups all-purpose flour
1½ teaspoons baking powder
½ teaspoon ground black pepper
1 (12-ounce) can undiluted evaporated milk

4 large cloves garlic, minced
⅓ cup chopped cilantro
⅓ cup finely sliced green onion
½ teaspoon crushed dried oregano leaves
Vegetable oil for deep frying
Mojo Isleño (See page 7)

1. *Soaking salt cod:* Place the salt cod in a medium bowl with cold water to cover for 4 to 8 hours, depending on the thickness and quality of the cod. Change the water every hour to remove saltiness. (If, after soaking, the cod is still very salty, place it in a saucepan with water to cover. Bring to a boil, remove from the heat, and let soak, covered, about 30 minutes. Drain.) Remove any skin or bones. Using the hands, gently squeeze salt cod to remove excess water. Shred and set aside until ready to use.

2. *Preparing batter:* In a bowl, whisk together the flour, baking powder, and pepper. Gradually add the evaporated milk, ½ cup at a time, mixing well after each addition to avoid lumps. Stir in the garlic, cilantro, green onions, oregano, and shredded salt cod; mix well.

3. *Frying:* In a deep fryer, heat sufficient oil to 375°F. Gently drop batter by rounded tablespoons into the oil. Fry a few at a time, about 5 to 7 minutes, or until golden and crisp. (Remove scattered pieces of fried batter between each batch). Drain on paper towels. Serve hot with Mojo Isleño.

NOTE: Salt cod can be soaked overnight in 1 gallon water or vigorously simmered over high heat for approximately 15 to 30 minutes instead of soaking in cold water.

MAKES 30 SERVINGS (PORTION SIZE: 1 FRITTER)

During street fiestas, particularly the fiestas patronales honoring a town's particular namesake saint, street vendors sell salt cod fritters wrapped in cone-shaped paper so that customers can enjoy these savory treats while strolling through the town. Originally brought to the Americas by the Spaniards and Portuguese, salt cod is considered a real delicacy. Each Latin American country has a signature dish and Puerto Rico certainly is famous for these addictive little fried balls of salt cod seasoned with cilantro, green onion, oregano, and garlic. One is never enough!

MOJO ISLEÑO

DIPPING SAUCE / PUERTO RICO

ISLAND ''OLIVE'' SAUCE

This traditional Puerto Rican sauce is often served with a variety of Caribbean island fritters, from the classic tostones de plátano (plantain chips) to Bacalaítos Fritos (Codfish Fritters) Try this savory sauce over fried, grilled, or baked fish fillets as well.

½ cup virgin olive oil
1 medium yellow onion, minced
 (about 1 cup)
¾ cup (10-ounce can) roasted red peppers, cut into tiny slices, with their juice

18 manzanilla olives, sliced
2 tablespoons capers
2 cups (16-ounce can) tomato sauce
2 bay leaves
1½ tablespoons vinegar
Salt to taste

In a small skillet, warm the oil over medium heat. Add the onion and sauté until soft. Stir in the peppers, olives, and capers and continue sautéing for 2 minutes. Add the tomato sauce, bay leaves, and vinegar. Bring to a boil, lower the heat, and simmer 15 minutes uncovered. Season to taste with salt.

MAKES 3 ½ CUPS

BOLAS DE ESPINACA
FAMILY OUTING / SOUTHWEST

SPANISH SPINACH FRITTERS

When my nephew was playing football in high school, the parents and relatives of the players would bring their munchies for the trip. These spinach fritters were always a favorite!

TERESA M. BENAVIDES

2 (10-ounce) packages frozen chopped spinach
1 cup grated Parmesan cheese
2 cups packaged herb-flavored stuffing mix
¼ to ½ cup chopped green onions

½ cup roasted and peeled diced green chile (canned or fresh)
½ cup toasted piñones (pine nuts)
6 eggs, beaten
12 tablespoons (1½ sticks) butter, melted

Cook and drain the spinach as directed on the package; let cool. In a bowl, combine the spinach, cheese, stuffing mix, onion, chile, and pine nuts; mix well. Stir in the beaten eggs and melted butter until the mixture is evenly moistened. Preheat the oven to 350°F. Using a tablespoon, drop spoonfuls of the batter onto a greased cookie sheet. Bake 10 to 15 minutes, or until lightly browned.

MAKES ABOUT 3 DOZEN FRITTERS

CACHAPAS DE CARABOBO (MAÍZ)

CORN PANCAKES WITH CREAM AND CHEESE

The Carabobo Indians of Venezuela cultivated the precious corn which is the basis for these cachapas. I recall our family outings to the countryside when I prepare this recipe, for it was there that we would nibble on these freshly prepared corn cakes hot off the griddle while waiting for our main meal. My brothers and I would race to snatch as many as we could. Then we would roll the warm cachapas around pieces of fresh country cheese or smother them with cream.

AYAN ALONZO

10 ears of yellow corn (about 5 cups kernels)

1/4 cup heavy cream, plus additional as needed

1 egg

2 tablespoons harina Pan (precooked white cornmeal) (see page 3) or all-purpose flour (optional)

2 tablespoons sugar

1/4 teaspoon salt

Oil or butter for frying

12 ounces Gouda cheese, cut into 12 sticks (optional)

1. *Batter:* Grate the corn, using a coarse grater, or slice the kernels off the cob, purée in a blender, and press through a sieve. (This should yield about 3 cups.) Combine the purée in a mixing bowl with 1/4 cup of cream, the egg, harina Pan, sugar, and salt. Mix the ingredients to form a pourable batter; let rest 15 minutes.

2. *Cooking:* Heat a griddle or cast-iron skillet. Pour 1 teaspoon of oil on the griddle. Pour about 1/4 cup of batter over the oil onto the griddle. Fry the cachapa, turning once, until lightly browned and firm on both sides. Remove from the griddle and serve with heavy cream, or wrap cachapa around a slice of cheese, if desired.

SERVING SUGGESTION: These are pleasant eaten instead of bread with a meal. They make an attractive cocktail nibble, miniaturized (about 3 inches across) and wrapped around a piece of farmer cheese, Muenster, or Gouda.

MAKES 12 SERVINGS (PORTION SIZE: 1 PANCAKE)

SURULLITOS DE MAÍZ

DEEP-FRIED CORN STICKS

2 cups water
1 teaspoon salt
1½ cups yellow cornmeal
1 cup grated Cheddar cheese

Oil for deep frying
Mojo Isleño (Island "Olive" Sauce,
page 7)

1. *Preparing dough:* Bring the water and salt to a boil in a medium saucepan. Whisk in the cornmeal. Reduce the heat and cook 5 minutes, stirring constantly with a wooden spoon. When the mixture follows the spoon around the pan, remove from heat. Immediately stir in the cheese; continue stirring until melted.

2. *Forming surullitos:* Knead the cooked dough on a cutting board until smooth; divide into 24 equal-sized balls. Roll the balls into cigar-shaped sticks about ½ inch thick in the center and tapered at the edges.

3. *Frying:* In a deep fryer, heat sufficient oil to 380°F. Carefully drop in a handful of surullitos. Fry 4 to 5 minutes, or until golden and thoroughly cooked. Remove with a slotted spoon; drain on paper towels and serve hot with sauce.

MAKES 24

In Puerto Rico, June 24 marks El Día de San Juan Bautista, the most celebrated saint's day of the year. At midnight on the Eve of San Juan, Puerto Ricans gather by the sea. Joining hands, friends walk backward, immersing themselves in water in the hope of good fortune for the coming year. It is an eve of festivity, fun, and of course food. All-day beach picnics abound, and the aroma of Puerto Rican snacks fills the air. Almojábanas, (deep-fried meat-cheese balls), surullitos, (deep-fried cornmeal-cheese sticks), and bacalaítos (deep-fried salt cod fritters) are just a few of the festive foods enjoyed by Puerto Ricans.

CEVICHE DORADO

DOLPHINFISH CEVICHE

This recipe reminds me of my childhood, when my parents would take my brothers and me out to the pier and jetties along the southern California coastline as a change of scene from our home in East Los Angeles. Perhaps it was those excursions that were the basis for my love of fishing, a sport I was able to translate into a profession as the host of "Sports Fishing with Dan Hernandez."

DAN HERNANDEZ

1 pound dorado (mahi mahi or dolphinfish fillets; see Note), bones removed, cut into bite-sized pieces

¾ cup lime juice (about 8 limes)

1 (14½-ounce) can diced tomatoes, drained

1 white onion, chopped (about ¾ cup)

⅔ cup chopped cilantro

1 (4-ounce) can diced jalapeño chiles, drained

1 (10-ounce) package frozen peas, thawed

1 (5-ounce) jar small pimiento-stuffed green olives, drained

Salt

Small tostadas (fried corn tortillas)

Hot sauce (optional)

1. *Marinating fish:* Place the fish pieces in a shallow nonreactive container; pour in sufficient lime juice to cover. Refrigerate covered overnight.

2. *Mixing and serving:* The next day, drain off the lime juice. Stir in the tomatoes, onion, cilantro, chiles, peas, and olives. Add fresh lime juice and salt to taste. Serve with tostadas and hot sauce, if desired.

NOTE: While this firm, flavorful fish is properly called dolphin, in order to avoid confusion with the mammal of the same name, the Hawaiian term *mahi mahi* or the Spanish word *dorado* is becoming more widespread in use.

SERVING SUGGESTION: For a poolside party, serve Dorado Ceviche with a platter of tropical fruits and vegetables (strawberries, pineapple, jicama, cucumbers, and melon). Sprinkle the fruit with lime juice, mild chile powder, and salt. Miniature fried taquitos, served with Fiesta Guacamole (Party Avocado Dip, page 15), and Ensalada de Nopales (Cactus Salad, page 17) will round out your afternoon buffet.

MAKES 8 CUPS

Seviche de Camarón

ECUADOREAN SHRIMP COCKTAIL

I love New Year's Eve! Our entire family gathers to usher in a new year and acknowledge the good fortune we have had as a family. Without fail, my mother prepares this shrimp seviche in great quantities. Twelve or fifteen shrimp are easy to enjoy prior to our celebration dinner. Maybe it's the unique Ecuadorean marinade or just the fact that I associate this evening with this seviche. Whatever the reason, I am pleased to be able to share a part of our culture. ¡Provecho!

JORGE JARRÍN

SHRIMP

1½ teaspoons salt
5 pounds uncooked large shrimp,
   shelled and deveined (see Note)

MARINADE

4 cups fresh-squeezed orange juice
1 cup ketchup
½ cup fresh-squeezed lemon juice
3 tablespoons Worcestershire sauce
½ cup minced white onion
½ cup minced green onions
¼ cup chopped cilantro leaves
½ teaspoon salt
¼ teaspoon ground black pepper
Hot sauce (optional)
Maíz tostado (toasted corn or popcorn,
   see Note)

1. *Cooking shrimp:* In a large pot, bring 3 quarts of water to a boil with the salt. Add the shrimp. Return to a boil, reduce the heat to a rapid simmer, and cook until the shrimp are pink, 3 to 5 minutes. Immediately remove from the heat and drain; rinse under cold water.

2. *Preparing marinade:* In a nonreactive bowl, mix together the orange juice, ketchup, lemon juice, Worcestershire sauce, onions, cilantro, salt, and pepper. Season with hot sauce, if desired. Add the cooked shrimp; cover and refrigerate overnight or at least 6 hours. Serve with toasted corn or popcorn.

NOTE: One 5-pound box of frozen shrimp will yield about 110 large shrimp. . . . Maíz tostado or roasted corn is large hominy-like kernels of corn that have been toasted, similar to popcorn in taste and to corn nuts in texture.

MAKES 15 SERVINGS (PORTION SIZE: ABOUT 10 PIECES)

Cebiche de Almejas

PANAMANIAN CLAM CEBICHE

Try this for a unique flavor sensation. Baby clams are poached in milk, then marinated in a lemony mustard sauce with a hint of dill. Minced onion and crisp baby peas add bite and color to this party dish.

2 cups milk
9 pounds small clams, shucked (about 3 cups meat) (see Box)
¾ cup finely chopped onion
¼ cup prepared yellow mustard
1 tablespoon chopped dill pickle

½ teaspoon ground black pepper
½ teaspoon salt
¾ cup fresh-squeezed lemon juice
½ cup frozen baby peas, thawed
¼ cup cilantro leaves (optional)

1. *Poaching clams:* In a medium saucepan, heat the milk to a rapid simmer; add the clams. Return to a rapid simmer and cook 1 additional minute. Drain, discarding the milk. Chop the clams fine and place in a glass bowl with clam juices. Makes about 3 cups.

2. *Mixing and marinating cebiche:* Stir the onion, mustard, pickle, pepper, salt, lemon juice, peas, and cilantro into the clams. Cover and refrigerate at least 3 hours before serving. Makes 4 cups.

SERVING SUGGESTION: Serve Cebiche de Almejas with saltine crackers or toasted pumpernickel bread as a party buffet item or fill Belgian endive spears, radicchio leaves, or Boston lettuce cups with this colorful cebiche for an attractive party presentation.

MAKES 8 SERVINGS (PORTION SIZE: ½ CUP)

To shuck a clam, hold the clam securely in the palm of the left hand with the arc side toward your fingers. Using a clam knife or a dull dinner knife, run the blade along the seam between the two shells; force the knife between the shells toward the hinge until you can pry the shell open. Sever the connecting muscles and separate the shells.

Guaca-Salsa con Totopos

DIPPING SAUCE / MEXICO

AVOCADO-SALSA DIP WITH FRIED CORN TORTILLA CHIPS

Every time I prepare this salsa I think of Mexico City and my sister-in-law, who gave me this very simple recipe. Today, I am able to share it with my coworkers at Mujeres Latinas en Acción, a social services agency dedicated to women and children. Whenever we have any kind of event involving food they insist that I prepare the guaca-salsa, and if I don't, I know I'm in a lot of trouble!

MARIA G. VILLA

1 pound (about 15 small) tomatillos
1 medium white onion, quartered
2 ripe avocados (see Note)
½ cup cilantro leaves
7 to 10 jalapeño chiles, rinsed,
  stemmed, and halved

1 cup water
3 large cloves garlic
2 teaspoons salt
Totopos (fried corn tortilla chips)

1. Remove husks from the tomatillos and rinse them under warm water to remove stickiness. Slice in half.

2. Place the tomatillos, onion, avocados, cilantro, jalapeños, water, garlic, and salt in a blender container or food processor bowl. Purée at medium speed for about 1 minute, until smooth yet thick. Season to taste. Serve guaca-salsa with totopos.

NOTE: If available, use the pebbly dark Hass or the smooth green Fuerte avocado, grown throughout California and Mexico. Prized for its rich flavor and creamy texture, the Hass avocado ranges in color from dark green to green-black when ripe. To ripen, place in a sealed paper bag and keep in a dark room or pantry. Once ripe, refrigerate. The smooth skinned Florida avocado has less flavor, the advantage being less fat and calories!

SERVING SUGGESTION: Guaca-salsa can be used as a condiment with different meats or served with Mexican antojitos (little snacks), such as totopos (fried tortilla chips), taquitos, quesadillas, nachos, and tostadas.

MAKES 5½ CUPS

Fiesta Guacamole
DIPPING SAUCE / MEXICO

PARTY AVOCADO DIP

20 ripe Hass or Fuerte avocados
2 medium white onions, minced
   (about 2 cups)
10 cloves garlic, minced, or substitute
   1 tablespoon garlic salt
10 serrano chiles, minced

⅓ cup mayonnaise
6 fresh limes, halved
Salt
1 bunch cilantro leaves, stemmed,
   cleaned, and chopped (about 1
   cup)

Halve the avocados; remove pits and scoop the pulp into a medium bowl. Add the onion, garlic, chiles, and mayonnaise. Mash the ingredients together with a fork until blended. Squeeze the juice of 4 to 6 limes into the guacamole to season; mix well. Add salt to taste and refrigerate until ready to serve. One hour before serving, stir in the cilantro.

MAKES 3 QUARTS

Salsa de Molcajete
DIPPING SAUCE / MEXICO

FRESH TOMATO SALSA

6 ripe and juicy medium tomatoes
2 to 4 fresh jalapeño chiles, stem and
   seeds removed
5 cloves garlic
¼ teaspoon dried oregano leaves

Salt to taste
½ medium white onion, cut up
¼ bunch cilantro leaves, stems removed, cleaned and chopped

In a saucepan, combine the tomatoes and chiles with water to cover. Bring to a boil and blanch for no more than 3 minutes, or until tomatoes are just soft; drain. Place the garlic, oregano, and salt in a molcajete (stone mortar). Using a tejolote (pestle), grind the ingredients together. Add the tomatoes, chile, onion, and cilantro. Continue grinding and mixing to the desired consistency. Season to taste with salt.

MAKES 3 CUPS

I n Spanish, the word "entrada" means "each of the more substantial dishes served at the table." These individual servings of rather substantial food play an important role in the culinary character of Latin America.

The Latin meal pattern reflects the lifestyle of its people. Breakfast is not typically a substantial meal. In most countries, businesses close in the early afternoon, allowing people several hours to enjoy the day's main meal at home with their families or partake in a leisurely business lunch. The rest of the day's food falls into the category of a light meal or snack.

These light meals aren't restricted to daytime. In all Latin countries, an early evening paseo (walk) is a national pastime. Families, friends, and couples, arm in arm, stroll through the town square, streets, or parks, chatting, laughing, and acknowledging one another with a smile. At some point, a snack or light meal will be enjoyed at a sidewalk café, restaurant, or street stand.

ENSALADA DE AGUACATE Y TOMATE
FAMILY GET-TOGETHERS / VENEZUELA

AVOCADO AND TOMATO SALAD

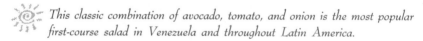 *This classic combination of avocado, tomato, and onion is the most popular first-course salad in Venezuela and throughout Latin America.*

2 heads romaine or butterhead lettuce, rinsed
3 small Hass or Fuerte avocados, peeled and sliced
4 large ripe beefsteak tomatoes, blanched, peeled, and quartered

½ white onion, sliced into thin rings
⅓ cup Spanish or virgin olive oil
4 tablespoons red wine vinegar
½ teaspoon salt
½ teaspoon ground black pepper

1. Tear the inner lettuce leaves into bite-sized pieces; wrap in paper towels. Refrigerate all ingredients until ready to use.

2. Just before serving, arrange the crisp lettuce leaves on a serving platter. Top with avocado, tomato, and onions; set aside. In a small bowl, mix the olive oil, vinegar, salt, and pepper. Pour over the salad and serve.

MAKES 6 SERVINGS

Ensalada de Nopales (Nopalitos)

ENTERTAINING / MEXICO

CACTUS SALAD

For those who haven't experienced the tasty nopal (cactus paddle), this festive salad brings out its best flavors in a marinade of olive oil, lime juice, garlic, and jalapeño chile.

2 (32-ounce) jars nopales, drained, rinsed, and cut into 1-inch strips, or 6 cups fresh nopales (see page 38)

1 large white onion, cut into thin 1-inch strips (about 2 cups)

5 large cloves garlic

3 marinated jalapeño chiles, stemmed

1 teaspoon salt (optional)

½ cup olive oil

½ cup fresh-squeezed lime juice

4 (14½-ounce) cans chopped tomatoes, drained

1 bunch cilantro leaves, stemmed, cleaned, and chopped

Crumbled fresh feta, fresco, or cotija cheese

Lime wedges and tortilla chips to garnish

1. *Marinating cactus:* In a mixing bowl, combine *nopales* (cactus) and onion. Set aside. In a mortar and pestle, mash garlic and jalapeños into salt. Stir in olive oil and lime juice until blended; let stand 15 minutes. Pour dressing over nopales and onions; mix well, cover, and refrigerate.

2. *Finishing and serving:* Before serving, stir tomatoes and cilantro into nopales mixture. Sprinkle with crumbled cheese and offer with lime wedges and tortilla chips, if desired.

SERVING SUGGESTION: Use nopalitos as a colorful salad to accompany barbecued meats or as a first course served on tostadas, or chop all the ingredients and use as an appetizer dip. As an idea for a outdoor grill party, barbecue whole cleaned and trimmed cactus paddles until tender and lightly charred. Slice into short strips and add warm to a prepared salad or use as a taco filling. Toss before serving.

MAKES 8 SERVINGS (PORTION SIZE: 1 CUP)

Ensalada Rusa

OUTDOOR ASADO / ARGENTINA

RUSSIAN SALAD

This has always been a favorite buffet dish at our famous asados (outdoor Argentine barbecues), or it can be served as a first course at a formal dinner. The finest restaurants throughout Argentina offer this classic salad, which is named after its Russian-style dressing.

GEORGINA VIGILATO

SALAD

1 cup peeled and diced carrots
1 teaspoon salt
4 cups peeled and diced potatoes
   (about 2 pounds)
1½ cups frozen peas, thawed

2 cups diced cooked chicken
1 cup finely diced ham
5 hard-cooked eggs, chopped
30 small pimiento-stuffed green olives
   (about ⅓ cup)

RUSSIAN DRESSING

1½ cups good-quality purchased
   mayonnaise
1 tablespoon prepared horseradish

¼ cup ketchup
2 tablespoons olive juice (optional)

GARNISH

Chopped parsley, pimiento slices,
   green olives, and sliced hard-cooked
   eggs

1. *Assembling salad:* In a pot, boil the carrots 5 minutes over medium high heat with water to cover and salt; add the potatoes. Continue to cook until just soft; drain and allow to cool. Combine the potatoes, carrots, peas, chicken, ham, eggs, and olives in a large bowl; toss gently to mix.

2. *Preparing dressing:* In a separate bowl, mix together the mayonnaise, horseradish, ketchup, and olive juice, if desired. Gently combine the dressing with the salad ingredients. Season to taste. Refrigerate until chilled.

3. *Serving:* Place the salad in a serving bowl. Garnish the rim with parsley, pimiento slices, olives, and hard-cooked eggs.

MAKES 9 SERVINGS (PORTION SIZE: ¾ CUP)

SALADA DE PALMITO

FAMILY GET-TOGETHERS / BRAZIL

HEARTS OF PALM SALAD

The slender, ivory-colored, and delicately flavored hearts of palm are very popular among Brazilians, who feature them in appetizers, soups, salads, rice dishes, and entrees. In this salad, the hearts of palm are nicely contrasted against mustard, onion, and cheese for a slightly sweet taste.

VEGETABLE SALAD

1 (15-ounce) can hearts of palm, drained and diced (about 1½ cups)

1 (16-ounce) can pitted medium black olives, drained

1 (10-ounce) package frozen peas

½ cup minced red onion

3 ripe tomatoes, cut into wedges

⅓ cup chopped parsley

DRESSING

⅓ cup red wine vinegar

1 teaspoon prepared yellow mustard

4 cloves garlic, passed through a press

¼ teaspoon ground black pepper

½ cup virgin olive oil

8 ounces feta cheese, cubed

1. *Assembling salad:* Combine the hearts of palm, olives, peas, onion, tomatoes, and parsley in a mixing bowl.

2. *Preparing dressing:* In a separate bowl, whisk together the vinegar, mustard, garlic, and pepper until blended. Stir in the oil and season to taste.

3. *Marinating and serving:* Pour the dressing over the vegetables. Refrigerate for several hours. Toss the feta cheese into the salad and serve.

SERVING SUGGESTION: A beautiful salad, attractively served, Salada de Palmito makes a substantial first-course salad to be followed by a main-course soup and bread. Or serve as a luncheon entree tossed with cooked seashell pasta and bay shrimp. This savory salad can also be used to accompany a slice of pâté in lieu of the usual cornichons.

MAKES 8 SERVINGS (PORTION SIZE: ¾ CUP)

APPETIZERS AND FIRST COURSES   •   19

Ensalada de Verdura Picada

FAMILY GET-TOGETHERS / ECUADOR

ECUADOREAN CHOPPED VEGETABLE SALAD

This is the perfect celebration vegetable salad, with colors and flavors to brighten any plate or buffet. The lemon vinaigrette complements most Ecuadorean seafood dishes.

TERESA SOTO

3 fresh beets, peeled and diced (about 2 cups)

4 carrots, peeled and diced (about 2 cups)

2 medium potatoes, peeled and diced (about 2 cups)

½ cauliflower head, broken into florets (about 4 cups)

1 small red onion, cut into thin 1-inch strips

Juice of 6 lemons (about 1¼ cups)

1 cup frozen peas, thawed

½ cup chopped cilantro leaves

Olive oil

Salt and ground black pepper

1. *Cooking vegetables:* In a small pot, cover the beets with water and cook until just tender; drain. Place the carrots and potatoes in a second saucepan with salted water to cover. Cook uncovered over medium high heat for 7 minutes; add the cauliflower, cover, and cook until the vegetables are just tender. Do not overcook.

2. *Marinating onions:* While the vegetables are cooking, rinse the sliced onion under cold running water. Place onions and lemon juice in a shallow container; toss to mix well. Set aside for 20 to 30 minutes.

3. *Tossing and serving:* Combine the beets, carrots, potatoes, cauliflower, marinated onions with lemon juice, peas, and cilantro in a serving bowl. Gently toss to combine. Drizzle olive oil over vegetables to taste. Season with salt and pepper. Toss before serving.

SERVING SUGGESTION: Serve this colorful vegetable salad with Tacos de Abulón (Abalone Steak Tacos, page 76) and Arroz Blanco Cubano (Cuban White Rice, page 145) for an exotic, colorful, and delicious afternoon meal.

MAKES 8 SERVINGS (PORTION SIZE: 1½ CUPS)

20   •   APERITIVOS Y ENTRADAS

Ensalada de Hongos Marinados

MARINATED MUSHROOM SALAD

1 cup olive oil
2/3 cup tarragon vinegar
10 cloves garlic, minced
3 tablespoons chopped fresh tarragon

1 teaspoon salt
1 1/2 to 2 pounds small mushroom
    caps, cleaned and stemmed
6 cups spinach leaves (optional)

In a bowl, whisk together the oil, vinegar, garlic, tarragon, and salt until blended. Pour over the mushrooms; cover and refrigerate. Marinate 4 hours or overnight, tossing occasionally. Clean, wash, and pat dry the spinach leaves. Top with mushroom mixture and serve immediately.

MAKES 6 SERVINGS (PORTION SIZE: 3/4 CUP)

Ensalada de Habas

MARKET DAY / MEXICO

FAVA BEAN SALAD

4 cups shelled and cooked habas (fava
    beans)
1 cup finely chopped white onion
2 cups chopped ripe tomatoes
1/2 bunch parsley, chopped (about
    1/2 cup)
1/4 cup capers or green olives

1/2 teaspoon dried oregano
1/2 cup olive oil
1/4 cup fresh-squeezed lime juice
2 cloves garlic, minced
1/2 pound feta cheese, cubed
Croutons to garnish

In a bowl, mix together the beans, onion, tomatoes, parsley, capers, oregano, olive oil, lime juice, and garlic. Refrigerate 1 to 2 hours, tossing occasionally. Sprinkle with feta cheese and croutons.

MAKES 8 CUPS

ENSALADA CÉSAR

CAESAR SALAD

Created in the 1920s by Alex-César Cardini near Tijuana, Mexico, Caesar salad is today prepared in countless ways. This recipe features a lighter, egg-free dressing and an arrangement suitable for a tardeada (afternoon party).

DRESSING
½ cup olive oil
1½ tablespoons red wine vinegar
3 tablespoons fresh-squeezed lemon
 juice
5 anchovy fillets
2 large cloves garlic, minced
1 teaspoon prepared mustard
Salt and black pepper

2 large heads romaine lettuce, rinsed,
 separated, and chilled
4 ounces crumbled cotija or feta
 cheese
1 cup croutons
Lemon wedges and anchovy fillets to
 garnish

1. *Blending dressing:* In a blender, combine the oil, vinegar, lemon juice, anchovies, garlic, and mustard and blend until smooth. Season to taste with salt and pepper. Transfer to a small bowl and set aside at room temperature or cover and refrigerate.

2. *Arranging salad and serving:* Select inner romaine leaves (spears) and arrange attractively on a platter. Drizzle the dressing over the spears and generously sprinkle with cheese and croutons. Garnish the platter with lemon wedges and anchovy fillets before serving.

SERVING SUGGESTION: At your next tardeada (late afternoon fiesta) serve this attractive Caesar Salad as an appetizer. Select only the smallest romaine leaves or use Belgian endive. Sprinkle with small croutons and crumbled cheese. Your guests can simply pick up a garnished romaine leaf as a refreshing hors d'oeuvre.

MAKES 4 SERVINGS (SERVING SIZE: 2 CUPS SALAD AND 2 TABLESPOONS DRESSING)

VIGORÓN

FAMILY MEAL / NICARAGUA

CABBAGE AND YUCCA SALAD
WITH PORK CRACKLINGS

Delicious and addictive, this popular Nicaraguan salad has many variations—tomatoes may be added, the chile may change—but the yucca, raw cabbage, and chicharrón (pork cracklings) make this recipe authentic.

1½ pounds frozen yucca or cassava
½ teaspoon salt
3 cups finely shredded cabbage
1 small white onion, sliced thin
¼ cup white wine vinegar
Juice of 3 lemons (about ⅓ cup)

1 to 2 fresh green or red chiles, sliced into thin slivers or minced
½ pound chicharrón (fried pork rinds), warmed and broken into small pieces
Cilantro sprigs

1. *Cooking yucca:* In a saucepan, combine the frozen yucca with salt and enough water to barely cover. Bring to a boil, lower the heat, and cook until tender, about 15 minutes. Drain and cover to keep warm.

2. *Preparing cabbage mixture:* In a salad bowl, mix the cabbage and onion with vinegar, lemon juice, and green chile to taste. Let marinate 15 minutes, tossing occasionally.

3. *Assembly:* To serve, place warm yucca on the bottom of a serving platter. Cover with dressed shredded cabbage and generously top with chicharrón. Garnish with cilantro.

MAKES 8 SERVINGS

> You can find chicharrones (the crisp brown skin of fried or roasted pork, also known as cracklings) at a carnicería (a Hispanic meat market) or oftentimes a tortillería (a Mexican tortilla deli) in Latin neighborhoods. To warm, place chicharrones in a paper bag, seal, and microwave on high for 1 minute.

APPETIZERS AND FIRST COURSES • 23

Pupusas Salvadoreñas con Curtido
FAMILY GET-TOGETHERS / EL SALVADOR

CORN GRIDDLE CAKES WITH PICKLED CABBAGE

My mom makes the best pupusas in the world, which is why she had such a loyal clientele when she would sell them at the bus stop to help make ends meet. Every day was the same routine: At 4 A.M. she used to go the bus stop and she would not come home until midnight. As a nurse, I have a great desire to care for people, especially those who are not so fortunate. My mother taught me this by example. This is her recipe.

TELMA PALOMEQUE DE SOTO

CURTIDO (PICKLED CABBAGE)
1 medium cabbage, shredded
2 carrots, shredded
1 small red onion, sliced thin
4 cups cider vinegar
4 cups water
1 tablespoon dried oregano leaves, crushed

2 teaspoons crushed red chile flakes
1 red bell pepper or 4 ajíes dulces
  (sweet red peppers), sliced thin
1 tablespoon salt

PORK AND POTATO FILLING
3 pounds pork butt, trimmed and cut into small pieces
1 teaspoon salt
1 pound tomatoes (about 3 medium)
½ small white onion, sliced

½ teaspoon dried oregano leaves
¼ teaspoon ground black pepper
3 whole cloves
1 large russet potato

CORN DOUGH
5 pounds masa (freshly ground corn dough)

1 cup vegetable oil

1. *Preparing the curtido:* In a large bowl, combine the cabbage, carrots, onion, vinegar, water, oregano, chile flakes, red bell pepper, and salt until well mixed. Transfer to a glass or plastic 1-gallon jar. Secure with the lid and agitate to mix well. Let marinate at least 1 day. Makes 1 gallon. *This mixture will keep up to 1 month in the refrigerator.*

2. *Preparing meat for filling:* In a small pot, combine the pork with water to cover by 2 inches and salt to season. Bring to a rapid simmer. Partially cover and cook until the pork is tender and the water has almost evaporated, about 40 minutes. Uncover; reduce the heat to very low and let the pork fry in its own fat until golden. Remove from the heat.

3. *Simmering the filling:* Put the tomatoes, onion, oregano, black pepper, and cloves in a blender container. Purée until smooth. Pour the blender contents into the saucepan with the pork. Place over medium heat, stirring the purée with a wooden spoon to loosen bits of browned pork on the bottom of the pot. Remove from the heat and, using 2 forks, shred the meat. Bring the mixture to a boil again. Lower the heat and cook uncovered over medium heat for 10 minutes, or until thickened.

4. *Finishing the filling:* Place the potato in a small pot with water to cover. Bring to a boil and cook until tender, 20 to 30 minutes. Remove from the heat, drain, and peel. Mash the potato or press it through a sieve. In a bowl, combine the pork mixture with $^1/_2$ to $^3/_4$ cup of the mashed potato; mix thoroughly. Makes about 4 cups filling.

5. *Forming and cooking pupusas:* Mix the masa with the oil until very soft. Form into 25 small balls and cover with a damp cloth. Pat each ball with the palms of your hand until flattened. Place a generous tablespoon of meat mixture in the center of each round. Carefully enclose the filling by pressing the edges of the masa up over the filling. Press the edges of masa together to seal the ball. Lightly pat the masa ball (with enclosed filling) until flattened to $^3/_8$-inch thickness. Place the pupusas on a heated greased griddle; cook until speckled brown. Turn once and continue cooking until speckled and puffed. Remove; top with curtido and serve.

SERVING SUGGESTION: El Salvador's most popular snack is similar to a thick corn tortilla stuffed with cheese, or in this version, pork and potatoes. Be sure to top the hot pupusas with a curtido, a colorful pickled vegetable mixture of cabbage, carrots, and onion. For party hors d'oeuvres, prepare miniature $2^1/_4$-inch pupusas up to 1 week ahead and freeze. Heat thawed pupusas in a 350°F oven for 20 minutes, or until heated through. Serve hot.

MAKES 25 SERVINGS (PORTION SIZE: 2 PUPUSAS)

CHILE VERDE EN ESCABECHE
HOLIDAYS / MEXICO

PICKLED GREEN CHILES

This special family recipe is one of many contained in an old book that has been passed on to me by my aunt, and to her by her mother. The cover is worn out from years of use, but I use the book to this day, passing on a piece of our culture to my own daughters.

ESPERANZA VIADES

CHILES
8 fresh poblano or pasilla green chiles

TUNA FILLING
2 (9-ounce) cans tuna, drained
1/3 cup frozen peas, thawed
1/4 cup mayonnaise

1/4 cup Mexican cream or heavy cream
1/4 teaspoon salt (optional)
1/4 teaspoon ground black pepper

ESCABECHE (PICKLING SAUCE)
2 cups olive oil
3 cloves garlic, halved
2 white onions, sliced thin
2 bay leaves
1 cinnamon stick
1 teaspoon coriander seed
12 whole cloves

1 teaspoon dried oregano leaves, crushed
1 1/3 cups cider vinegar
2 carrots, julienne cut and blanched
1 teaspoon salt
1 teaspoon ground black pepper
1 teaspoon sugar

GARNISH
16 radish flowers

16 scallion flowers

1. *Roasting and peeling chiles:* To remove the skin of the chiles, first blister the chiles over a fired grill or place directly on a heated griddle, turning frequently with tongs. When the skins are charred, blistered, and somewhat blackened, remove from griddle. (Take care not to burn through to the flesh.) Immediately place the roasted chile into a plastic bag that has been covered with a damp cloth. Repeat the process until all 8 chiles are roasted. After the chiles have steamed 20 minutes, peel off the skin under cold running water, being careful not to tear the chile. With a small sharp

knife, make a 3-inch slit on one side of the chile. Carefully remove the seeds and veins under running water. Set aside until ready to stuff.

2. *Preparing tuna filling:* In a small bowl, combine tuna, peas, mayonnaise, and cream; mix well. Season with salt and pepper to taste. Using a small spoon, carefully stuff each chile with 1/4 cup of the tuna filling; cover and refrigerate.

3. *Escabeche (pickling sauce):* In a medium skillet, warm the olive oil over medium low heat. Fry the garlic, onion, bay leaves, cinnamon stick, coriander seed, cloves, and oregano about 5 minutes, until onion is just soft. Do not overcook. Add vinegar and carrots to the skillet. Bring to a quick boil, reduce the heat, and simmer covered for 5 minutes. Season with salt, pepper, and sugar. Cover and keep warm. Makes 4 cups.

4. *Assembly:* Place the chiles, stuffed with tuna filling, in a rectangular 7 × 9 × 2½-inch dish. Pour warm escabeche over the chiles. Let stand at room temperature until cooled. Cover and refrigerate overnight, basting occasionally with vinaigrette. Serve at room temperature, garnished with radish and onion flowers.

SERVING SUGGESTION: Enjoy Chiles Verdes en Escabeche with frijoles refritos (refried beans) and bolillos (Mexican rolls) as a special late-night holiday dinner, or serve as part of a festive holiday buffet.

MAKES 8 SERVINGS (PORTION SIZE: 1 CHILE)

In Mexico, dried red chiles or fresh green chiles are marinated in a savory escabeche (pickled dressing). Use your imagination and try a variety of interesting stuffings, such as smoked chicken, seasoned beans, herbed cheeses, or a picadillo (beef with nuts and fruit). . . . Chiles poblanos are a thick-skinned dark green, almost blackish triangular-shaped chile ranging in flavor from mild to hot. Since they retain their shape after roasting, chiles poblanos are used for stuffing. In areas of the United States, chiles poblanos are also known as chiles pasillas.

ESCABECHE DE PESCADO FRITO
PARTY BUFFET / URUGUAY

PICKLED FRIED FISH

This dish is often prepared in Uruguay for a simple family meal served with a green salad and hearty bread. We especially love to make it with freshwater fish.

JACQUES DOGHRAM

FISH
3 pounds firm-fleshed white fish such as orange roughy, red snapper, or sea bass, cut into fillets (see Note)
Salt

Freshly ground black pepper
Flour for dusting
3 tablespoons butter or lard

ESCABECHE (PICKLING SAUCE)
1 cup olive oil or vegetable oil
2 medium onions, sliced thick
½ red bell pepper, cut into strips
½ green bell pepper, cut into strips

¼ teaspoon dried oregano leaves
2 bay leaves
⅓ cup white wine vinegar

GARNISH
12 parsley sprigs
12 lemon wedges

Capers and green olives (optional)

1. *Frying fish:* Season the fish with salt and pepper and dredge in flour, shaking to remove the excess. Melt the butter in a skillet over medium heat and sauté the fish until lightly browned on both sides. Cover and cook for a few minutes until the fish is no longer opaque. Transfer to a shallow serving platter and keep warm.

2. *Preparing escabeche:* Heat the oil in a medium skillet. Add the onions and pepper strips and cook over low heat until the onions are lightly browned. Stir in the oregano and bay leaves; cook for a minute longer. Stir in the vinegar; bring to a boil and cook 1 minute. Pour the escabeche over the fish. Serve immediately, garnished with parsley and lemon wedges. Sprinkle with capers and green olives, if desired.

NOTE: Select fish of equal size to ensure even cooking of fillets.

MAKES 8 SERVINGS

Mixtas

STREET FOOD / GUATEMALA

SAUSAGE WRAP

One of my fondest memories of Guatemala City is strolling through the busy city streets and stopping for a mixta, a cross between an American hot dog and a Mexican taco. To this day, whenever I have a craving, I can whip up a quick mixta and somehow feel satisfied and closer to home.

MARCELLA CABRERA

1 package kosher or all-beef hot dogs (about 8) or sausages

16 thin corn tortillas

AVOCADO SALAD
2 ripe avocados, peeled and pitted
Juice of 1 large lime (about ¼ cup)
⅓ cup finely minced white onion
½ teaspoon crushed oregano leaves, toasted (see Note)

1 teaspoon salt
¼ teaspoon ground black pepper

1. *Hot dogs:* In a saucepan, combine the hot dogs with water to cover. Bring to a boil; lower the heat and simmer for 10 minutes, until plump. Drain.

2. *Avocado salad:* Combine the avocados, lime juice, onion, oregano, salt, and pepper in a small bowl. Using a fork, mash until blended, yet not so well as to lose all texture. Adjust seasoning to taste. Chill.

3. *Serving:* Heat corn tortillas on a comal (griddle) until speckled brown. Place one hot dog on 2 stacked tortillas and top with a heaping spoonful of avocado salad. Fold the tortilla over the hot dog and eat like a taco.

CHICKEN MIXTAS
Substitute 2 cups of warm shredded chicken combined with 1 cup shredded cabbage and carrots for 8 hot dogs.

NOTE: To toast oregano, heat a heavy skillet and toast oregano lightly, stirring until aroma is released. Immediately remove from skillet.

MAKES 8 SERVINGS (PORTION SIZE: 1 MIXTA WITH ¼ CUP SALAD)

EMPANADAS DE RES

OUTDOOR ASADO / ARGENTINA

ARGENTINE BEEF TURNOVERS

I still associate the wonderful smell of the empanadas frying with my mother's gentle comforting voice. It brings back those words that used to make me so happy: "Well done, you get empanadas today!" Today my daughter, Bronwyn, not only enjoys eating these treats but is very skilled at forming the traditional gaucho "Argentina cowboy" rope tie to steal the pastry.

IRENE ALBINA ROSETTI DE BARI

PASTRY DOUGH
2 cups all-purpose flour, or as needed
1 package active dry yeast
1 teaspoon salt

1 cup lukewarm water (110° to 115°F)
Oil for frying

BEEF FILLING
2 tablespoons vegetable oil
1 cup minced onion
1 pound lean ground beef
1 (8-ounce) can tomato sauce
1½ cups water
4 hard-cooked eggs, chopped coarsely

⅔ cup raisins
1 teaspoon pimentón (ground sweet red pepper) or Hungarian paprika
½ teaspoon salt
¼ teaspoon ground cumin
16 pimiento-stuffed olives

1. *Mixing pastry:* In a mixing bowl, combine the flour, yeast, and salt and mix thoroughly. Add water, mixing with hands to form a soft dough. Cover with a damp cloth and let rest at least 4 hours or refrigerate overnight.

2. *Preparing beef filling:* In a medium skillet, warm the oil over medium heat. Add the onion and sauté until soft, about 5 minutes. Add the beef and cook until browned, stirring frequently. Stir in the tomato sauce and water. Continue cooking uncovered, stirring occasionally, until the liquid has evaporated. Remove from the heat. Stir in the eggs, raisins, paprika, salt, and cumin. Season to taste according to preference. Set aside.

3. *Rolling out dough:* Turn the dough out onto a work surface that has been lightly coated with vegetable oil. Roll with an oiled rolling pin or pat with your hands until it is ⅛ to ¼ inch thick. Cut out circles, using a 4- to 5-inch saucer. Form scraps into a ball and reroll.

4. *Forming turnovers:* Spoon a generous tablespoon of filling (depending on the size of the empanada) on center of a dough circle; place an olive on the filling. Lightly moisten the edges of the dough with cold water. Fold dough over the filling, expelling as much air as possible, and seal, forming a crescent-shaped empanada.

5. *Frying:* In a small skillet, heat 2 inches of oil to 375°F. Fry the empanadas, not more than 3 at a time, for 2 to 3 minutes, turning once, until golden brown. Remove with a slotted spoon and drain on absorbent towels. Serve immediately or place on baking sheet, uncovered, in 200°F oven until ready to serve.

NOTE: To create the traditional gaucho (Argentine cowboy) "rope" tie along the arc of empanada, first turn 1/2 inch of one corner edge up toward the top of the curved arc. Fold over the next 1/2 inch of the edge. Make a rough triangle over the first fold. Repeat this folding around the edge, pressing each fold tight, as you proceed. Tuck the last fold under the empanada.

SERVING SUGGESTION: To create a menu for an Argentine-style parrillada or asado (outdoor mixed grill), select your favorite cuts of meat, poultry, and sausages to grill over hot coals or mesquite. For an appetizer serve these Empanadas de Res along with Ensalada Rusa (Russian Salad, page 18). Let guests select their meat from a large platter. Serve Salsa para Asados (Roasted Meat Sauce, page 113), baguettes, and an assortment of three or four different cold salads—a green garden salad, a marinated hearts of palm salad, a crunchy coleslaw, carrot-raisin salad, or a pasta salad would all be appropriate choices.

MAKES 16 SERVINGS (PORTION SIZE: 1 EMPANADA)

Little luncheon cafés known as empanaderías specialize in these popular turnovers, offering dozens of sweet and savory fillings, each filling oftentimes dictating the shape and seal of the empanada. For example, chicken empanadas would actually be shaped like little fat hens. Argentine empanadas are famous throughout the world, and this recipe is a good example of how scrumptious they can be.

EMPANADAS DE POLLO
OUTDOOR ASADO / URUGUAY
•
URUGUAYAN CHICKEN TURNOVERS

As a parrillero (grill master) at an asado (country barbecue), I have several rules. First, I never serve beef empanadas as appetizers, as they kill your hunger for the incredible feast of beef, lamb, and mutton I am preparing. Second, my asados are always served by noon—not 1:00 or 2:00 P.M. as so often occurs with a young parrillero. The guests should enjoy the meal while their appetites still cry out and the wine has not overflowed. And finally, the women should always be served first—as in the old days—with respect and appreciation for all the other days of the week they have served us.

JACQUES DOGHRAM

PASTRY DOUGH
4 cups all-purpose flour
2 packages active dry yeast
2 teaspoons salt

2 cups water

Oil for frying

CHICKEN FILLING
½ cup olive oil
1 white onion, cut into thin ½-inch-
  long strips (about 1½ cups)
1 minced jalapeño chile
1 red bell pepper, chopped fine
2 large ripe tomatoes, diced
¼ cup chopped fresh oregano leaves
⅓ cup chopped fresh basil
1 tablespoon ground white pepper

1½ teaspoons salt
½ teaspoon ground cumin
2 bay leaves
⅓ cup well-seasoned chicken broth
  (see page 33)
3 cups shredded chicken (see page 33)
3 hard-cooked eggs, chopped
¼ cup pimiento-stuffed green olives,
  halved (about 20)

1. *Pastry:* In a mixing bowl, combine flour, yeast, and salt; thoroughly mix. Add water, mixing with hands to form a soft dough. Cover with a damp cloth and let rest at least 4 hours or refrigerate overnight.

2. *Chicken filling:* In a saucepan, heat the olive oil over medium low heat; sauté the onion and jalapeño until soft, about 10 minutes. Add the red pepper and continue cooking an additional 10 minutes, stirring frequently to avoid browning the onion. Add the tomatoes, oregano, basil, white

pepper, salt, cumin, bay leaves, and chicken broth. Cook over medium heat until the tomatoes release their juices and partially disintegrate. Stir in the chicken; lower the heat and simmer 10 minutes covered. The filling should be moist; if dry, add a few spoonfuls of broth. Before using the filling, stir in the eggs and olives. One cup of chicken filling will make about six 5-inch empanadas or 4 entree empanadas.

3. *Rolling out dough:* Turn the dough out onto a work surface that has been lightly coated with vegetable oil. Roll with an oiled rolling pin or pat with your hands until it is ⅛ to ¼ inch thick. Cut out circles, using a 4- to 5-inch saucer. Form scraps into a ball and reroll.

4. *Forming turnovers:* Spoon a generous tablespoon of filling (depending on the size of the empanada) on the center of the circle. Lightly moisten edges of dough with cold water. Fold the dough over the filling, expelling as much air as possible, and seal, forming a crescent-shaped empanada.

5. *Frying:* In a small skillet, heat 2 inches of oil to 375°F. Fry empanadas, not more than 3 at a time, for 2 minutes, turning once, until golden brown. Remove with a slotted spoon and drain on absorbent towels. Serve immediately or place on a baking sheet, uncovered, in a 200°F oven until ready to serve.

SHREDDED COOKED CHICKEN AND BROTH
To prepare cooked chicken, place a 3½-pound broiler-fryer in a pot with 1 coarsely chopped onion, 2 bay leaves, 3 cloves garlic, a cut-up carrot, and a cut-up celery stalk. Add water to barely cover and salt and pepper to season. Bring to a boil, skimming any foam that surfaces with a strainer. Lower the heat and simmer covered for 35 minutes. Cool. Shred the chicken; discard skin and bones. Makes about 3 cups shredded chicken and 4 cups broth.

SERVING SUGGESTION: This filling, when prepared correctly, is juicy and alive with flavor so it needs no additional dipping sauce. As an Argentine luncheon entree, serve with a pasta salad and an Ensalada de Palmito (Hearts of Palm Salad, page 19). Lemon tarts would make a light ending to this simple and elegant meal.

MAKES 6 CUPS OR ENOUGH FILLING FOR 3 DOZEN LUNCHEON EMPANADAS

CALDUDAS

JUICY BEEFSTEAK TURNOVERS

I consider caldudas, juicy steak turnovers, everyday street food. Although caldudas is slang for juicy, *this crisp thin pastry is the ideal envelope for that succulent steak and potato filling. Eat these fast to avoid spilling the juices!*

PABLO VALDES

STEAK AND POTATO FILLING

2 tablespoons vegetable oil

1 teaspoon paprika

1 ¼ pounds finely minced trimmed sirloin or rib-eye steak

½ teaspoon salt

½ teaspoon black pepper

1 medium onion, chopped fine (about 1 cup)

1 teaspoon pimentón picante (hot ground red pepper) or chile powder

½ teaspoon dried oregano leaves

½ cup beef stock

2 tablespoons Madeira (optional)

1 medium potato, boiled, peeled, and diced (about 1 cup)

⅓ cup raisins

15 black or green olives

3 hard-cooked eggs, sliced into 18 wedges

DOUGH

4 cups all-purpose flour

1 teaspoon salt

3 egg yolks

12 tablespoons (1 ½ sticks) butter or lard, melted

1 ⅓ cups water

3 tablespoons white wine vinegar

1 egg beaten with 2 tablespoons milk

1. *Preparing filling:* In a frying pan, warm the oil and paprika over medium heat. Stir in the meat seasoned with salt and pepper and fry until the meat is seared. Add the onion and sauté until soft. Stir in the chile powder, oregano, beef stock, Madeira if desired, potato, raisins, and olives. Continue cooking, stirring occasionally, until the flavors combine, about 5 minutes. Do not overcook the meat. Makes 3 ½ cups.

2. *Mixing dough:* Stir the flour and salt into a large bowl. Make a well in the center of the flour; place the yolks and melted butter in the well and

mix gently with your hands until blended. Slowly add water and vinegar, blending until dough is soft and sticky. Knead the dough gently by folding in half, patting down, and folding again. The dough is ready once the mixture no longer sticks to the hands but leaves them clean.

3. *Forming and filling empanadas:* Divide the dough into 18 even pieces. Using the palms of your hands, flatten each piece into a disc; roll out with a rolling pin to make a 5-inch circle about $1/4$ inch thick, using extra flour on the hands and rolling pin to prevent sticking (or, using a medium bowl, press down to cut out a perfect 5-inch circle). Spoon 2 to 3 tablespoons of filling on one side of the circle; add a slice of egg. Fold the dough over; crimp the edges with a fork, making sure to apply enough pressure to seal. Brush each empanada with a glaze made by beating egg with milk. Arrange on a baking sheet and bake in a 400°F oven 20 to 25 minutes, until lightly brown.

SERVING SUGGESTION: Although empanadas are enjoyed as a snack throughout Latin America, these hearty steak and potato turnovers are a satisfying first course to a grilled or roasted seafood meal such as Corvina con Acelgas y Frijoles Blancos (Roasted Sea Bass with Swiss Chard and White Beans, page 78) followed by an Ensalada César (Caesar Salad, page 22).

MAKES 18 SERVINGS (PORTION SIZE: 1 EMPANADA)

This Creole-style filling with its olives, raisins, and ají (chile) is called a *pine*, a savory-sweet ground or chopped meat filling. In this version any tender cut of meat with a good amount of marbling can be minced and quickly seared. If you are adventurous, omit the potato or reduce the amount for a more authentic juicy filling.

Tortilla Española de Papa con Alioli

SPANISH POTATO OMELET WITH GARLIC MAYONNAISE

If you enjoy pan-fried potatoes and onions, you will love this typical Spanish tortilla, or omelet. Don't be fooled by its simple list of ingredients—the artful preparation of an authentic tortilla requires quite a bit of skill.

½ cup virgin olive oil
½ cup canola oil
5 large potatoes, peeled and cut into
  ¼-inch slices
1 tablespoon salt
1 large white onion, sliced thin (about
  1½ cups)

5 large cloves garlic, minced
6 large eggs
Salt and pepper
Alioli (Garlic Mayonnaise) (see page
  37)

1. *Cooking potatoes:* Warm the olive and canola oil in a 9- or 10-inch non-stick skillet over medium heat. Add the potato slices ½ cup at a time, sprinkling with salt and coating with oil before the next addition. Stir the onion and garlic into the potato, mixing well. Cook covered over medium heat, turning potatoes occasionally, until they are tender. Do not brown or burn.

2. *Preparing egg and potato mixture:* While the potatoes are cooking, beat the eggs in a large bowl until foamy. Season to taste with salt and pepper; set aside. Once the potatoes have cooked, pour them into a colander to drain, reserving about ⅓ cup of oil. Place the potatoes in a large bowl and gently stir in the beaten eggs until mixed. Let the mixture rest 10 minutes.

3. *Frying:* Heat the reserved oil over medium high heat in the same skillet used to fry potatoes. When the oil is very hot, pour in the potato mixture. Lower the heat to medium and shake the pan often to prevent sticking. When the potatoes begin to brown underneath, invert a plate of the same size over the skillet. Flip the omelet onto the plate; add another 2 tablespoons of oil to the skillet, warm the oil over medium high heat, then slide the tortilla back into the skillet. Lower the heat and continue cooking

about 5 minutes, or until eggs have completely set. Transfer to a platter and serve hot or at room temperature.

ALIOLI (Garlic Mayonnaise)

To prepare alioli, purée 15 cloves crushed garlic, 2 egg yolks, $1/2$ teaspoon salt, and 2 tablespoons lemon juice in a blender. While the blender is running, slowly pour in $1/4$ cup olive oil until the mixture is creamy and thick (about 3 minutes). Continue to slowly pour an additional 1 cup oil (about 5 minutes). Refrigerate.

SERVING SUGGESTION: Top the tortilla with a generous dollop of alioli and sprinkle with parsley and diced pimiento. Serve at a party buffet, allowing each guest to slice his or her own wedge.

MAKES ONE 9-INCH TORTILLA

Although the Spanish tortilla is simply a potato omelet, preparation of this 2-inch-thick omelet requires patience. It's worth the investment in a few nonstick skillets. Once you've mastered the technique you'll flip the tortilla from one skillet into the next!

Huevos Revueltos con Nopalitos

BREAKFAST / MEXICO

SCRAMBLED EGGS WITH CACTUS

4 eggs
1 tablespoon milk
1/4 teaspoon salt (if using fresh nopales)
1/4 teaspoon ground black pepper
2 tablespoons butter
3 slices onion, separated into rings

1/2 cup bottled nopales (cactus), rinsed, drained, and cut into 1-inch strips, or fresh cooked (see below)
1/4 cup shredded longhorn Cheddar cheese
Corn or flour tortillas
Hot sauce

1. In a small bowl, beat the eggs lightly with the milk, salt, and pepper.

2. Melt the butter over medium low heat in a heavy skillet. Add the onion and fry gently without browning for about 1 minute. Stir in the nopales and continue cooking until heated through, about 2 minutes.

3. Pour the beaten eggs into the skillet and cook, turning the mixture over gently, until the eggs are just set and still moist (not dry)—about 4 minutes. Immediately turn onto a platter, garnish with the shredded cheese, and serve with warmed tortillas accompanied by hot sauce.

SERVING SUGGESTION: Begin your almuerzo with a platter of fresh fruit sprinkled with lime juice. Serve the eggs and tortillas with frijoles refritos (refried beans), followed by coffee and a pan dulce (sweet bread).

TO CLEAN AND BLANCH FRESH NOPALES
Select firm thin paddles (about 1/4 inch thick). Use a pair of tongs and a paring knife to carefully cut off the tiny thorns. Remove the thick base and discard. Rinse and cut into 1-inch-long strips. Place in rapidly boiling water with a few sterilized copper pennies or green onions to help eliminate the viscous juices and a pinch of baking soda to preserve the color. Blanch just until tender—about 5 minutes. Rinse several times in cold water to remove their viscous juices. Refrigerate until ready to use.

MAKES 2 SERVINGS

Arepas de Huevo

CORN GRIDDLE CAKES WITH EGG

For the Christmas holiday, my family would often travel to the coastal city of Cartagena and stay in a beachside cabin. Each morning we would enjoy these arepas de huevo, along with sorbete, a frothy fruit and milk beverage, or a jugo, a refreshing fruit and water beverage. We especially loved selecting our fruit for the morning drink from the assortment in the ollas (clay pots) balanced on the heads of the vendors passing by.

PATRICIA CIFUENTES

2 cups harina Pan (precooked white cornmeal) (see page 3)
1 cup all-purpose flour
1 cup cornmeal
1 tablespoon sugar
1 teaspoon salt

1 cup grated sharp Cheddar cheese (about ¼ pound)
Vegetable oil for frying
8 eggs
8 teaspoons salted water

1. *Preparing dough:* In a medium bowl, mix together the harina Pan, all-purpose flour, cornmeal, sugar, and salt. Stir the cheese and 2 cups of water into the flour mixture. Gently knead to form a dough. Add a little more water, if necessary. On a floured board, turn out the dough. Continue to knead until soft and pliable. Cover and let rest 20 minutes.

2. *Forming and frying arepas:* Divide the dough into 10 equal-sized balls. On top of a damp kitchen towel, flatten each ball to the shape and size of a fat English muffin (about 3 inches across and ½ inch thick). Heat 3 inches of oil in a pot, wok, or deep fryer to a temperature of 380°F. Fry the arepas one by one for 3 minutes, reserving the last 2 arepas. As they are cooked, remove them from the oil and drain.

3. *Stuffing and frying:* Using a small knife, make a slit on one side of an arepa. Gently squeeze to open further. Slip 1 raw egg and 1 teaspoon of salted water into the arepa. Using some of the dough from the last 2 arepas, seal the slit. Return the arepas to the hot oil and fry until golden.

MAKES 8 SERVINGS (PORTION SIZE: 1 AREPA)

Chiles Rellenos de Queso

CHEESE-STUFFED CHILES IN TOMATO SAUCE

I consider my mother an artist in the kitchen. Cooking was her way of expressing herself as an individual and a way of expressing her feeling beyond words as a caring mother and wife. While I was living in Brazil, she would send me a care package with all the Mexican ingredients I would be craving. My new friends had opened their arms, homes, and kitchens to make me feel welcome. I knew of no better way to return the gesture than with the time and patience it took in preparing this favorite family recipe. The aroma alone of the toasting chiles enticed my friends and even drew strangers into the kitchen from the street. My friends immediately understood the symbolism of receiving a gift of well-prepared food.

MARIA L. GUTIÉRREZ

CHILES
6 fresh poblano or pasilla chiles
8 ounces Monterey Jack cheese, cut
   into 6 thick rectangles
⅓ cup all-purpose flour

4 egg yolks
4 egg whites
Vegetable oil for frying

TOMATO SAUCE
2 pounds (about 14) ripe plum
   tomatoes
1 white onion, chopped coarse
2 cloves garlic, minced
¼ cup vegetable oil
1 cup water

1 chicken bouillon cube
2 bay leaves
½ teaspoon salt
½ teaspoon ground black pepper
½ teaspoon dried oregano leaves
   (optional)

1. *Roasting, peeling, and stuffing chiles:* To remove the skins, first blister the chiles over a fired grill or place directly on a heated griddle, turning frequently with tongs. When the skins are charred, blistered, and somewhat blackened, remove from the griddle. (Take care not to burn them through to the flesh.) Immediately place the roasted chiles in a plastic bag; close the bag and cover it with a damp cloth. Repeat the process until all 6 chiles are roasted. After the chiles have steamed 20 minutes, peel off the skin under cold running water, being careful not to tear the chile. With

a small sharp knife, make a 3-inch slit on one side of each chile. Gently remove the seeds and veins under running water. Carefully insert cheese into the chiles. Dust chiles with ¼ cup of the flour until well coated.

2. *Preparing batter:* In a small bowl, beat the egg yolks to a lemon-yellow color. In a separate bowl, beat the egg whites until they form soft peaks (do not overbeat). Sprinkle the remaining 3 tablespoons of flour over the beaten whites; add the yolks and gently fold together until blended.

3. *Frying chiles:* In a large skillet, heat ¼ inch oil over medium high heat. Gently place one chile at a time into the egg mixture to coat. With a large slotted spoon, carefully place the chile in the hot oil. Fry until golden brown, turning once. Drain on paper towels.

4. *Preparing sauce:* To roast tomatoes, heat a greased or seasoned griddle over medium high heat. Place tomatoes on griddle and cook about 2 minutes, or until peel has charred and blackened. Continue cooking and turning until tomato is evenly charred and softened; remove from griddle and proceed with recipe. In a blender container, purée the tomatoes, onion, and garlic. In a large skillet, heat the oil over medium high heat. Stir in the blended tomato purée, cooking until the purée changes to a brighter red-orange color. Add the water, bouillon cube, bay leaves, salt, black pepper, and oregano if desired. Bring to a boil; reduce the heat. Simmer uncovered 5 to 10 minutes, until reduced but not thickened. Remove the bay leaves. *(At this point the chiles and broth can be stored in the refrigerator for up to 5 days before using.)*

5. *Serving:* Add the fried chiles to the simmering tomato broth; continue to cook until the chiles are heated through. To serve, place a fried chile onto 6 individual plates and cover with sauce.

MAKES 6 SERVINGS (PORTION SIZE: 1 CHILE WITH ½ CUP BROTH)

These traditional chiles rellenos are lightly battered and fried. Too much egg white batter holds in the oil and masks the flavor of the cheese and chile. Ideally, the batter should be the consistency of scrambled eggs.

CHILES RELLENOS DULCES DE NUEVO MEXICO

CHRISTMAS / NEW MEXICO

SWEET NEW MEXICAN CHILES RELLENOS

These New Mexican–style "chiles rellenos"—spicy fritters rather than the traditional stuffed chiles—were synonymous with Thanksgiving or Christmas in the Benavides household. The ritual would begin with my mother and grandmother getting together each year to make this time-consuming recipe and ended with the entire family savoring each and every delicious bite. Made with stewed tongue meat that is ground with roasted green chiles, allspice, and sugar, these delicacies are battered and fried to look like chiles rellenos. It is not uncommon to add raisins, cinnamon, and pine nuts and use the stuffing to fill sweet empanadas (turnovers).

TERESA M. BENAVIDES

1 beef tongue (about 3 pounds)
2 bay leaves
Salt
2 cups roasted, peeled, and chopped green chiles (between 12 and 18 chiles depending on size)

½ cup sugar
2 teaspoons ground allspice
8 eggs, separated
2 tablespoons flour, plus additional for dusting
Oil for deep frying

1. *Stewing tongue:* In a pot, combine the tongue with 12 cups of water, the bay leaves, and 1 tablespoon of salt. Bring to a boil; lower the heat, skim off foam, and simmer 2½ hours, or until tender. Cool; reserve broth. Skin and trim the tongue, cutting away the root, small bones, and gristle. Cut the meat into 1-inch pieces and finely shred or grind in a meat grinder or food processor.

2. *Preparing filling:* In a bowl, combine the shredded tongue, chopped green chiles, sugar, allspice, and 2 teaspoons of salt; thoroughly mix, adding reserved tongue broth to moisten if necessary. Form into 2-inch-long by ½-inch-wide "cigars." Set aside.

3. *Mixing batter:* In a separate bowl, beat the egg yolks until creamy. In another bowl, beat egg whites to the soft peak stage; fold in the beaten yolks and 2 tablespoons of flour.

4. *Frying:* In a deep skillet or fryer, heat 3 inches of oil to 375°F. Dust each cigar-shaped relleno with flour, pass through the egg batter, and gently drop into hot oil. Fry a few at a time, turning once, until golden brown. Remove the rellenos with a slotted spoon and drain on absorbent towels. Keep warm.

VARIATION

Grind 2 cooked and peeled beef tongues with 2 cups sugar, 1 teaspoon salt, 2 teaspoons ground cinnamon, 1 teaspoon ground allspice, 1 table-spoon vanilla extract, 1 cup raisins, and 1½ cups toasted pine nuts. Stir in 2 cups roasted, peeled, and chopped green chiles, adding enough re-served tongue broth to moisten. Let mixture marinate 2 hours before using to prepare Sweet New Mexican Chiles Rellenos or empanaditas (little turnovers).

SERVING SUGGESTION: Serve these fritters as part of a Santa Fe Christmas buffet along with Empanaditas Santa Fe (Santa Fe Mincemeat Turnovers, page 172), bizcochitos (anise cookies), Tamales Rojos (Red Chile and Pork Tamales, page 128) and Pozole (Pork, Chicken, and Hominy Soup with Red Chile, page 100) during the "Las Candelarias" Christmas festivities.

MAKES 30 SERVINGS (PORTION SIZE: 1 SWEET RELLENO)

> From the luminarias—beautiful lanterns made by placing a candle in a paper bag anchored with a layer of desert sand—to the posadas pageant when family and friends roam from home to home singing carols and feasting on traditional foods, a Southwestern Christmas is not to be forgotten.

CHAPTER TWO

PLATILLOS FUERTES: AVES, CARNES, MARISCOS, Y PESCADOS

MAIN DISHES: POULTRY, MEATS, AND SEAFOOD

*F*rom chicken to seafood, the recipes in this chapter provide a cross section of celebration dishes and cooking methods throughout the Americas.

Domestically raised poultry, whether chicken in Mexico or turkey in Central America, tends to be served at informal family celebrations, whereas game birds, especially duck, squab, quail, and wild turkey as well as rabbit, common features of the Latin landscape, are hunted enthusiastically and prepared for small, intimate gatherings. And as in Spain, a marinated stuffed turkey is the hallmark of Christmas dinner.

GALLINA EN FRICASÉ
FAMILY GET-TOGETHERS / PUERTO RICO

CHICKEN FRICASSEE

This recipe represents my mother and her very special way of adding a magical flavor to everything she cooks. As often as I prepare Gallina en Fricasé for our family dinners, my son reminds me that it's not quite like Grandma's. She doesn't use measurements, but there is a certain rhythmic precision to her preparation of this traditional Puerto Rican fare. Family get-togethers, whether at a simple weekday dinner or at a festive holiday table, give me the opportunity to share our rich cultural heritage with my children just as my mom shared it with hers.

FRANCES FLORES PELL

1 broiler/fryer, about 2½ to 3 pounds, cut into serving pieces
2 cloves garlic, crushed or passed through a press
1 teaspoon salt
1 teaspoon ground black pepper
1½ teaspoons dried oregano leaves
2 tablespoons vegetable oil
1 medium onion, cut into ½-inch strips
2 cups (16-ounce can) tomato sauce

½ cup red or white wine or water
½ teaspoon dried mustard
1 tablespoon white wine vinegar
3 tablespoons dark brown sugar
1 tablespoon Worcestershire sauce
½ cup chopped pimientos morrones (roasted red peppers) (optional)
¾ cup frozen green peas (optional)
Cooked white rice

(continued on next page)

1. *Seasoning chicken:* Rinse the chicken under cold running water; pat dry with paper towels. Rub the chicken pieces with crushed garlic; sprinkle with salt, pepper, and oregano.

2. *Frying chicken:* Heat the oil in a large skillet or dutch oven. Pan-fry the chicken over medium heat, turning occasionally, until golden brown. Remove the chicken to a platter; cover and keep warm.

3. *Simmering fricasé:* Add the onion to the skillet; sauté until soft, stirring to loosen the browned bits stuck to the bottom of the pan. Stir in the tomato sauce, wine, mustard, vinegar, brown sugar, and Worcestershire sauce. Return the fried chicken to the skillet. Bring the sauce to a boil, lower the heat, and simmer covered about 40 minutes. Ten minutes before serving, add the pimientos and peas, if desired.

SERVING SUGGESTION: Accompany Gallina en Fricasé with steamed white rice. Arrange the chicken on a serving plate and ladle the sauce over. Round out the meal with Ensalada de Aguacate y Tomate (Avocado and Tomato Salad, page 16).

MAKES 4 SERVINGS (PORTION SIZE: 2 PIECES CHICKEN AND $^1/_2$ CUP SAUCE)

Gallina en Fricasé is a classic Puerto Rican chicken stew eaten at informal yet hearty family meals. This island adaptation of the classic French fricassee varies widely from family to family. Based on the occasion or family preference, Gallina en Fricasé can be saucy or chunky, flavored with wine or water. Ingredients can include green bell pepper, potatoes, mushrooms, olives, capers, and even dried prunes.

MOLE RANCHERO

CHICKEN IN A RED COUNTRY-STYLE MOLE SAUCE

This recipe is from Las Moras, a little ranch in Mexico. I can still picture my father, using a pair of horses to pull the plow and plant the corn which my mother would then cook on a chiminea (adobe stove) using logs to make the fire. This recipe, passed down from generation to generation, would be prepared on very special occasions. Whenever I make this special recipe it brings back warm memories of my family and the hard, but happy times.

VICTORIA CÁZARES

CHICKEN AND BROTH

1 broiler/fryer chicken, cut into serving pieces, or 6 legs and thighs (hind-quarters) (about 3½ to 4 pounds)
1 teaspoon salt

1 small onion, halved
2 cloves garlic, peeled
1 extra-large chicken bouillon cube

MOLE SAUCE

¼ pound dried California red chile peppers (about 6)
½ avocado pit
1 medium white onion, peeled and sliced 1 inch thick
3 large cloves garlic
⅓ cup sesame seeds
⅓ cup vegetable oil
5 saltine crackers

2 fresh bay leaves (or 3 dried)
5 whole black peppercorns
3 whole cloves
1 tablet (about 2 ounces) Mexican chocolate
3½ to 4½ cups well-seasoned chicken broth, heated
Sesame seeds and cilantro sprigs to garnish

1. *Preparing chicken and broth:* Rinse the chicken under cold running water. Bring 8 cups of water and the salt to a boil in a pot with the onion halves, garlic, and bouillon. Add the chicken and return to a boil, skimming off the foam that rises to the surface. Lower the heat and simmer, partially covered, 25 minutes, until the chicken is just cooked. Set aside.

2. *Toasting ingredients:* Heat a greased griddle or cast-iron skillet over medium heat until hot. Place the chiles on the griddle and toast, pressing

(continued on next page)

them down with a kitchen towel or spatula. Remove the chiles from the griddle when they have changed color (do not permit them to blacken). Set aside. Place the avocado pit, onion slices, and garlic cloves on the griddle. Toast, turning occasionally, until speckled brown; remove from the griddle. Using a spatula, clean the griddle by scraping off any burnt particles. Place the sesame seeds on the griddle over low heat and stir constantly until golden brown. Remove to a plate immediately.

3. *Frying ingredients:* On the same griddle or skillet, heat 2 to 3 table-spoons of the oil over medium high heat. Pan-fry the crackers and bay leaves until lightly browned; remove to the plate. Add the peppercorns and cloves and continue frying for 1 minute, being careful not to burn.

4. *Preparing mole paste:* Pass the chocolate tablet with the toasted and fried ingredients (chile, avocado pit, onion slices, garlic, crackers, bay leaves, peppercorns, and cloves) through a meat grinder; place in a bowl. Stir in 1½ cups of the warm chicken broth until ingredients have dissolved. *If a meat grinder is unavailable, pulverize the chocolate, avocado pit, bay leaves, peppercorns, and cloves in a spice grinder. Place the pulverized ingredients in a food processor bowl or blender with the chiles, onion, garlic, crackers, and 1½ cups of warm chicken broth; purée until smooth and velvety.*

5. *Preparing mole sauce:* In a pot, warm the remaining 3 tablespoons of oil over medium high heat. Pour in the mole paste and fry for a few minutes, stirring constantly. Stir the remaining broth into the mole, stirring until well blended. Bring to a boil; lower the heat to medium low and cook, partially covered, 5 minutes. Season to taste. The sauce should be the consistency of heavy cream. To thin, stir in additional broth.

6. *Serving:* Place the chicken pieces in the mole sauce. Cook over medium low heat until heated through, about 10 to 15 minutes. Arrange chicken pieces on each plate. Pour sauce over chicken and lightly sprinkle with sesame seeds. Garnish with cilantro sprigs.

SERVING SUGGESTION: Serve Mole Ranchero with Sopa de Arroz (Mexican Rice, page 145), Frijoles de la Olla (Pinto Beans "From the Pot," page 154), corn tortillas, and a salad of your choice.

MAKES 6 SERVINGS (PORTION SIZE: 1 CHICKEN QUARTER AND ABOUT 1 CUP SAUCE)

Manchamanteles

CHICKEN STEWED IN FRUIT AND RED CHILE

Chicken

1 broiler/fryer (3 ½ to 4 pounds), cut into serving pieces, plus 4 chicken breast halves

1 onion, halved
2 bay leaves
Salt and ground black pepper to taste

Fruit and Red Chile Sauce

5 ancho chiles, stemmed (see Notes)
3 pasilla chiles, stemmed, or chiles chipotle
4 tablespoons lard or vegetable oil
1 slice bolillo (Mexican roll) or French bread
½ cup blanched almonds
2 cinnamon sticks
3 cloves garlic, peeled and left whole
1 cup (8-ounce can) tomato sauce
2 to 3 bolitas de chorizo (segments of Mexican sausage), casings removed (about ½ cup)

2 medium onions, diced (2 cups)
5 to 6 cups well-seasoned chicken broth
5 fresh *sweet* pineapple slices, about 1 inch thick, cut into chunks, or 1 (15-ounce) can crushed pineapple with syrup
4 small Pippin apples, cored, peeled, and sliced
2 bananas, peeled and sliced
10 pickled serrano chiles
3 tablespoons vinegar
1 teaspoon salt

1. *Cooking chicken:* Place the chicken in a pot with water to barely cover. Add the onion halves, bay leaves, and salt and pepper. Bring to a boil, skimming off any foam that surfaces with a strainer. Lower the heat and simmer covered for 30 minutes. Let the chicken cool in its own broth.

2. *Toasting sauce ingredients:* Heat a cast-iron skillet over medium heat until very hot. Place the chiles on the griddle and toast, pressing down with a kitchen towel or spatula. Remove the chiles from the griddle when they have changed color (do not allow to blacken). Set aside.

3. *Frying:* In a dutch oven, melt 2 tablespoons of the lard over medium heat. Fry the bread, turning once, until toasted; remove from the skillet

(continued on next page)

and set aside. Fry the almonds, cinnamon, and garlic until completely golden or toasted. Remove from the skillet. Fry the tomato sauce for 2 minutes, stirring, to dissolve browned bits on skillet bottom.

4. *Puréeing ingredients:* Place the toasted and fried ingredients (chiles, bread, almonds, cinnamon, garlic, and tomato sauce) in a meat grinder or a food processor and purée until smooth and thick. Set aside.

5. *Preparing sauce:* In the same pot used for frying the bread, fry the chorizo in the remaining 2 tablespoons of lard over medium heat, stirring to break up the chorizo into bite-sized pieces and to color the lard. Using a slotted spoon, lift out the chorizo and set aside. Sauté the onions in the same skillet as the chorizo, stirring until soft and yellow. Add the puréed mixture to the skillet and continue frying until thick. Stir in the broth, pineapple, apples, bananas, chiles, vinegar, and salt. Bring to a boil; lower the heat and simmer covered 1 hour, or until the fruits have disintegrated. (Add additional hot chicken broth during the cooking process if necessary.) Taste for seasoning, adding sugar or additional vinegar if necessary.

6. *Finishing:* Place the chicken and cooked chorizo pieces in the sauce. Cook over medium low heat uncovered until the chicken is heated through and the sauce is the desired consistency. Serve immediately.

NOTES: Chile ancho means "broad or wide" chile which refers to its large triangular shape. It is used in sauces for its flavor (semi-hot) and color. Look for a dried brick-red chile with wrinkled skin. . . . The term chile pasilla can refer to many varieties of chiles from the fresh green pasilla chile grown in California (called poblano in Mexico) to the dried long light red chile chilaca or the very hot smoked chile.

SERVING SUGGESTION: Serve Manchamanteles on a large platter garnished with Plátanos Maduros Fritos (Fried Sweet Plantains, page 168) and pineapple slices. Baked sweet potatoes, steamed white rice, and corn tortillas would nicely complement the sweet-tart succulent flavors of the manchamanteles sauce.

MAKES 6 SERVINGS (PORTION SIZE: 2 CHICKEN PIECES AND 1 CUP SAUCE)

GUINEO ASADO CON JUGO DE LIMÓN Y PIMIENTA NEGRA

OUTDOOR GRILL / MEXICO

ROASTED QUAIL WITH LEMON PEPPER SAUCE

I have many fond childhood memories of summers spent with my grandparents, uncles, aunts, and cousins on our family ranch in Baja California. I remember late afternoon meals of quail and rabbits which my uncles would hunt in the open range. We would use green tree branches and skewer three or four quail on each branch. Then we would all sit around an open fire, roasting our quail. Looking back, I didn't have a clue about the incredible gourmet feasts we enjoyed as part of our Baja lifestyle.

LAURA VALVERDE SANCHEZ

8 wild quail, cleaned
8 cloves garlic, flattened
16 sprigs fresh thyme
16 sprigs fresh marjoram
8 fresh bay leaves
8 teaspoons olive oil
Salt and ground black pepper to taste

2 cups fresh-squeezed lemon juice
2 tablespoons freshly ground black pepper
Minced cilantro leaves
Whole radishes, cleaned
Minced white onion
Minced serrano chiles

1. *Preparing quail:* Stuff each quail with 1 clove of garlic, 2 sprigs each of fresh thyme and marjoram, 1 fresh bay leaf, and 1 teaspoon of olive oil. Rub salt and pepper into quail skin; refrigerate until ready to cook.

2. *Grilling:* Place quail on an oiled grill 8 inches above red hot mesquite. Grill 8 minutes, turn, and continue grilling until cooked through.

3. *Serving:* While the quail is cooking, combine the lemon juice and black pepper in a small saucepan. Quickly bring to a simmer and remove from the heat. Place the quail on a shallow serving platter and sprinkle with cilantro leaves and garnish with radishes. Serve with lemon pepper sauce and offer small bowls of minced onion and minced serrano chiles.

N O T E : If possible, ask your butcher for fresh bone-in quail, which has a sweeter meat than the boned or frozen varieties.

MAKES 4 SERVINGS (PORTION SIZE: 2 QUAIL)

FRICASÉ DE GUINEO

GUINEA FOWL FRICASSEE

When I cook this dish and smell the aromas, I am filled with memories of my mother and grandmother in the kitchen back in Cuba. Every time I make Fricasé de Guineo I cry, remembering those days now long gone; that's probably why my son calls this "the crying fricassee." He loves the dish, and when we eat it, he tells me he pictures my story in his mind.

ESTRELLA CRUZ GALLEGO DE VALDES AND FRANK CAIRO

1 guinea fowl, cut into 4 serving pieces, or 4 quail, whole or halved

Salt and black pepper to taste

6 cloves garlic, minced

1 teaspoon adobo seasoning (see Note)

1 cup jugo de naranja ágria (sour orange juice), or a 50-50 mixture of orange and lime juices

1/4 cup olive oil

1 large onion, sliced thin

4 red potatoes, peeled and sliced thin (about 1 1/2 cups)

2 cups good-quality red wine

1/2 cup raisins

1. *Preparing guinea fowl:* Rinse the meat and pat dry. Place in a glass bowl and season with salt and pepper, garlic, and adobo. Pour juice over the meat; cover and refrigerate for about 3 hours. Drain, reserving the marinade.

2. *Sautéing:* Heat the oil in a large skillet over medium high heat. Sauté the onion rings until soft; remove from the skillet. Fry the meat in the same oil, turning until golden, about 5 minutes per side. Place the onions over the meat and pour in the reserved marinade. Bring to a quick boil, lower the heat, cover, and vigorously simmer for 5 minutes.

3. *Finishing:* Stir in the potatoes, wine, and raisins. Cover and simmer 25 minutes, stirring occasionally, until the meat is tender. Immediately remove from heat.

NOTE: Adobo is a seasoning mix of salt, black pepper, oregano, and garlic.

MAKES 4 SERVINGS (PORTION SIZE: 1/4 FOWL AND SAUCE)

PATO A LA CONI

CELEBRATION / CUBA

DUCK À LA CONI

Whenever my day is filled with memories of Cuba, I think immediately of Uncle Bebe (Cuban for "Baby"; my grandparents disliked "Junior"), who took me duck hunting at the early age of six. Our beloved cook Masita's preparation of the ducks we brought home ignited my love for this delicacy.

CONSUELO GUERRA OLIVER DE MARTINEZ

1 (3- to 4-pound) duck, cut up
1 cup fresh jugo de naranja ágria
   (sour orange juice), or a 50-50 mixture of orange and lime juices
1 cup white wine
3 tablespoons olive oil
4 cloves garlic, minced
1 large onion, sliced
1 green bell pepper, sliced thin

1 yellow or red bell pepper, sliced thin
3 tomatoes, diced
2 bay leaves
½ cup canned tomato-vegetable juice
20 pimiento-stuffed green olives
12 small pitted black olives
1 tablespoon chopped parsley
½ teaspoon ground black pepper
½ teaspoon salt

1. *Marinating:* In a nonreactive bowl, combine the duck, orange juice, and white wine. Cover and refrigerate for 1 hour, turning once. Remove from the marinade and pat dry. Reserve the marinade for the sauce.

2. *Sautéing and searing duck:* Heat the oil in a deep skillet over medium high heat. Fry the duck until browned, turning as needed. Add the garlic, onion, peppers, tomatoes, and bay leaves and sauté 2 minutes.

3. *Cooking:* Stir the reserved marinade and tomato juice into the skillet. Cook covered over medium low heat for 45 minutes. Remove the duck from the skillet; cover and keep warm. Stir in the olives, parsley, pepper, and salt. Cook uncovered for 10 minutes until the sauce has reduced. Adjust seasoning; return duck to skillet and cook until thoroughly heated.

SERVING SUGGESTION: Serve this exquisite dish with Cuban white rice and an asparagus salad with roasted red bell pepper. Also, a robust Spanish red wine accompanies this lovely dish splendidly.

MAKES 4 SERVINGS (PORTION SIZE: ¼ DUCK AND SAUCE)

Pavo Salvadoreño en Especias

SALVADORAN ROASTED SPICED TURKEY

☀ *I remember the scent of the spiced turkey roasting in our oven during the Christmas season. For Christmas or New Year's dinner our family would enjoy this traditional turkey accompanied by the spiced sauce, a lovely rice and asparagus dish, a green salad, and vegetables. The Salvadoran turkeys were always so flavorful and juicy, perhaps due to the constant basting!*

MARTA MONAHAN

TURKEY

1 fresh hen turkey (about 15 pounds)
½ pound (2 sticks) butter, softened
⅓ cup prepared mustard

⅛ cup cider vinegar
2 teaspoons salt
1 teaspoon dried thyme

RECADO (SEASONING)

1¼ cups sesame seeds
⅓ cup pepitoría (hulled pumpkin seeds)
3 dried chiles pasas or chiles pasillas, stems removed (see Note)
8 bay leaves
8 whole cloves

1 (2-inch) cinnamon stick
1½ teaspoons dried oregano leaves
1 teaspoon dried thyme
2 slices French bread
3 medium tomatoes
2 medium white onions, peeled
8 cloves garlic, peeled

1. *Preparing turkey:* Remove the giblets from the turkey cavity and set aside for another use. Rinse the bird under cold running water and pat dry. In a small bowl, mix the butter, mustard, vinegar, salt, and thyme to form a paste. Rub the turkey, inside and out, with the paste. Refrigerate covered until ready to use.

2. *Toasting ingredients:* Heat a lightly greased griddle over medium heat. Toast the sesame and pumpkin seeds, stirring frequently, being careful not to burn; place in a medium bowl. Toast the chiles pasas, bay leaves, cloves, cinnamon stick, oregano, and thyme, stirring until lightly colored and fragrant. As the ingredients are toasted, place in the bowl with the toasted seeds. Pour 3 cups of boiling water over the ingredients; cover and soak 15 minutes. In small batches, grind the toasted ingredients in a

blender container or in the workbowl of a food processor until completely smooth.

3. *Roasting ingredients:* Toast the bread until dry; crush into crumbs. You should have about ³/₄ cup. Place the tomatoes and onions on a heated griddle. Roast, turning as needed, until the tomatoes have blackened and the onions are lightly charred. In a blender container, purée the bread, tomatoes, onion, and garlic until smooth.

4. *Finishing recado sauce:* Stir the tomato purée into the toasted seed paste until blended. Combine with 3 quarts of water and mix. If the recado isn't completely smooth and satiny, strain through a wire mesh sieve.

5. *Roasting turkey:* Place the turkey in a roasting pan. Roast breast side up in a preheated 375°F oven for 20 minutes. Turn breast side down and continue roasting for 15 minutes. Pour the recado sauce over the turkey. Continue roasting at 350°F for about 3¹/₂ hours, basting often, until completely cooked. Carve turkey and serve with plenty of sauce.

NOTE: Chile pasa is a dried, red Salvadoran chile pod similar to the Mexican pasilla chile.

SERVING SUGGESTION: For a Christmas buffet, serve the pavo en especias with its own sauce, accompanied by a rice and asparagus casserole and a watercress and pear salad. For vegetables, try sautéed acorn squash with red bell pepper and onion and steamed broccoli with walnut butter. A tropical fruit trifle (made with sponge cake, coconut pudding, and guava, mango, or pineapple purée) would be a spectacular ending.

MAKES 16 TO 18 SERVINGS (PORTION SIZE: 8 OUNCES)

> This turkey dish is not stuffed. The turkey is basted in a recado (sauce) of traditional Salvadoran spices and herbs. The turkey is cooked breast side down, and its juices mix with the recado, forming a lovely sauce which actually braises rather than roasts the bird. This cooking method produces a succulent holiday bird.

Pavo del Día de Acción de Gracias

THANKSGIVING DAY TURKEY

When they moved to this country from Mexico, our parents wanted us to take part in all the North American holidays, like Thanksgiving. My mom was grateful to receive her family's traditional recipe for el pavo navideño (Christmas turkey), which shortly became part of our Thanksgiving Day feast. My father was so proud to be able to raise his children to be North American citizens, yet at the same time he taught us Spanish, Mexican history and culture, and the universal value of decency. These are the things, along with this recipe, that I hope to pass along to my own daughter.

ISABEL SALINAS

TURKEY

1 fresh turkey hen (about 15 pounds)

8 tablespoons (1 stick) butter, softened

Salt and ground black pepper

1½ teaspoons grated nutmeg

8 cloves garlic, diced fine

1 liter (4 cups) port wine

STUFFING

1½ pounds ground pork

8 tablespoons (1 stick) butter

¾ cup chopped white onion

4 cloves garlic, minced

½ cup chopped green bell pepper

½ cup chopped red bell pepper

1½ cups chopped celery

1 (14½-ounce) can stewed tomatoes with juice, cut up

⅓ cup chopped parsley

1½ pounds pork butt, trimmed, cooked, and shredded (about 2 cups)

2 tablespoons sazonador Maggi's (seasoning sauce) (see Note)

1 teaspoon grated nutmeg

1 teaspoon ground cinnamon

Salt and ground black pepper to taste

½ cup raisins

½ cup small pimiento-stuffed green olives

2 Mexican or French rolls (each about 6 inches), toasted

3 cups port wine

1 cup chopped hazelnuts or walnuts

1 cup biznaga (cactus candy), diced, or diced cooked chestnuts

2 small green apples, stemmed

2 bay leaves

1. *Preparing and roasting turkey:* Remove the giblets and neck from the turkey cavity and set aside for another use. Rinse and thoroughly dry the turkey. Rub the skin with a paste made of the softened butter, salt, pepper, and nutmeg. Rub the body and neck cavities with the finely diced garlic. Place the turkey in a deep container and pour the port over it. Cover and refrigerate. Marinate for 24 hours, turning the bird occasionally. Discard the marinade before stuffing the turkey.

2. *Preparing stuffing:* In a saucepan, combine the ground pork with water to cover. Bring to a boil, lower the heat, and cook uncovered for 20 minutes, or until thoroughly cooked; drain. In a pot, melt the butter over medium high heat. Sauté the onion, garlic, bell pepper, and celery until soft. Add the tomatoes and parsley and cook about 10 minutes, stirring occasionally. Add the cooked ground pork, shredded cooked pork, seasoning sauce, nutmeg, cinnamon, salt, pepper, raisins, and olives. Stir until thoroughly mixed. Let the mixture cook, stirring occasionally, until the flavors have combined, about 20 minutes. Meanwhile, moisten the toasted rolls with 1 cup of the port. Stir the soaked rolls, hazelnuts, and biznaga into the meat mixture. Remove from the heat, let cool, and refrigerate until ready to use. Makes 2½ quarts.

3. *Stuffing and roasting turkey:* Stuff each turkey cavity—the neck and the body—with one apple and the meat stuffing; truss. Place the turkey in a roasting pan. Roast uncovered for 2 hours at 350°F, breast side down, basting occasionally with the pan juices. When the turkey is half-cooked, turn breast side up and pour 2 cups of the port into the roasting pan with 1 to 2 cups of water and the bay leaves. Cover lightly with foil and roast for an 2 additional hours, basting occasionally. When the turkey is cooked (approximately 20 minutes per pound cooking time), remove from the oven and let it rest 20 minutes before carving.

NOTE: Maggi's seasoning sauce is a very important condiment used in Mexico to flavor meats, sauces, marinades, and dressings. Known as Maggi's, this bottled condiment can be found in markets specializing in international products.

MAKES 12 SERVINGS (PORTION SIZE: 6 OUNCES TURKEY AND 1 CUP STUFFING)

In Latin countries which raise cattle, the preparation of beef dishes for special celebrations is a culinary art. Argentina, Uruguay, and Paraguay enjoy their asados or churrascos (meat grills), and in northern Mexico and the North American Southwest, marinated, grilled, or barbecued beef is the specialty.

Mutton, lamb, and goat all play a prominent role on the Latin American table, and are traditionally reserved for special occasions such as birthdays, weddings, or Sunday dinners. Pork is also extremely popular and cooked in every manner throughout the continent. A well-marinated and slow-roasted pork leg is the preferred meat for Christmas dinner, especially in the Caribbean, Venezuela, and Colombia.

PECETO ASADO CON TALLARINES
SUNDAY DINNER / ARGENTINA

OVEN-ROASTED EYE OF ROUND WITH FETTUCCINE

With eight children to care for, my mother pretty much disliked cooking. Yet she always managed to hire excellent cooks. (My sister and I used to play house in the kitchen, chopping parsley and carrots to keep ourselves occupied.) Sunday was a family day. After attending church we would come home to our special meal, such as this peceto asado, an eye-round roast cooked until tender with a tuco, an Argentine tomato sauce. The wonderful meat juices were poured over the homemade tallarines (fettuccine noodles).

MARIA TERESA ENDARA ALIAGA VIERCI

TUCO (TOMATO SAUCE)
1/3 cup vegetable oil
1 medium onion, chopped
1/2 green bell pepper, sliced into short
   strips
2 tomatoes, seeded and chopped
   (about 1 1/2 cups)

2 heaping tablespoons tomato purée
1 cup well-seasoned beef broth or
   puchero stock (see page 112)
1 fresh bay leaf or 2 dried
Salt

ROAST

1 beef eye round roast (about 4
  pounds)
4 cloves garlic, passed through a press
⅓ cup olive oil
1 teaspoon salt
1 teaspoon ground black pepper

1 tablespoon rosemary leaves, crushed
½ cup wine or water (optional)
8 servings cooked tallarines (fettuccine, linguine, or spaghettini),
  about 8 cups

1. *To prepare tuco (sauce):* Heat the oil in a medium skillet. Sauté the
onion over medium high heat until soft. Add the green pepper and continue sautéing for 1 minute. Stir in the tomatoes and cook uncovered
until the tomatoes release their juices. At this point, stir constantly until
the juices have evaporated. Add the tomato purée, beef broth, and bay
leaf. Bring to a boil; lower the heat and simmer for 10 minutes uncovered
to thicken slightly. Season to taste with salt.

2. *Marinating beef:* Trim any excess fat from the roast. In a mortar, mash
the garlic and mix with the oil, salt, pepper, and rosemary leaves, forming
a paste. Rub the paste into the roast; cover with plastic wrap and refrigerate overnight.

3. *Roasting:* Place the beef in a shallow roasting pan and roast uncovered
at 325°F for about 1 hour. Pour the tomato sauce over the roast, mixing
with the pan juices. Continue roasting about 1½ hours, or until cooked
to preference, basting the meat every 20 minutes, adding ½ cup wine or
water if the sauce becomes dry.

4. *Serving:* Remove the meat from the pan; slice according to preference.
Arrange the slices on individual plates. Serve the tuco (basting sauce) over
cooked tallarines (fettuccine).

SERVING SUGGESTION: Accompany the peceto asado with buttered peas and roasted onions and garlic. For dessert, offer Dulce de
Leche (Milk Caramel, page 191).

MAKES 8 SERVINGS (PORTION SIZE: 3 SLICES BEEF AND
SAUCE)

BIRRIA DE RES

STEWED BEEF IN A MILD CHILE BROTH

Whenever I make birria my thoughts take me back to my own wedding. In the state of Jalisco, Mexico, traditional dishes are almost as much a ritual as the wedding itself—and birria is no exception. In this wedding version, beef replaces the traditional goat or mutton and is simmered in a chile broth flavored with cactus paddles. The meat is then shredded and served in a special tomato and meat sauce. The unmistakable bold, hearty flavor of birria is certainly welcomed by wedding guests and signifies a family's pride in the new union by their sharing of this earthy, time-honored, family specialty.

MARIA YOLANDA PEREZ

BIRRIA

6 dried pasilla chiles, stemmed and seeded

3 large ripe tomatoes (about 1 pound), cut up

¼ cup white vinegar

10 large cloves garlic, peeled

1 tablespoon salt

1 teaspoon sesame seeds

1 teaspoon dried oregano leaves, crushed

¼ teaspoon ground cloves

¼ teaspoon ground cumin

¼ teaspoon ground black pepper

5 pounds boneless beef shoulder clod, cut into 1-inch chunks

12 to 15 bay leaves (fresh or dried)

3 pencas de nopal (cactus paddles), needles removed, sliced lengthwise

BIRRIA SAUCE

3 ripe tomatoes

6 dried árbol chiles, stemmed and lightly toasted (see Note)

3 cloves garlic, flattened and peeled

½ teaspoon dried oregano leaves

½ teaspoon salt

2 cups reserved birria cooking liquid

GARNISHES

Finely chopped white onion

Cilantro leaves

Lime wedges

Corn tortillas

1. *Preparing and puréeing ingredients:* In a small saucepan, combine the pasilla chiles, tomatoes, and 2 cups of water. Cook covered over medium

high heat for 10 minutes. Remove from the heat and let steep, covered, for 5 minutes. Drain, reserving the cooking liquid. In a blender container, combine the cooked pasilla chiles and tomatoes with the vinegar, garlic, salt, sesame seeds, oregano, cloves, cumin, and black pepper. Blend until smooth, adding up to $1/2$ cup of the reserved cooking liquid if necessary. Set aside.

2. *Cooking beef:* Place the beef in a large stockpot with 8 cups of water. Arrange the bay leaves over the meat. Pour in the blended chile mixture. (The beef should be barely covered; if it is not, add additional water.) Cover with the sliced cactus paddles, cut side down. Bring to a boil; lower the heat and cook uncovered over medium low heat for $1^3/4$ hours, or until the meat is tender. Remove the meat from the pot and cut or shred into $1^1/2$-inch pieces. Reserve at least 2 cups of the cooking liquid to prepare birria sauce. If desired, scrape cooked inner cactus from the paddles into a small bowl; cover and keep warm.

3. *Preparing birria sauce:* Combine 2 cups of water, the tomatoes and the árbol chiles in a saucepan. Bring to a boil; lower the heat and cook for 15 minutes uncovered. Let cool. Place the cooked tomatoes, árbol chiles, and their cooking liquid in a blender container with the garlic, oregano, and salt. Purée the mixture until it is velvety smooth. Pour the blender contents into the saucepan with the tomatoes. Stir in the reserved 2 cups of birria cooking liquid. Cook over medium heat, stirring occasionally, until warm.

4. *Serving:* Place portions of the meat in shallow soup bowls or rimmed plates. Ladle birria sauce over the meat and sprinkle with finely chopped white onion and cilantro. Place a lime wedge on each plate (squeeze lime juice over the meat if desired). Serve with cooked cactus and corn tortillas.

NOTE: Chiles de árbol are dried red chiles about 2 inches long and very hot.

SERVING SUGGESTION: Serve Birria de Res with the traditional accompaniments of Frijoles de la Olla (Pinto Beans "From the Pot," page 154) and Sopa de Arroz (Mexican Rice, page 145), flour tortillas, and tequila.

MAKES 8 TO 10 SERVINGS (PORTION SIZE: 5 OUNCES MEAT AND $1/2$ CUP SAUCE)

GUISO DE CHILE COLORADO

FAMILY GET-TOGETHERS / SOUTHWEST

NEW MEXICAN RED CHILE STEW

Late each summer, after chile harvest season, homes and roadside stands of New Mexico blossom with the state's most famous symbol—bright red chile ristras. As autumn changes to winter, home cooks pluck their ristras to prepare the traditional chile colorado—red chile stew. And there is nothing like a plate of rich chile colorado served with beans, rice, and flour tortillas to bring our family together.

MELANY SHEA

1 package (about 18) dried New Mexico red chiles
2 large cloves garlic
1 small white onion
Salt and ground black pepper

1 teaspoon all-purpose flour
2 pounds (about 6) bone-in pork chops
3 large russet potatoes, cut into ½-inch dice (about 2 cups)

1. *Soaking pods and seasoning chile purée:* Lightly rinse the chiles under running water. Wearing gloves, remove the seeds, stems, and veins (the more seeds and veins you leave in, the hotter the sauce will be). Place the chile pods in a pot and cover with boiling water. Cover and let the chiles soak until plump, about 20 minutes. Drain, reserving 2 cups of soaking liquid. In small batches, blend the softened chiles, garlic, onion, ½ teaspoon each of salt and pepper, and the flour until just smooth, using reserved liquid if necessary. Strain the chile purée through a wire mesh sieve and discard stray seeds and skin. Purée should be consistency of tomato paste.

2. *Frying and simmering meat:* Remove the pork meat from the bone; set the bones aside. Cut the meat into 1-inch pieces; season with salt and pepper. In a large skillet, fry the meat and bones in their own fat over medium heat. After the pork has browned, pour the chile purée into the skillet. Bring to a boil; add the potatoes. Lower the heat and simmer covered until the potatoes are tender, about 20 minutes. Season to taste with salt, pepper, or garlic.

MAKES 8 SERVINGS (PORTION SIZE: 1 CUP)

Fajitas

GRILLED SKIRT STEAK

Here is the story of fajitas as my father told it to me: Years ago, on the plains of what is now south Texas and northern Mexico, scrawny cattle had to exist on what little grass and water they could find. As a consequence, the meat from these range cattle was tough. The ranch owners would save the best cuts for the family, and the ranch hands were often given the less desirable cuts, like the fajita, or skirt steak. The ranch hands would butterfly, season, and marinate the meat briefly in lime juice to tenderize it. They would then grill the steaks over an open fire of mesquite wood, which was plentiful in these areas. In the 1960s and '70s, word of the ranch hands' ingenuity spread from the border towns of Laredo and Brownsville to the bigger cities of San Antonio and Houston. Before you knew it, fajitas had become a craze.

SYLVAN RODRIGUEZ

2 tablespoons seasoned meat tenderizer

1 tablespoon ground black pepper

1 tablespoon salt

3 pounds fajitas (skirt steaks), trimmed and butterflied open 3/8 inch

6 large cloves garlic, passed through a press

Juice of 3 limes (about 1/3 cup)

1/4 cup teriyaki sauce

1 dozen small flour tortillas

1. *Seasoning fajitas:* In a small bowl, combine the tenderizer, black pepper, and salt. Place one layer of steaks flat in a glass dish and rub the garlic into the meat (2 cloves per 1 pound of meat). Generously sprinkle with the seasoning mixture followed by the lime juice. Continue the process with the remaining steaks. Cover and marinate for 2 hours in the refrigerator. Add the teriyaki sauce, mix well, and marinate 1 additional hour. (If fajitas are marinated too long, they take on a sour flavor from the lime juice.)

2. *Grilling:* Grill the meat at least 4 inches above red hot mesquite for about 4 minutes, basting often with the marinade. Turn the meat and grill for an additional 2 minutes. *Be careful not to allow the sugar in the teriyaki sauce to burn.* Slice the meat against the grain and serve with heated flour tortillas.

MAKES 6 SERVINGS (PORTION SIZE: 2 FAJITAS)

CARNE PUYADA

VEGETABLE-STUFFED BEEF POT ROAST

Special occasions call for this recipe, which takes me back to my home in Colombia. My grandmother Istemenia taught me how to make this dish; it was her favorite recipe for baptisms, holidays, birthdays, or when someone special came to visit us for a few days or to have dinner with us. The aroma when I'm making Carne Puyada makes my neighbors come over to my house to ask, "What are you cooking? You have to give me the recipe!" Thanks to my grandma, I can now continue the family traditions with my daughters.

GIOMAR VELOZ

½ large green bell pepper, sliced
½ large red bell pepper
½ large yellow bell pepper
1 large carrot, peeled
2 medium white onions
1 stalk celery
½ cup beer
1 beef eye round roast, trimmed (about 3 to 4 pounds)

½ cup red wine
2 bay leaves
2 large cloves garlic, minced
1 teaspoon salt
1 tablespoon whole black peppercorns or ½ teaspoon ground black pepper
½ teaspoon bijol powder (yellow coloring) (optional)

1. *Stuffing roast:* Slice the bell peppers, carrot, onions, and celery into long thin strips. Place the vegetables and beer in a shallow bowl; marinate for ½ hour. With a long thin knife, make a 1-inch-wide hole lengthwise through the center of the roast, from one end to the other. Stuff the vegetable strips into the cavity, making sure the hole is completely filled. Dice the unused vegetable strips and reserve marinade.

2. *Braising:* Preheat the oven to 325°F. Place the roast in a dutch oven with the wine, bay leaves, garlic, salt, peppercorns, 2 cups of water, and the bijol. Add the reserved marinade and diced vegetables to the pot. Cover and braise, adding more water as needed, approximately 2 hours, until tender. Remove from oven and let cool 5 minutes.

3. *To serve:* Slice and arrange on a shallow platter with remaining meat juices and diced vegetables.

MAKES 6 SERVINGS

Ropa Vieja

FAMILY GET-TOGETHERS / CUBA

SHREDDED FLANK STEAK WITH SAUCE

As a child living in Cuba, food was scarce and flank steak was a real luxury, leaving my parents no choice but to purchase this precious cut of beef through the black market. Our arrival to New York meant leaving behind friends and my cherished ropa vieja. I quickly learned that ropa vieja was served only on specific days of the week; one Cuban restaurant would have it on Tuesday, the other Thursday, and it was made at home on Sundays. I wonder if that's why I was the only five-year-old in kindergarten who knew the days of the week?!

CARMEN FRANCHI DE ALFARO

ROPA VIEJA

1 pound flank steak
1 onion, chopped (about 1 cup)
½ green bell pepper, cut into strips
4 cloves garlic, crushed
½ teaspoon salt

1 tablespoon dry white wine
½ cup beef broth
¼ cup green peas
1 (2-ounce) jar sliced pimientos and juice

SOFRITO (SEASONING)

3 cloves garlic, minced
1 medium onion, chopped fine
¼ cup olive oil
½ green bell pepper, chopped fine
1 carrot, chopped fine

½ cup tomato sauce
¼ cup water
2 teaspoons vinegar
⅛ teaspoon ground oregano
¼ teaspoon salt

1. *Cooking flank steak:* Place the meat in a pot with water to cover, the onion, bell pepper, garlic, and salt. Bring to a boil and cook uncovered for 15 minutes. Reduce the heat to medium low; cover and simmer for 2 hours, or until tender. Strain the cooking liquid and reserve. Shred the steak.

2. *Cooking ropa vieja:* Sauté the garlic and onion in oil over medium heat until the onion is soft. Stir in the bell pepper, carrot, tomato sauce, water, vinegar, oregano, and salt; cook 10 minutes. Add the meat, wine, and broth. Bring to a boil, lower heat, and simmer covered for another 10 minutes. Stir in the peas and pimientos with juice; season to taste.

MAKES 4 SERVINGS (PORTION SIZE: 1⅓ CUPS)

GUISO DE COLA
QUINCEÑERA / PANAMA

OXTAIL STEW

Originally from Spain, land of the bull, oxtail stew is also known as rabo de toro, or tail-of-the-bull stew. The very flavorful tail of the bull or ox produces a rich, fork-tender stew with a delicious wine-infused sauce. At my quinceñera (coming-out party), the dish was prepared in large quantities and served with saffron rice.

JACKIE ALHAMBRA LÁVALOS

4 pounds oxtail, cut into 2-inch pieces
Salt and ground black pepper
Flour for dusting
⅓ cup olive oil
4 cloves garlic, minced
⅓ cup chopped ham
1 large onion, chopped (1¾ cups)
3 carrots, peeled and diced (1 cup)

2 stalks celery, sliced
2 bay leaves
1 teaspoon dried thyme leaves
1 to 2 cups dry white wine
1 extra-large beef bouillon cube
1 cup frozen peas (optional)
Minced fresh parsley and minced garlic

1. *Browning oxtail:* Generously season the oxtail with salt and pepper; dredge in flour, shaking to remove excess. In a dutch oven, fry the oxtail pieces in oil until completely browned. Remove from the skillet.

2. *Simmering stew:* In the same skillet, sauté the garlic and ham for 2 minutes. Add the onion and continue sautéing over medium heat until the onion is soft, stirring to detach browned bits of meat from the skillet bottom. Add the carrots, celery, bay leaves, and thyme; cook an additional 5 minutes. Return the meat to the skillet and stir in the wine, bouillon cube, and water to cover. Bring to a boil, reduce the heat, and simmer covered 3 to 3½ hours, or until the oxtail is very tender. Adjust seasoning if necessary. Remove the meat from the skillet and cover to keep warm.

3. *Finishing and serving:* Skim excess fat from the sauce in the skillet. Press the sauce through a sieve and return to the skillet. Cook until smooth and thickened. Return the meat to the skillet; add the peas and cook just long enough to heat. Sprinkle each serving with minced parsley and minced garlic.

MAKES 4 TO 6 SERVINGS (PORTION SIZE: 1 TO 1½ CUPS)

CHORIZO TEQUILA

MEXICAN SAUSAGE WITH TEQUILA

There is no better way to quiet a Sunday-morning appetite than with our family's very own tequila chorizo! Whether prepared for Superbowl Sunday, Easter Sunday, or family breakfast celebrations, it is the breakfast of kings.

EVA PERERIA

24 New Mexico dried red chiles (or a combination of 12 California and 12 New Mexico)

1½ pounds ground beef

1½ pounds ground pork

8 cloves garlic, minced or passed through a press

2 tablespoons dried oregano leaves, crushed

1 tablespoon salt

1 cup tequila

½ cup red chile powder

1. *Preparing chiles purée:* To soak and soften chiles, follow directions on page 62. Combine the softened chiles with 1 cup of the soaking liquid in a blender. In small batches, purée until smooth, about 4 minutes per batch. Do not overblend or the chile purée will become bitter. Strain the purée through a wire mesh sieve. Add additional cooking liquid to make 3 cups of purée. Set aside.

2. *Seasoning meat:* In a nonreactive bowl, mix together the beef, ground pork, garlic, oregano, and salt. Refrigerate for 1 hour.

3. *Marinating:* Pour tequila over the seasoned meat. Using your hands, mix tequila into the meat until thoroughly combined. Marinate an additional hour. Mix the chile powder and chile purée into the seasoned meat. Cover the bowl and refrigerate overnight.

4. *Cooking:* Sauté the tequila chorizo 10 minutes in a heavy skillet over medium heat until cooked. Chorizo will keep between 3 to 5 days tightly wrapped in plastic and refrigerated at between 32°F to 37°F. If desired, freeze 1-pound portions of the chorizo in freezer bags up to 2 months.

MAKES ABOUT 4 POUNDS OR 12 SERVINGS (PORTION SIZE: 6 OUNCES)

Lechón Asado

ROAST SUCKLING PIG

Christmas Eve always means a wonderful feast in the de Cárdenas home, with the whole family participating. Early in the morning, my dad picks up the suckling pig from the butcher. Once home, he prepares his special basting sauce, Mojo Criollo, which he rubs on the pig inside and out. While the pig roasts all day in the outdoor pit barbecue, the men—my father, brothers, cousins, and friends—stand around, smoking cigars, snacking, and laughing while they carefully guard our evening dinner. By 7 o'clock we begin with an assortment of appetizers that change from year to year: Italian, Chinese, French.... a green salad begins the meal. Then we step up to a gigantic buffet. The suckling pig has been sliced and is served on several platters, one with the chicharrón, or crisp pork skin; one with the rib steaks; and finally one with the cut-up chunks of marinated roasted meat and juices. An aromatic roasted turkey with stuffing, Cuban black beans, white rice, and yuca frita con mojo (fried yucca with a garlic sauce) make up the selection of side dishes. Later in the evening as we watch the children open gifts, we enjoy eating a croquembouche served with Cuban coffee. Midnight Mass shortly follows, and the Christmas Day festivities begin again the next morning!

MARIA DE CÁRDENAS

1 small (15-pound) suckling pig, prepared by the butcher for roasting
30 cloves garlic
¼ cup salt
2 tablespoons dried oregano leaves
2 tablespoons ground black pepper (optional)

1 tablespoon ground cumin
4 bay leaves
2 cups jugo de naranja ágria (sour orange juice), or a 50-50 mixture of fresh lime juice and orange juice
1 cup dry sherry (optional)
3 large onions, sliced thick

1. *Marinating:* The day before serving, pierce the meat all over with the tip of a knife. In a mortar, mash the garlic, salt, oregano, pepper, and cumin into a paste. Transfer the paste to a nonreactive bowl and stir in the bay leaves, sour orange juice, and sherry until well mixed. Place the pig in a large roasting pan and pour in the marinade; top with onions. Cover with plastic wrap and refrigerate overnight, turning the meat several times.

2. *Roasting:* About 5 hours before serving, preheat the oven to 350° F. Place the roasting pan with suckling pig on the bottom rack. Roast 1 hour, turning the pig to brown on all sides. Reduce the temperature to 325°F; baste the pork with the marinade and cover loosely with aluminum foil. Cook for another 3 hours or so, turning the meat over and basting frequently with marinade. Remove the foil during the last 30 minutes of roasting and continue roasting until the skin is dark brown and crispy. If you are using a meat thermometer, the internal temperature should be 180°F before removing pork from oven. Allow between 6 and 8 hours cooking time if you use an outdoor barbecue or ground pit.

3. *Serving:* When completely cooked, carefully remove the pig to a serving platter and allow to stand, covered with the foil, 15 minutes before carving. Serve with the meat juices and marinade.

SERVING SUGGESTION: Serve the lechón with Frijoles Negros (Cuban Black Beans, page 152), Arroz Blanco Cubano (Cuban White Rice, page 145), Yuca Frita Con Guasacaca (Fried Yucca with Avocado Vinaigrette, page 165), doused with Mojo Criollo (Creole Garlic Sauce, recipe follows).

MAKES 20 SERVINGS (PORTION SIZE: 6 OUNCES)

MOJO CRIOLLO (Creole Garlic Sauce)

Mash 20 cloves garlic and 2 teaspoons salt into a paste, using a mortar and pestle. Stir in 1 1/2 cups sour orange juice, 1 cup minced onion, and 1 teaspoon oregano; let sit at room temperature for 30 minutes or longer. In a saucepan, heat 1 1/2 cups Spanish olive oil just to the boiling point and remove from the heat. Whisk in the garlic–orange juice mixture until well blended. Serve at room temperature or use as a marinade.

MAKES 1 QUART

PUERCO EN SALSA VERDE

FAMILY GET-TOGETHERS / MEXICO

PORK IN GREEN CHILE SAUCE

I am five years old, and my mom has gone to Riverside to Grandma's house with my newborn sister. I am wearing Mom's apron, standing on a chair at the kitchen table, rolling out crooked tortillas for my dad's lunch. His black lunchbox and thermos sit next to a small pot of beans and a bowl of green chile and pork, which Mom had prepared the night before. I sometimes think this memory is the bridge between my childhood and who or what I was supposed to become when I grew up—the caretaker, the nurturer.

ALMA GONZALES THOMAS

2 pounds trimmed pork butt, cut into
1-inch cubes
1 teaspoon salt
1 pound tomatillos, husks removed
6 large cloves garlic, peeled
3 bunches green onions (1½ cups)
1 bunch cilantro, cleaned, stemmed,
and chopped (about 1 cup)

4 serrano chiles
½ fresh jalapeño chile, stem removed
2 yellow güero chiles
Minced garlic to taste
Salt and black pepper to taste

1. *Cooking pork:* Cook meat according to the directions on page 25.

2. *Making salsa verde:* In a pot, combine the tomatillos, garlic, 1 cup of the onions, half the cilantro, 2 of the serrano chiles, the jalapeño chile, the güero chiles, and 4 cups of water. Simmer uncovered for 20 minutes. Strain, reserving the cooking liquid. Place the solids in a blender container with 2 cups of the reserved liquid. Leave the lid partially opened to allow steam to escape. Purée until smooth.

3. *Simmering:* Return the pot with the pork pieces to the stove; pour in blended chile. Cook over medium heat about 10 minutes, stirring to loosen any fried bits of pork stuck to the bottom of the pan. Mince the remaining serrano chiles and stir in, along with the remaining onion and cilantro. Season to taste with garlic, salt, and pepper. Serve hot.

MAKES 6 SERVINGS (PORTION SIZE: 1 CUP)

Jamón de Año Nuevo

NEW YEAR'S BAKED HAM

Throughout the Americas, glazed baked ham is the centerpiece of a party buffet or Sunday comida (large afternoon meal). The pineapple, sherry, brown sugar, and mustard glaze make this ham particularly festive.

3 tablespoons cornstarch
½ cup packed brown sugar
2 tablespoons butter
1 (16-ounce) can pineapple rings or mango halves, drained, syrup reserved
1 cup dry sherry

2 tablespoons prepared yellow mustard
1 ready-to-eat cured half ham (about 6 pounds)
25 whole cloves
1 (4-ounce) jar maraschino cherries, drained

1. *Preparing marinade:* In a saucepan, dissolve the cornstarch in 1 cup of cold water; add the brown sugar, butter, and pineapple syrup (about ¾ cup). Cook over low heat, stirring constantly with a wooden spoon (cornstarch will not stick to wood), until the mixture has thickened, about 10 minutes. Immediately stir in the sherry and mustard until blended. The sauce should be the consistency of pourable cream; dilute with water or additional sherry if needed. Remove from the heat. Makes about 2 cups.

2. *Garnishing ham and baking:* Using a paring knife, score the ham fat in a large crisscross pattern ⅛ inch deep, forming a diamond-shaped lattice. To decorate, push a clove into the center of each diamond. Arrange pineapple rings over the scored surface of the ham, securing with toothpicks. Position a cherry in the center of each pineapple ring. Place the ham in a roasting pan; baste with sherry marinade. Bake in a preheated 350°F oven for 12 to 15 minutes a pound, basting every 20 minutes. Serve hot.

SERVING SUGGESTION: It is not uncommon to serve Tamales Rojos (Red Chile and Pork Tamales, page 128) on the same buffet with Frijoles de la Olla (Pinto Beans "From the Pot," page 154) and a baked glazed ham with ensalada de papa (potato salad). It actually is quite an amazing and complementary potpourri of flavors.

MAKES 15 SERVINGS (PORTION SIZE: 6 OUNCES)

PERNIL HORNEADO

CHRISTMAS / COLOMBIA

ROASTED FRESH HAM

A roasted pork leg (fresh ham) always signals a special occasion in Latin America. Smaller towns are host to a community of families who participate in the pit roasting, with one family contributing the wood, the other the pork. Other families round out the feast with an assortment of side dishes and desserts.

1 (8-pound) pork leg (fresh ham)
1 (12-ounce) can beer
1 cup cider vinegar
⅓ cup jugo de naranja ágria (sour orange juice), or substitute a 50-50 mixture of orange and lime juices
4 green onions, chopped (about ¾ cup)
12 garlic cloves, chopped
2 teaspoons coriander seeds

2 tablespoons chopped mint leaves
2 teaspoons crushed oregano leaves
6 bay leaves, ground in a coffee grinder
2 teaspoons dried thyme
1 teaspoon grated nutmeg
1 tablespoon salt
1 teaspoon ground black pepper

1. *Marinating pernil (pork leg):* Pierce the meat all over with the tip of a sharp paring knife; place in a nonreactive container. Combine the remaining ingredients in a nonreactive bowl and pour over the meat. Cover and refrigerate overnight, turning the meat several times.

2. *Roasting:* Preheat the oven to 325°F. Transfer the roast and marinade to a roasting pan and cook for 2 to 3 hours, basting often, or place the meat in a clay pot, seal, and put in an oven preheated to 250°F for 4 hours. Thirty minutes before serving, open the pot and crisp the skin under the broiler.

SERVING SUGGESTION: For a traditional Colombian feast, serve Pernil Horneado with Frijoles Cargamantos (Cargamanto Red Beans with Pork, page 155), Arroz Blanco Cubano (Cuban White Rice, page 145), and Plátanos Maduros Fritos (Fried Sweet Plantains, page 168).

MAKES 12 SERVINGS

SECO DE CHIVO

ECUADOREAN KID OR GOAT STEW

I remember my grandmother preparing Seco de Chivo on Sundays, the day my aunts, uncles, and cousins would come to our home for their weekly visit. This dish brings back memories of those family reunions.

ELIZABETH JIMÉNEZ

1½ tablespoons achiote oil or vegetable oil
1 cup sliced green onions
1 cup chopped green bell pepper
½ cup chopped parsley
½ cup chopped cilantro
1½ teaspoons achiote paste
2 cloves garlic, minced
2 pounds bone-in goat or lamb chops, cut up

1 teaspoon salt
½ teaspoon ground black pepper
½ teaspoon ground cumin
2 (14½-ounce) cans whole tomatoes and juice
1 (12-ounce) can golden lager or amber beer

1. *Sautéing:* Warm the oil in a pot over medium heat. Sautè the onions, bell pepper, parsley, cilantro, achiote, and garlic a few minutes. Season the meat with salt, pepper, and cumin. Add to the skillet and fry until browned.

2. *Simmering:* Purée the tomatoes in a blender until smooth; pour into the skillet with beer. Bring to a boil; lower the heat and simmer uncovered 25 to 30 minutes, or until the meat is tender and sauce thickened.

MAKES 6 SERVINGS (PORTION SIZE: 1⅓ CUPS)

Seco means dry; the term here refers to a thickened-sauce dish rather than a soupy stew. Although the ingredients are not exotic, the flavor of the savory beer-stewed sauce complements the full-flavored tender goat. The original recipe calls for naranjillas, small sour oranges; however, a golden lager beer produces a similar taste.

ARVEJADO DE CORDERO

SUNDAY DINNER / CHILE

CHILEAN PEA AND LAMB STEW

This dish reminds me of my dad. Because he worked with the airlines he would be away quite often. Whenever he came home he would prepare a family meal. Arvejado de Cordero was one of his specialties, as it is mine.

PABLO VALDES

LAMB STEW
3 tablespoons olive oil
3 cloves garlic, flattened
1 tablespoon pimentón (ground red pepper) or substitute paprika
1 teaspoon ground black pepper
3 pounds trimmed lamb shoulder (stewing meat), cut into 1-inch pieces
1 large white onion, chopped fine

2 tablespoons all-purpose flour
2 cups water or beef broth
1 teaspoon salt
1½ cups red table wine
⅓ cup grated raw potato
1 (16-ounce) package frozen peas, thawed
2 eggs, lightly beaten
⅓ cup chopped parsley

FRENCH-FRIED POTATOES
6 russet potatoes
Oil for deep frying

Salt
Minced parsley to garnish

1. *Braising lamb:* In a dutch oven or large skillet, heat the oil and sauté the garlic over medium low heat until it is browned; remove garlic from the skillet and discard. Add the paprika, black pepper, lamb, and onion. Stir constantly until the lamb is seared and onions are soft. Add the flour and cook for 2 minutes, stirring and scraping any bits of browned meat from bottom of pan. Stir in the water, salt, wine, and potatoes. Cover and simmer about 1 hour, stirring occasionally, until lamb is tender.

2. *Frying potatoes:* Twenty minutes before serving, prepare the French fries. Peel and slice the potatoes into long, thin sticks. Heat sufficient oil in a deep fryer to 380°F. Carefully drop in the potato sticks in small batches and fry until golden brown. Lift out with a slotted spoon and drain on absorbent towels to remove excess oil. Season with salt and keep warm and crisp in a 250°F oven.

3. *Finishing:* When the lamb is tender, add the peas and return to a rapid simmer. Cook until just tender. With a slotted spoon, lift the meat and peas into a serving dish; cover and keep warm. Season the sauce to taste, adding additional liquid if necessary. Stir the beaten eggs and parsley into the remaining sauce. Lower the heat and simmer, stirring constantly, until the sauce has thickened somewhat. Do not boil or the sauce will separate.

4. *Serving:* Pour the warm sauce over slices of lamb and the peas. Top each serving with a handful of French fries sprinkled with chopped parsley.

SERVING SUGGESTION: Serve this hearty yet elegant meal with a spinach–red onion salad and hard-cooked egg salad with hot dressing or a shredded beet and carrot salad with a mint vinaigrette. Enjoy!

MAKES 8 SERVINGS (PORTION SIZE: 5 OUNCES AND 1 CUP SAUCE WITH VEGETABLES)

Arvejado means peas, and the literal translation of this recipe title is pea stew with lamb. Since Chile is blessed with an abundance of fresh vegetables year-round, fresh peas are quite common. However, frozen peas will substitute nicely; just be careful not to overcook them.

South America, the Caribbean, Central America, and Mexico all share a passion for seafood—from simple to elaborate ceviches and grilled or pan-fried fish, to magnificent cioppino-style enchilados and mariscadas. Once the hallmark of the Lenten season, dried shrimp and salt cod are now popular celebration foods year-round, particularly in Brazil, Mexico, and the Caribbean.

Tacos de Abulón

SEASIDE OUTING / MEXICO

ABALONE STEAK TACOS

Summertime at my grandparents' ranch was always fun. With several families spending the entire summer vacation, I always had cousins to play with. We would often pile into several trucks and drive a few miles to the caves along the Baja coastline. Once we set up camp, the moms would prepare breakfast, while we kids would gather the abalone from the rocks in the shallow waters of the caves. After hours of play, our afternoon comida would be served. Although there was plenty of other food, pan-fried abalone was in abundant supply—cooked campfire-style in the shell or sautéed with onions and chile and served as tacos.

LAURA VALVERDE SANCHEZ

4 abalone or 1 pound abalone steaks
2 eggs, lightly beaten
Salt and ground black pepper
2 teaspoons lime juice

1/4 cup all-purpose flour
1/2 cup fine bread crumbs
Butter and vegetable oil for frying
Chopped cilantro to garnish

FRESH SALSA
1 cup minced white onion
1/4 cup lime juice
1/2 cup finely chopped cilantro leaves
1 tablespoon minced serrano chile

1/4 teaspoon salt
Corn tortillas
Avocado slices
Bottled hot sauce

1. *Cleaning and tenderizing abalone in the shell:* With a cleaver, hit the top of the abalone shell with one or two stunning blows. Place on a flat surface with the row of holes facing up. Insert an abalone iron, screwdriver, or cleaver down inside the shell to pry or pop the meat loose. Pull all the guts away from the smooth round muscle and discard (or use as fish bait). Rinse the abalone under cold running water and submerge in ice water. Once the round muscle has flattened, trim away the tentacles, head portion, heel, skin, and dark meat. (These parts can be ground and used in chowders, sausages, and stuffings.) At this point the smooth white steak should be exposed. Lightly pound the smooth muscle with a mallet until the meat is soft but not broken. If desired, lightly score the abalone in a crisscross pattern with a sharp knife.

2. *Fresh salsa:* In a shallow plate or bowl, combine the onion and lime juice; let stand 20 minutes to marinate. Stir in the cilantro leaves, chile, and salt.

3. *Sautéing abalone:* In a small bowl, beat together the eggs, salt, pepper, and lime juice. Dredge the abalone steaks in the flour, shaking to remove excess. Dip into the beaten eggs, then press both sides into the crumbs. Refrigerate at least 1 hour. Heat butter mixed with equal parts of oil over medium high heat in a large heavy skillet. Add the steaks and pan-fry about 20 to 30 seconds on each side. Do not overcook or the steaks will be tough. Immediately remove from the heat and serve.

4. *Serving:* Place the hot breaded abalone steaks on a serving plate garnished with cilantro. Serve with hot corn tortillas, avocado slices, hot sauce, and fresh salsa. Allow each guest to cut abalone steaks and make their own tacos.

SERVING SUGGESTION: All that is needed to finish off this exquisite meal is frijoles refritos (refried beans), a coleslaw of your choice, and ice-cold beer.

MAKES 6 SERVINGS (PORTION SIZE: 2 TACOS)

CORVINA CON ACELGAS Y FRIJOLES BLANCOS

SUNDAY DINNER / CHILE

ROASTED SEA BASS WITH SWISS CHARD AND WHITE BEANS

My many travels throughout Latin America have exposed me to the rich cultural and gastronomic diversity of Mexico, the Caribbean, and Central and South America. When I first visited Chile, however, I was struck by the geographic similarities to my own California: majestic mountains, a robust coastline and an expansive desert, all of which produced a bounty of fruits and vegetables and amazing seafood. I immediately felt at home. This dish is my best recollection of the first meal I ever had in Chile; it carries with it fond memories of a gracious and elegant people.

EMMA CARRASCO

FRIJOLES BLANCOS (WHITE BEANS)
1 pound dried small white beans

1 medium onion, halved

1 whole head garlic, cleaned and
  halved horizontally

1½ teaspoons salt

1 bunch fresh sage, rinsed

ACELGAS (SWISS CHARD)
4 bunches Swiss chard, rinsed and
  stems removed (about 5 cups,
  trimmed)

¼ cup virgin olive oil

12 cloves garlic, chopped fine

⅓ cup toasted pine nuts

Freshly ground black pepper to taste

Lemon wedges

CORVINA (OVEN-ROASTED SEA BASS)
2 (4-pound) sea bass, with heads and
  tails scaled and dressed

Olive oil

Salt and ground black pepper

Fresh sage leaves

1. *Preparing white beans:* Sort the beans through your hands to pick out any small stones or debris. Rinse in cold water and place in a 6-quart pot. Add the onion halves, garlic, and enough water to come at least 3 inches above the level of the beans. Discard any beans that float. Slowly bring the pot to a rapid simmer over medium heat, about 30 minutes.

Lower the heat, skim, cover, and continue simmering for about 2½ to 3 hours, until the skins of the beans curl when gently blown on. Stir in the salt and sage and continue cooking for ½ hour. *(At this point, the beans when pressed between your fingers should be creamy and the cooking liquid slightly thickened and colored. The bean broth should be about 2 inches above the cooked bean level.)* During the cooking process, stir the beans occasionally, adding additional hot water if needed.

2. *Swiss chard:* Rinse the chard. Remove the stems, reserving them for another purpose. In a stockpot, heat 2 quarts of water to boiling. Drop the Swiss chard leaves into the water, return to a boil, and cook uncovered for 1 minute. Immediately drain and place in a large bowl of ice water. Gently squeeze excess moisture out of the chard leaves and chop the leaves. Heat the oil in a large skillet. Add the garlic, stirring until the aroma is released. Add the chard and sauté, stirring frequently, about 3 minutes. Stir in the pine nuts and black pepper until thoroughly mixed. Serve hot garnished with fresh lemon wedges.

3. *Oven-roasted sea bass:* Preheat the oven to 400°F. Rinse the whole bass under cold running water; rub the fish inside and out with a damp cloth and place in a small roasting pan with rack. Rub the fish inside and out with olive oil. Generously season with salt and pepper. Fill the cavities with fresh sage leaves and truss with skewers. Arrange the fish, bellies down, on a well-greased rack and bake (roast) uncovered for 35 minutes, or until crisp and golden brown. To test doneness, press the fish; it should feel firm but spring back.

4. *Finishing:* Carefully lift the rack from the roasting pan, being careful not to break the fish. Stir the beans; spoon beans and their juices onto a shallow serving platter. Remove the trussing from the fish cavities and discard the sage. Arrange the fish on the beans and stuff the cavities with warm sautéed chard. Serve immediately.

SERVING SUGGESTION: Enjoy this as an ideal summertime outdoor dinner, beginning with a bowl of gazpacho with bread sticks as a first course. Follow with the roasted sea bass, and for dessert offer Bizcochuelo (Spongecake with Fruit and Cream, page 196) served with a Cafezinho (Demitasse Coffee, page 202).

MAKES 6 SERVINGS

TORTITAS DE CAMARÓN EN SALSA DE CHILE ANCHO CON QUELITES

LENT / MEXICO

DRIED SHRIMP FRITTERS IN A CHILE ANCHO SAUCE WITH SPINACH

Although tortitas are considered a Lenten dish because they contain no meat, my mother, Gregoria Huerta, used to prepare this flavorful meal year-round. Dried shrimp is easy to store and very little goes a long way to feed your family a rich and satisfying meal. I like to serve tortitas de camarón in a light chile sauce characteristic of our beloved Guadalajara.

ANGELINA ESPINOSA

SALSA DE CHILE ANCHO (CHILE BROTH)

3 dried pasilla chiles, stemmed and rinsed

2 dried guajillo chiles, stemmed and rinsed

2 large cloves garlic, peeled

1 teaspoon salt

1 tablespoon vegetable oil

TORTITAS (DRIED SHRIMP FRITTERS)

3 eggs

1 (2-ounce) package ground dried shrimp

1 tablespoon all-purpose flour (optional)

Oil for frying

ESPINACA (SPINACH)

1 pound spinach, or substitute verdolagas (purslane)

½ teaspoon salt

Pinch baking soda (optional)

1. *Preparing chile broth:* In a small pot, combine the chiles, garlic, and salt with water to barely cover. Bring to a rapid boil, remove from the heat, cover, and let soak 20 minutes. Place the chiles, garlic, and cooking liquid in a blender container and purée until smooth. Strain, discarding the seeds and skins. In a small skillet, warm the oil over medium high heat. Pour in the chile purée and cook for 10 minutes, stirring occasionally. Makes 4 cups.

2. *Shrimp fritters:* In a small bowl, beat the eggs until frothy. Add the dried shrimp and flour if desired. Continue beating until well mixed. Let

stand 5 minutes. Meanwhile, heat sufficient oil for deep frying to 375°F in a deep fryer or skillet. Once the oil is hot, beat the batter to remix and drop a tablespoon of batter into the oil. Fry for 2 to 3 minutes, or until golden; turn and continue frying 1 minute. Lift out of the oil with a slotted spoon and drain on absorbent towels. Makes 12 tortitas.

3. *Cooking spinach:* Rinse the spinach under cold running water; trim away any thick stems. In a pot, heat 2 quarts of water to boiling; add the salt and baking soda. (Baking soda helps preserve color.) Add the spinach and cook uncovered for 5 minutes, or until just tender. Drain and add to the chile ancho broth. Combine the fritters with the spinach and broth; serve hot.

NOTE: In Mexico and the North American southwest, *quelites* refers to any wild greens, from wild spinach, chard, mustard greens, or verdolagas.

SERVING SUGGESTION: A flavorful, earthy dish, this Lenten dish specialty is served with Sopa de Arroz (Mexican Rice, page 145) and tortillas de harina (flour tortillas).

MAKES 4 SERVINGS (PORTION SIZE: 3 FRITTERS AND 1 1/3 CUPS BROTH AND SPINACH)

> The Lenten season is distinguished by the abundance of meatless dishes, one of the most recognized being tortitas de camarón, which has many regional variations based on the type of chiles and greens available.

FANESCA

LENTEN STEW

Every Good Friday, my parents would spend what seemed like hours preparing fanesca. My father told us that all the ingredients in the fanesca represent what the Roman soldiers fed to Jesus of Nazareth and other prisoners before their crucifixion. The soldiers basically mixed the leftovers from the week's food in a bowl. In Ecuador we eat fanesca in remembrance of Him.

TERI SOTO

BACALAO (SALT COD)
1 pound bacalao seco (salt cod)

VEGETABLES AND LEGUMES
2 cups cubed pumpkin or zapallo
  (winter squash or acorn squash)
1/4 head green cabbage
2 to 4 cups freshly scraped yellow
  corn kernels (about 4 ears)
1 cup baby green peas
1 cup canned white or yellow whole
  hominy
1 (14-ounce) can hearts of palm,
  sliced (about 1 1/2 cups)

1 cup cut-up green beans (optional)
1/2 cup dried lentils, sorted and cooked
1/2 cup dried habas (fava beans),
  sorted and cooked
1 cup dried pinto or pink beans, sorted
  and cooked
1/2 cup canned garbanzo beans

SOFRITO (SEASONING) AND VEGETABLES
1/2 cup achiote oil or 8 tablespoons
  (1 stick) butter, melted
4 large cloves garlic, minced
1 small white onion, minced (3/4 cup)
6 green onions, sliced thin (about 1
  cup)
2 green bell peppers, diced (about
  1 1/2 cups)
1 cup diced tomatoes
1/2 teaspoon oregano, crushed
1/2 teaspoon ground black pepper

1/4 teaspoon ground cumin
1/4 teaspoon salt
1/2 cup peanut butter dissolved in 2
  cups water
1/2 cup chopped peanuts
8 ounces cream cheese, cut into cubes
4 cups whole milk
2 tablespoons chopped cilantro leaves
4 hard-cooked eggs, peeled and
  quartered
Chopped parsley to garnish

1. *Soaking salt cod:* Soak salt cod following the directions on page 6. Cut the fish into ½-inch pieces. Set aside.

2. *Cooking pumpkin and cabbage:* In a medium saucepan, combine the pumpkin with water to cover. Bring to a boil, lower the heat, and cook covered for 30 minutes, or until the pumpkin is very soft and begins to break apart. Add the cabbage and continue cooking uncovered until tender. Remove from the heat and set aside. Do not drain.

3. *Sofrito (sautéing ingredients):* Heat the achiote oil in a large pot over medium high heat. Add the garlic and sauté for 1 minute. Stir in the onions and bell peppers; continue sautéing until the onions are soft. Add the tomatoes, oregano, black pepper, cumin, and salt and cook for 3 minutes. Pour in the peanut butter that has been dissolved in water, add the peanuts, and stir until thoroughly mixed.

4. *Cooking vegetables:* Add the corn, peas, hominy, hearts of palm, green beans, lentils, habas, and pinto and garbanzo beans to the pot with the sofrito. Bring to a boil, lower the heat, and vigorously simmer for 20 minutes uncovered. Add the squash-cabbage mixture (with cooking liquid) and the drained salt cod. Return to a boil, lower the heat, and simmer covered 10 minutes.

5. *Finishing fanesca:* Stir the cream cheese and 2 cups of the milk into the vegetables. Cook uncovered for 10 minutes over medium heat, stirring occasionally, until the cheese has dissolved. Add the cilantro leaves and remaining 2 cups of milk. Continue cooking until heated through. If fanesca is too thick, add additional milk. Serve fanesca in shallow bowls garnished with egg and parsley.

SERVING SUGGESTION: For a traditional lenten Good Friday supper, serve Fanesca with a good-quality bread, followed by Humitas en Chala (Steamed Fresh Corn and Basil Humitas, page 118) and Ecuadorean Café Tinto (Demitasse Coffee, page 202).

MAKES 12 SERVINGS (PORTION SIZE: 1 ⅓ CUPS)

Bacalao a la Vizcaína

VIZCAÍNA-STYLE SALT COD STEW

I always had a love-hate relationship with my mother's bacalao. The night that she soaked her salted codfish, the scent would transform the house into a fishing pier! It was a bittersweet feeling, because I knew that the next day we would be feasting on the best bacalao in the world.

MARIA ELENA SALINAS-RODRIGUEZ

2 pounds bacalao (salt cod)
2 quarts milk for soaking
2 medium white onions (about 1 cup chopped and 1 whole quartered)
10 cloves garlic (5 cloves minced and 5 cloves crushed)
1 large green bell pepper, seeded and cut up
1 cup water or dry sherry
½ cup olive oil
1 (14½-ounce) can diced tomatoes and juice

1 (16-ounce) can tomato sauce
1 tablespoon wine vinegar
1½ pounds russet potatoes, boiled, peeled, and sliced (about 3 cups)
4 ounces chiles güeros en escabeche (pickled yellow chiles)
1 cup small pimiento-stuffed green olives
1 cup finely chopped parsley

GARNISH
⅓ cup chopped parsley
1 (4-ounce) jar sweet red pimientos, drained and chopped

8 to 12 French bread slices, sautéed in olive oil until browned (optional)

1. *Soaking salt cod:* In a large bowl, combine the salt cod with cold water to cover. Soak for 3 hours, changing the water twice. Place the drained bacalao and half the milk in a saucepan. Bring to a rapid simmer and cook 15 minutes; drain. Continue soaking in the remaining fresh milk. When ready to use, gently squeeze the cod to rid it of excess milk. Shred, removing the skin and bones, and set aside.

2. *Blending:* Combine the quartered onion, the 5 minced garlic cloves, the bell pepper, and water or wine in a blender container. Purée until smooth and set aside.

3. *Sautéing:* In a large skillet or pot, warm the oil over medium high heat. Sauté the remaining garlic until golden. Remove the garlic and lower the heat to medium. Add the remaining onion and continue sautéing until golden, about 20 minutes. Pour the blender contents into the skillet. Bring to a boil, lower the heat, and cook 5 minutes, or until slightly reduced. Stir in the diced tomatoes and juice, the tomato sauce, and vinegar. Cook 20 minutes for flavors to combine.

4. *Finishing:* Stir the shredded salt cod, potatoes, yellow chiles, olives, and parsley into the sauce. Cover and cook over low heat for an additional 30 minutes. Taste and adjust seasoning to your preference, adding additional chiles en escabeche, if desired.

5. *Garnishing:* Before serving, sprinkle the parsley and pimientos over the bacalao. For an authentic touch, fry French bread in olive oil until browned. Arrange toasted bread slices on top of the dish. Serve with white rice.

NOTE: Salt cod can be vigorously simmered over high heat for approximately 15 to 30 minutes instead of soaking 3 hours in cold water. It may then be drained and prepared with milk as in step 1.

SERVING SUGGESTION: Bacalao a la Vizcaína is a traditional dish served for the Christmas Eve or Christmas Day dinner in Mexico. Serve bacalao for any celebration dinner, accompanied by a fresh garden salad, rice, and rolls.

MAKES 8 TO 12 SERVINGS (PORTION SIZE: 1 TO 1¹/₂ CUPS)

Vizcaína is a Basque city in Spain famous for their preparation of this dish. You'll find one or more versions of the bacalao in every Spanish-speaking country. One of the distinctive sights throughout Latin America is the flat slab of dried salt cod hanging or stacked up by the bale in open marketplaces, ready for cutting off portions. Oftentimes you will find bacalao in small wooden boxes or displayed in a refrigerated case. The main difference between the two is that the packaged or refrigerated salt cod is usually boneless and meatier; the thin whole fish has more bones and requires more soaking time to remove the salt.

Pescado con Salsa Fría de Nuez

FAMILY GET-TOGETHERS / PERU

FISH WITH COLD WALNUT SAUCE

This dish hails from the Peruvian city of Arequipa, where fiery dishes are commonplace. The cold walnut sauce balances out the spiciness of the recipe.

AJÍ-WALNUT SAUCE

4 dried árbol chiles or 2 to 3 fresh Peruvian rocoto chiles, seeds and stems removed and roasted

¾ cup chopped green onions, both white and green sections

2 large cloves garlic

1 cup walnut meats or roasted peanuts

1 cup grated Muenster cheese

½ to ¾ cup half-and-half

Salt and black pepper to taste

FISH

4 sea bass fillets or 4 whole trout (about 12 ounces each)

Salt and ground black pepper

⅓ cup all-purpose flour

2 tablespoons butter

2 tablespoons vegetable oil

Green olives or capers to garnish

1. *Blending sauce:* In a blender or food processor, purée the roasted chiles, green onions, garlic, walnuts, cheese, and half-and-half. The mixture should resemble a thick mayonnaise. Continue blending, pouring in additional half-and-half to create the consistency of thick cream. Season with salt and pepper. Cover and refrigerate until ready to use. Makes 3 cups.

2. *Pan-frying fish:* Rinse the fish under cold running water and pat dry. Generously season with salt and pepper. Dredge in flour, shaking off the excess. In a large skillet, melt the butter and oil over medium heat. Sauté the fillets approximately 4 minutes on each side, depending on thickness, or until the flesh is no longer opaque. Serve immediately accompanied by the cold walnut sauce. Garnish with green olives.

SERVING SUGGESTION: For an elegant dinner, serve cooked quinoa, Ensalada de Aguacate y Tomate (Avocado and Tomato Salad, page 16), rolls, and a crisp white wine.

MAKES 6 SERVINGS (PORTION SIZE: 1 LARGE FILLET AND ½ CUP SAUCE)

Mariscos Enchilado

SHELLFISH IN A SPICY CREOLE SAUCE

One of the few spicy dishes in the Cuban cuisine, enchilado was originally associated with a Cuban cangrejada (crabfest), a festival of dance and food. This more elegant version features shellfish which are lightly poached in a creole sauce.

¼ cup olive oil

5 cloves garlic, minced

1 medium onion, chopped fine (about ¾ cup)

1 large green bell pepper, chopped fine (about 1¼ cups)

1 to 2 serrano peppers, seeded and minced, or red chile flakes to taste

2 bay leaves

1 teaspoon dried oregano leaves, crushed

½ teaspoon dried thyme

2 large canned pimientos, blended

1 (16-ounce) can tomato sauce

1 cup beer

1½ teaspoons salt

1 teaspoon sugar

1 pound scallops

1 pound large shrimp, shelled and deveined

1½ pounds (three 8-ounce) lobster tails, shelled and cut into 4 pieces each

Finely chopped Italian parsley

Lemon slices

1. *Preparing sauce:* Heat the oil in a pot over medium high heat. Sauté the garlic until slightly golden. Add the onion, bell pepper, serrano peppers, bay leaves, oregano, and thyme. Cook for 3 minutes. Pour in the blended pimientos, tomato sauce, beer, salt, and sugar; mix well. Bring to a boil, reduce the heat, and simmer 10 minutes, or until the sauce thickens slightly.

2. *Cooking shellfish:* Add the scallops, shrimp, and lobster to the sauce. Cover and cook 4 minutes. Remove from the heat and keep warm.

3. *Serving:* Remove the bay leaves. Sprinkle with chopped parsley and serve garnished with lemon slices.

MAKES 6 SERVINGS (PORTION SIZE: 1½ CUPS)

Run Dunn

CHRISTMAS/NEW YEAR'S / BELIZE

BELIZIAN SEAFOOD COCONUT STEW

In Belize, if you lived in a village, Christmas gifts and fancy festivities were not common. Instead, our family used to make a ritual of the holiday meal. This was our gift. I learned as a child that gifts given from the heart are the true gifts of this season.

RENAI CLAYTON

8 tablespoons (1 stick) butter
8 ounces shallots, minced (about 1 cup)
½ cup minced green onions
1 up diced green bell pepper
4 serrano chiles, minced
4 bay leaves
3 (12-ounce) cans coconut milk
1 pound large shrimp, shelled and deveined
½ pound large scallops, halved

½ pound cooked crabmeat or fish fillets, shredded
3 tablespoons capers
1 tablespoon dried dill
½ teaspoon paprika
1 teaspoon vanilla extract
Salt and ground black pepper
2 (6-ounce) cans prepared Hollandaise sauce
½ cup canned sweetened condensed milk

1. *Preparing broth:* In a medium pot, melt the butter over medium high heat. Sauté the shallots, onions, bell pepper, chiles, and bay leaves 4 minutes. Pour the coconut milk into the pot and cook for 20 minutes, or until broth has reduced by one quarter.

2. *Poaching and seasoning seafood:* Stir the shrimp, scallops, and crabmeat into the simmering coconut broth; cover and cook 2 minutes. Stir in the capers, dill, paprika, and vanilla. Season to taste with salt and pepper. Cook, uncovered, over medium low heat until the flavors combine, about 10 minutes.

3. *Finishing:* In a small bowl, whisk together the Hollandaise sauce, condensed milk, and 2 cups of the coconut broth until smooth. Pour into the pot and continue cooking until heated through. Season to taste before serving.

MAKES 6 SERVINGS (PORTION SIZE: 1 CUP)

VATAPÁ

EASTER / BRAZIL

SHRIMP COCONUT STEW

We did not have a traditional Easter Sunday meal, but my mother would often prepare vatapá, one of the regional specialties from Bahía. I remember going to Easter Mass in my small village, and afterward sharing our food with less fortunate families. It was a tradition for these families to go from house to house receiving food as a gift from those more fortunate. As a child I had a sense of helping others and also a sense of my good fortune. What better act to perform on Easter Sunday, one of the most glorious days of the year?

FRANCESCA "FÁTIMA" GORDILS

¼ pound dried whole shrimp, shelled and soaked in water for 8 hours
¼ pound toasted peanuts (about ½ cup)

¼ pound cashew nuts, shelled and lightly toasted (about ½ cup)

COCONUT MILK
2 large coconuts

Hot water for blending

GARLIC SHRIMP AND FISH
½ cup *dendê* oil or vegetable oil (see Note)
2½ pounds large raw shrimp
8 cloves garlic, minced
½ teaspoon salt

1 pound whitefish fillets, cut into 2-inch cubes
Lime juice

COURT BOUILLON (FISH STOCK)
1 medium onion, quartered
½ pound fish heads

3 cloves garlic
Reserved shrimp shells

TEMPORO (SEASONING BASE)
¼ cup fresh cilantro leaves
1 small white onion
2 medium tomatoes
1 clove garlic
½ medium green bell pepper

1 California Anaheim green chile pepper or 2 serrano chiles, minced
¼ cup palm oil or peanut oil
1¼ cups rice flour
1 tablespoon finely grated ginger root

(continued on next page)

1. *Grinding ingredients:* In separate batches, grind the dried shrimp, peanuts, and cashew nuts in a food processor or spice grinder. Place each in small containers and set aside.

2. *Extracting coconut milk:* Follow the recipe below. You should have 2 cups of thick coconut milk and 2 cups of thin. Set aside.

3. *Garlic shrimp and fish:* In a large skillet, warm ¼ cup of oil over medium high heat. Pat the shrimp dry. Add the shrimp, 4 cloves of garlic, and ¼ teaspoon of salt to the skillet. Cook briskly, stirring constantly, until the shrimp turn pink. Cooking time will depend on the size of the shrimp. Repeat the process with the fish and cook until just done (fish meat will turn opaque). Shell and devein the shrimp and set aside; reserve the shells for court bouillon. Sprinkle shelled shrimp and fish with lime juice, tightly cover, and refrigerate.

4. *Court bouillon (fish stock):* In a large pot, combine 8 cups of water, onion, fish heads, remaining 4 cloves of garlic, and the reserved shrimp shells. Bring to a boil; lower the heat and simmer covered 1 hour. Strain; set aside. Makes about 6 cups.

5. *Temporo (seasoning base):* In a blender container, purée the cilantro, onion, tomatoes, garlic, and peppers until smooth, adding ½ cup of court bouillon if necessary.

6. *Simmering vatapá:* In a pot, warm the palm oil over medium heat. Add the temporo (see step 5) and fry 5 minutes, stirring frequently. Add 2 cups of thick coconut milk and 4 cups court bouillon. Bring to a boil, lower the heat, and simmer covered. While the stock is simmering, combine the remaining 2 cups of coconut milk with the rice flour and ginger root in a bowl. Slowly whisk in remaining 2 cups of hot court bouillon. Briskly stir ground peanuts and ground cashews into the pot. Season to taste with the ground dried shrimp, adding between ¼ to 1 cup depending on preference. Cook 15 minutes over very low heat, stirring often. Finally add the garlic shrimp and fish mixture and cook until thoroughly heated. Adjust seasoning to taste.

EXTRACTING COCONUT MILK
Using a sharp object, pierce through the 3 eyes of each coconut; drain, reserving the thin water. Place the coconuts in a preheated 400°F oven for about 15 minutes. Remove coconuts and place on a damp towel on

a kitchen countertop. Break the coconut shells, using a mallet or hammer. (The hard shell will separate from the meat.) In a food processor work-bowl, grate the coconut with the smallest shredding blade, using 2 cups of hot water, until shredded. This will make about 4 cups of pulverized meat. Press the coconut meat through a fine mesh sieve or squeeze and twist the meat through cheesecloth to extract the first thick milk, or coconut cream, about 2 cups. Set aside until ready to use. In a second bowl, pour 1 to 2 cups of hot water and the reserved coconut water over the coconut meat to extract the second, thinner coconut milk, about 2 to 3 cups. Set aside until ready to use.

NOTE: Dendê oil can be found in markets specializing in Caribbean or South American cuisine.

SERVING SUGGESTION: Serve Vatapá with steamed white rice and Hot Pepper-Ginger-Lime Sauce (see the variation under Môlho de Pimento com Limao, page 109).

MAKES 4 SERVINGS

The secret of this delectable Afro-Brazilian dish is the shrimp, both fresh and dried, and the milk of freshly grated coconut. It is a specialty of Bahía, where African cooking was developed to a high art. Eaten in its native habitat, stinging hot with crushed chiles, it is a unique experience not to be matched in any other country. There are many variations: the meat ingredient may be fish, chicken, or even pork; the nuts which enrich and flavor it may be peanuts, cashews, or almonds; and the thickening abent may be rice flour, cornmeal, or a mixture of cornmeal and cassava meal. But no matter what it's made of, all vatapás are made in the same fashion, of which this recipe is a good example.

CALAMARES RELLENOS "DOÑA RAQUEL"

CHRISTMASTIME / MEXICO

DOÑA RAQUEL'S STUFFED SQUID

This recipe dates back to the turn of the century, when my great-grandmother passed it on to my grandmother, Doña Raquel. It has been prepared at Christmastime for four generations. I remember how my grandmother would gather us all in the kitchen and give us each an assignment, according to our age. The youngest were allowed to peel the hard-cooked eggs or the almonds. When we were old enough to handle a knife, we were assigned chopping duty. At age seven, we were taught how to peel the squid; at age nine my grandmother's rite of passage allowed us to cook the dish entirely. Finally, by age ten, the women in my family were the stuffed squid experts!

MARIA ANTONIETA COLLINS

6½ pounds large squid
Juice of 3 lemons
Olive oil
2 white onions, minced
2 hard-cooked eggs, chopped

1 large sprig parsley, minced
1 (3-ounce) jar capers
4 cups milk
2¼ pounds blanched almonds
¾ cup white wine

1. *Preparing squid:* Slice off the heads and remove the ink sacs, cartilage, and transparent skin. Rinse the squid under cold running water. Place the squid in a glass bowl with the lemon juice while removing the tentacles with kitchen shears. Mince the tentacles; set aside.

2. *Preparing filling and stuffing:* Warm ¼ cup of olive oil in a large skillet over medium heat. Sauté the onions and minced tentacles until the onions are transparent. Stir in the eggs, parsley, and capers and continue frying for 1 minute; let cool. Drain the squid and stuff with the filling; set aside.

3. *Almond sauce:* In a blender container, combine the milk and almonds. Purée 4 minutes or until creamy; set aside.

4. *Cooking:* In a flameproof clay pot, warm 2 tablespoons of olive oil. Sauté the stuffed squid until browned. Add the wine and almond milk, cover, and cook 20 to 30 minutes over very low heat, or until tender.

MAKES 12 SERVINGS (PORTION SIZE: 5 SQUID AND SAUCE)

CHAPTER THREE

Platillos Fuertes: Sopas, Arroces, Tamales, Enchiladas, y Caserolas

Main Dishes: Hearty Soups, Stews, Rice Entrees, Corn Dishes, and Casseroles

Many of the classic stews and soups of Spain, such as the cocido, a meat, garbanzo, and vegetable stew, slow-cooked in an olla (earthenware pot), are the forebearers of the diverse hearty soups seen throughout Latin America. Some closely resemble the Spanish version while others venture into the flavors of "la cocina criolla" (the native or indigenous kitchen).

From simple to scrumptious, you'll find the basic cocido or boiled dinner under many different guises from the Argentine puchero to the Mexican caldo de res.

Besides boiled dinners, an assortment of hearty chowders and tasty soups define each country's unique, indigenous cooking style: Brazilian feijoada, the lorcos of Bolivia, Paraguay, Argentina, and Ecuador, the menudo and pozole of Mexico, to name a few. Even our own North American Southwest pozole, the quintessential New Mexican stew, and chile beans, a Tex-Mex classic, evolved from our shared frontier and traditions of many different cultures.

LORCO DE PAPA

FAMILY GATHERING / ECUADOR

ECUADOREAN POTATO SOUP

My father and I share the same voracious appetite for this hearty soup from Ecuador. Somehow it just hits the spot. As a young child I didn't care for avocados, yet in this recipe the cold avocado against the hot creamy soup was a perfect combination, especially during cold winter weekends. My mother now prepares this typical Ecuadorean recipe for special occasions and holidays.

JORGE JARRÍN

2 tablespoons vegetable oil
1 small onion, chopped
3 cloves garlic, minced
3 large russet potatoes, peeled and sliced (about 5 cups)
2 (10-ounce) cans chicken broth or 2¼ cups homemade
½ cup milk

1 cup chopped cabbage
3 eggs
1 (8-ounce) container cottage cheese
½ to 1 cup shredded white melting cheese: Monterey Jack, provolone, or mozzarella (about 4 ounces)
Avocado slices to garnish
Hot red-pepper sauce (optional)

1. *Cooking potatoes:* In a 1½-quart stockpot, warm the oil over medium high heat. Sauté the onion and garlic until soft. Add the potatoes and chicken broth. Bring to a boil, lower the heat, and cook covered until tender, about 30 minutes.

2. *Seasoning:* Stir the milk and cabbage into the potato mixture. Cook over medium high heat about 5 minutes, or until the cabbage is tender. Reduce heat to a bare simmer.

3. *Poaching eggs:* Break the eggs one at a time into a small bowl and slip them into the potato soup, being careful not to break the yolks. Cover and simmer 5 additional minutes.

4. *Thickening lorco and serving:* While the eggs are cooking, mix together the cottage cheese and shredded cheese; stir into the soup. At this point the soup should be thick and creamy. Garnish with avocado slices and season with hot sauce, if desired.

SERVING SUGGESTION: Serve a generous portion of this delicious, hearty soup with biscuits or a good-quality bread. Or use as an ample first-course soup, followed by a simply prepared fish (sautéed with butter, capers, and white wine) accompanied by a salad of greens and ripe tomato.

MAKES 4 SERVINGS (PORTION SIZE: 2 CUPS)

Lorco is one of those nourishing home-style soups that are seen throughout South America. In Argentina and Paraguay, a lorco can be made with wheat, corn, or cassava. Lorcos can include beef, pork, sausages, or even dried squash, in which case it's more of a feast-day specialty. This famous version from Ecuador is made with potatoes. In the Ecuadorean highlands, when milk, eggs, and cheese are not always available, the potatoes are cooked in water to a nourishing milky consistency and fresh ajíes (hot chiles) are added for flavor.

SOPA TARASCA

TARASCAN BEAN SOUP

The pride of our Mexican heritage was instilled in me by my parents. And what could be more Mexican than this soup made with the staples of the Mexican kitchen: tortillas, beans, chile, and avocado?

MARY GONZALEZ KOENIG

SOPA (SOUP)

2 medium tomatoes

2 dried pasilla or ancho chiles, stemmed and seeded

1 cup cooked pinto beans plus 1 cup pinto bean broth (see Frijoles de la Olla recipe, page 154)

3 tablespoons vegetable oil

3 large cloves garlic, minced

2 bay leaves

½ teaspoon dried thyme

½ teaspoon dried marjoram

¼ teaspoon ground black pepper

1 cup finely chopped white onion

4 cups well-seasoned chicken broth

Salt to taste

GARNISH

½ cup fresco or feta cheese

½ cup Mexican cream or crème fraîche

1 avocado, pit removed, peeled and cubed

2 dried pasilla or ancho chiles, stems and seeds removed, cut into strips and fried (see page 97)

6 corn tortillas, cut into strips and fried

1 cup shredded cooked chicken (optional)

1. *Toasting soup ingredients:* Place the whole tomatoes and chiles on a greased griddle over medium heat; toast, turning occasionally. Remove the chiles when they begin darkening and release their aroma; set aside. Continue toasting the tomatoes until soft and blackened. (If the temperature is too high, the tomato skin will break completely while blackening.) Set aside.

2. *Puréeing tomatoes and beans:* Place the toasted tomatoes in a blender container and purée until smooth. Pour into a small bowl and set aside.

In a separate batch, blend the toasted pasilla chiles, the pinto beans, and bean broth until smooth; set aside.

3. *Frying and simmering the sopa:* In a large skillet, warm the oil over medium low heat. Sauté the garlic, bay leaves, thyme, marjoram, and black pepper for 2 minutes. Add the onion and continue cooking until softened. Stir in the blended tomato purée and bring to a boil. Cook 3 to 5 minutes, stirring occasionally, until the purée has reduced and turned from orange to a bright red-orange. Stir in the chicken broth and blended bean purée; return to a boil. Lower the heat and simmer uncovered 15 to 20 minutes, or until desired consistency. Taste and adjust seasoning with salt and pepper. Remove the bay leaves. Add additional broth for a thinner soup.

4. *Serving:* Ladle the bean soup into shallow bowls. Allow guests to garnish the soup with crumbled cheese, cream, avocado, fried pasilla chile strips, and tortilla strips. If desired, offer shredded chicken to create a main-course soup.

FRIED CHILE STRIPS
Heat $\frac{1}{4}$ inch of oil in a heavy or cast-iron skillet. Fry the chile strips until crisp but not blackened. Remove and drain on absorbent towels.

SERVING SUGGESTION: For a colorful birthday dinner, begin your meal with a papaya salad with a lime vinaigrette dressing. Serve sopa tarasca accompanied by small bowls of garnishes. Conclude the festivities with a Bien Me Sabe (Layered Coconut Cream Torte, page 182) and a hot beverage of your choice.

MAKES 6 SERVINGS (PORTION SIZE: $\frac{3}{4}$ CUP)

This earthy bean soup, named for the Tarascan Indians, originates from the State of Michoacán, Mexico, distinguished for its rich and authentic regional cuisine. In the small town of Patzcuaro this regional soup is often referred to as sopa de tortilla (tortilla soup) and is appreciated for its rich smoothness (from the beans), its earthy intense flavor (from the roasting of the red chile and vegetables), and its textural contrast (from the myriad garnishes).

AJIACO

HOLIDAY PARTY / COLOMBIA

POTATO CHICKEN SOUP

It was a very cold afternoon when I last tasted a traditional ajiaco bogotano. It was at our friend's country home in the majestic mountains surrounding Bogotá, Colombia. Our hostess passed around a pitcher of fresh cream and small bowls of capers and olives which we spooned into our empty soup bowls. After placing a peeled avocado half in the bowl, we ladled the steaming Ajiaco over the condiments.

CLARITA LONDOÑO-CONNALLY

AJIACO

6 cups milk

2 pounds new potatoes, peeled and sliced ⅜ inch thick (about 5 cups)

2 pounds russet potatoes, peeled and sliced ⅜ inch thick

1½ pounds yellow criollo (yellow) potatoes or baby red potatoes, peeled and sliced ⅜ inch thick

1 broiler/fryer, cut up (about 4 pounds), or 2 pounds chicken breasts and 2 pounds hindquarters

2 bunches green onions, cleaned and sliced into ½-inch pieces

10 large cloves garlic, peeled

3 extra-large chicken-flavored bouillon cubes or 4 tablespoons chicken bouillon granules

Salt and pepper to taste

1 pound frozen corn (about 3 cups)

1 cup chopped canned white asparagus, or 2 bunches chopped guascas (see Note), optional

GARNISH

2 cups heavy cream

1 cup capers, drained

6 ripe Hass avocados, halved, pitted, peeled, and diced

1. *Simmering stock and cooking chicken:* In an 8-quart stockpot, combine the milk with 8 cups of water, the potatoes, chicken pieces, green onions, garlic, bouillon cubes, salt, and pepper. Bring to a boil over high heat (this will take between 20 and 30 minutes). Remove the foam with a wire mesh strainer during the cooking process. Lower the heat to medium and cook uncovered for 30 minutes, or until the chicken is thoroughly cooked.

98 • PLATILLOS FUERTES

2. *Shredding chicken:* Remove the chicken pieces and let cool. Pull the meat from the bones; discard skin and bones. Shred or cut the chicken into bite-sized pieces. Cover the meat and set aside. Makes about 5 cups.

3. *Finishing soup:* Meanwhile, continue cooking the stock uncovered for about 40 minutes, or until the potatoes have begun to break apart and thicken the broth. The soup should have a thin creamy consistency. Stir in the corn, cooked chicken, and asparagus, if desired. Continue cooking for 10 minutes. Season to taste.

4. *Garnishing:* Place 2 tablespoons of cream, 1 tablespoon of capers, and 1 avocado half in each bowl. Ladle hot soup into bowls and serve.

NOTE: Guascas, a green herb, is an essential ingredient in ajiaco. Colombian restaurants use canned white asparagus to duplicate guascas' distinct flavor.

SERVING SUGGESTION: For a holiday gathering Latin style, serve plenty of pasantes (appetizers) and beverages. After about an hour of drinks and hors d'oeuvres, begin your meal with a fresh marinated vegetable salad followed by Ajiaco. Let guests place the condiments in their bowls and ladle in the soup. Serve Ajiaco with good-quality French or Italian bread. End the meal—hours later—with an exotic budín de guayaban (guava bread pudding) and freshly brewed Colombian coffee.

MAKES 15 SERVINGS (PORTION SIZE: 1 1/2 CUPS)

Colombians use many varieties of potatoes in their diet, their traditional ajiaco calling for three types: the yellow criollo or amarillo potato, also known as the Yukon gold potato, which dissolves, providing a rich flavor and lovely color; the white grainy sabanero potato, which thickens the broth; and the pastuso potato, which holds its shape. The preceding recipe has been adapted using North American ingredients, providing a wonderful example of foreign culinary traditions coming into contact with local foods and creating new dishes and new flavors.

POZOLE

PORK, CHICKEN, AND HOMINY SOUP
WITH RED CHILE

Your fondest memories of home invariably include your mom's cooking. As a male member in a twelve-sibling family, I did not get the inside scoop or training on how to prepare our family's dishes. I did, however, remember how those dishes tasted. As such, after much trial and error and extensive culinary discussions with my sisters, I finally broke the code on my mother's pozole recipe. To this day, my sisters will say that I make the best pozole in the world!

VICTOR FRANCO

POZOLE (SOUP)

4 pounds pork neck bones, cut into 1½-inch pieces

1 tablespoon salt

1 broiler/fryer, cut into pieces (about 3 pounds)

5 ripe tomatoes

6 large cloves garlic, peeled

3 (30-ounce) cans white hominy, drained and rinsed

¼ to ½ cup mild California red chile powder

3 extra-large chicken-flavored bouillon cubes

1½ teaspoons crushed oregano leaves

GARNISH

½ head iceberg lettuce, shredded (about 3 cups)

1 medium onion, chopped fine (about 1 cup)

1 bunch radishes, cleaned and sliced thin (about 1 cup)

½ bunch cilantro, cleaned and chopped (about 1½ cups)

Lemon wedges

Bean Tostadas (see page 101)

1. *Simmering the pork:* In a large stockpot, combine the neck bones and salt with enough water to cover (about 10 cups). Bring to a rolling boil and cook uncovered for 30 minutes, adding additional water if necessary and skimming off foam as it accumulates.

2. *Preparing chicken and stock:* To the same stockpot, add the chicken. Reduce the heat to medium and cook uncovered an additional 30 minutes,

skimming as necessary. Remove the chicken pieces and let cool. When cool shred the chicken, discarding skin and bones.

3. *Preparing purée:* In a small saucepan, combine the tomatoes and garlic with water to barely cover. Cook covered over medium heat until the tomatoes are tender. Pour the tomatoes, garlic, and cooking liquid into a blender container. Partially cover the container with the lid, allowing steam to escape; purée until smooth. Makes about 3 1/2 cups tomato purée.

4. *Finishing soup:* Pour the blended tomato purée, shredded chicken, and hominy into the stockpot. Add the chile powder, bouillon cubes, and oregano; mix thoroughly. Continue cooking uncovered over medium heat for 30 minutes, or until the hominy has softened and flavors are blended. Season to taste with additional chile powder, pressed garlic, or salt depending on preference.

5. *Garnishing:* To serve, ladle the pozole into soup bowls and pass condiment bowls of lettuce, chopped onion, radishes, and cilantro for garnishing the soup. Offer each guest lemon wedges and bean tostadas.

BEAN TOSTADAS
Spread warm frijoles refritos (refried beans) over tostadas (crisp corn tortillas).

MAKES 8 SERVINGS (PORTION SIZE: 2 CUPS)

Pozole, a hearty soup of pork, chicken, and hominy simmered in a light red chile broth, is one of the best-known dishes of the tapatio kitchen, an affectionate term for the people of Guadalajara, Jalisco, also used to distinguish their authentic dishes. This streamlined version has all the rich flavor of the original recipe but can be prepared within two hours, compared to the typical all-day cooking process.

CALDO DE RES (COUDO)

BEEF AND VEGETABLE SOUP

Autumn has always been a favorite time of the year for me. The change of season reminds me of the many Saturday afternoons that my brothers and I spent helping my dad rake leaves and do the other chores necessary for preparing the yard for the cold months ahead. At the end of the day, we would go into the house to the warmth and comfort of a fresh bowl of caldo de res. The caldo filled not only our bodies, but also our souls. This recipe is from my mother, Florence Marmolejo Marquez, who learned it from her mother, Anastacia Gomez Marmolejo: a proud lineage of Mexican women who care about their family and community.

BARBARA MARQUEZ

CALDO (BROTH)
1 pound beef shank, sliced into 1½-inch-thick pieces
1 onion, quartered
4 to 6 cloves garlic, minced

2 medium russet potatoes, grated
1 small bunch cilantro, stems removed, cleaned and cut up
Salt to taste

BEEF AND VEGETABLES
2 pounds chuck roast or stewing beef, cubed
5 carrots, cut into 1-inch-thick rounds
2 ears corn, cuts into 4 pieces each
¾ cup diced tomatoes
2 small zucchini or yellow squash, cut into ¾-inch-thick pieces (about 2 cups)

4 medium russet potatoes, cut into chunks
1 small cabbage, quartered

GARNISH
Chopped cilantro leaves
Chopped green onions

Lemon wedges

1. *Preparing caldo (broth):* In a large stockpot combine the beef shank, onion, garlic, grated potatoes, cilantro, and salt with 6 quarts of water.

Bring to a boil, reduce the heat, and vigorously simmer for about 1 hour. (The grated potatoes should dissolve, thickening the broth.)

2. *Cooking meat and vegetables:* Add the cubed chuck to the broth. Lower the heat and simmer uncovered for 1 hour, or until the meat is tender. Add the carrots and corn; cook for 20 minutes. Add the tomatoes, squash, and potato chunks. Bring to a boil and cook 5 to 10 minutes, or until the vegetables are tender. Turn off the heat and add the cabbage to the broth. Cover and let steam 30 minutes. Season to taste.

3. *Serving:* In each bowl, place a ladleful of meat and broth, a piece of corn, a portion of cabbage, and 2 or 3 pieces each of carrots, zucchini, and potatoes. Offer cilantro and green onions as a garnish. Serve with lemon wedges.

NOTE: If desired, refrigerate Caldo de Res overnight. The next day, before serving, remove the layer of hardened fat. Reheat and serve. The caldo de res always tastes better the next day, even without the fat!

SERVING SUGGESTION: This dish is traditionally served with a small bowl of Sopa de Arroz (Mexican Rice, page 145), salsa de chile de arbol and tortillas de harina (flour tortillas).

MAKES 8 SERVINGS (PORTION SIZE: 2 CUPS)

Caldo de res is also known as cocido, a hearty soup of exceptional flavor that is really quite economical to prepare. Every family has its own recipe and its special mix of vegetables to add to the stock. Supermarkets specializing in Latin products package "cocido vegetables" together during the wintertime for convenience. Cocido's well-seasoned broth furnishes the base for many of the soups and sauces made during the week.

MENUDO

BEEF TRIPE AND HOMINY SOUP WITH RED CHILE

This is the recipe that launched our little take-out café called "The Menudo Pot ... y Mucho Más." As my first experience in the food business, I learned how each step of a recipe is as important as the ingredients themselves. During the day, family members would walk into the café, go straight back to the kitchen, stir, and taste the Menudo. There would always be a critique which I learned to interpret as an acknowledgment. To this day, our family and friends celebrate the New Year with a pot of this delicious soup.

DIANE CORDOVA CREYAUFMILLER

MENUDO (SOUP)
1 pata (calf's foot), cut into 2-inch sections by butcher (about 2½ pounds)
1 large white onion
1 whole head garlic, separated into cloves, peeled
2 tablespoons salt
7½ pounds menudo (beef honeycomb tripe)
2½ pounds librio (book or pocket tripe)
5 pounds nixtamal (hominy), soaked and rinsed

CHILE PURÉE
8 New Mexico dried red chile peppers (see Note)
8 California dried red chile peppers
4 cloves garlic
1 small white onion, halved
Salt

GARNISH
Minced white onion
Chopped cilantro leaves
Dried oregano leaves
Red chile flakes
Lemon wedges
Flour or corn tortillas

1. *Preparing stock:* In a large stockpot, combine the calf's foot with the onion, garlic, salt, and water to cover by 5 inches. Bring to a boil, lower the heat, and vigorously simmer covered for 1 hour. Skim occasionally and discard any foam that rises to surface.

2. *Cooking tripe and hominy:* Cut the tripe into small squares and add to the pot. Continue cooking, covered, 2 hours, stirring occasionally. Add the hominy and continue to cook, uncovered, over medium heat. Add additional hot water during the cooking process to maintain the water level at least 3 inches above meat. The menudo is completely cooked when the hominy is soft and tripe can be easily cut with a fork.

3. *Chile purée:* Lightly rinse the chiles under cold running water. Remove the seeds, stems, and veins. (The more seeds and veins, the hotter the sauce.) Place the chile pods in a large kettle with water to barely cover. Bring to a boil; remove from the heat. Cover and let soak until plump, about 20 minutes. Drain the chiles, reserving about 2 cups of soaking liquid. In small batches, blend the softened chiles with garlic, onion, and salt to taste until smooth, adding reserved soaking liquid until the purée has the consistency of pourable cream. Strain the chile purée through a fine sieve; discard stray seeds and skin.

4. *Seasoning:* Pour the strained chile purée into the menudo according to your preference. Bring menudo to a boil, lower the heat, and simmer 20 minutes uncovered. Season with salt to taste.

5. *Serving:* Accompany menudo with small bowls of onion, cilantro, oregano, chile flakes, and lemon wedges to garnish soup. Serve with hot tortillas.

N O T E : Adjust the spice and color of Menudo by the type of chile used. New Mexico chile tends to be a dark brick-red with a fiery flavor. Usually, California chile pods produce a bright red color and mild flavor.

MAKES 15 SERVINGS (PORTION SIZE: 1 1/2 CUPS)

Menudo, one of Mexico's great soups, is one of the few traditional dishes that does not vary greatly regionally. Nixtamal (cured corn), beef hoof, and tripe are the 3 main ingredients, slowly simmered to create a nourishing broth oftentimes seasoned with a chile purée. The type of chile used depends on the recipe origin—in this case California and New Mexico.

Feijoada Completa

BRAZILIAN BLACK BEAN AND MEAT STEW

In Brazil, we work to live. There is nothing that a Brazilian loves more than to play, laugh, and enjoy life—especially on Saturday, which is Feijoada Day. Everyone seems to know which family or friend is preparing a feijoada. It is a dish that takes time and patience to prepare, so you always acknowledge the hostess and receive this dish as a gift.

FRANCESCA "FÁTIMA" GORDILS

TONGUE

1 beef tongue, fresh or smoked (about 3½ pounds)

2 bay leaves

1 onion, halved

1 small head garlic, halved

1 tablespoon salt

1 teaspoon ground black pepper

1 tablespoon liquid smoke (optional)

BEANS AND MEAT STEW

5 cups (2 pounds) dried black beans, sorted and rinsed

1 pound carne seca, cecina, or carne de xargue (salted beef)

1 pound longaniza-style chorizo (Mexican sausage) or pork chorizo

6 spicy linguiças (pork sausages), about 2 pounds

½ pound unsliced bacon

½ pound smoked pork loin

½ pound cured ham or salt pork, cut up

1 salted pig's foot (optional)

4 pig's ears (optional)

1 pound calabaza (pumpkin) or yellow winter squash, peeled and cubed

3 chayotes (vegetable pears), peeled and cubed

FEIJOADA SAUCE

2 tablespoons vegetable oil

1 medium white onion

4 green onions, sliced

3 malagueta or serrano chiles, minced

4 cloves garlic, minced

ACCOMPANIMENTS

Fresh sliced pineapple

Fresh sliced oranges

2 bunches collard greens, braised with green onions

Steamed white rice

Farofa branca (toasted manioc flour) (see Note)

Môho de Pimento com Limao (Hot Pepper-Lime Sauce, see page 108)

1. *Cooking tongue:* Place the tongue in a pot with water to cover, bay leaves, onion, garlic, salt, and black pepper. (If using fresh tongue, add liquid smoke to the pot.) Bring to a boil; lower the heat and simmer covered 2 to 2½ hours, or until very tender. Let cool in the broth. Strain, reserving 1 cup broth. Remove the skin and gristle from tongue; keep warm.

2. *Stewing beans and meats:* Place the beans with 4 inches of water to cover in a separate stockpot. Bring to a boil, lower the heat, and simmer 1 hour. Place the salted beef, chorizo, linguiça, bacon, smoked pork loin, ham, pig's foot and ears, if desired, pumpkin, and chayote into the pot. Add additional hot water to just cover meats and return to a rapid simmer. Cook 1½ to 2 hours, or until the beans are tender, adding additional hot water to keep the ingredients barely covered.

3. *Preparing feijoada sauce:* In a skillet, heat the oil and sauté the onions and chiles over medium heat. Add the reserved tongue cooking liquid, garlic, and 3 cups of strained black beans from the stockpot. Bring to a boil, lower the heat, and cook uncovered 10 minutes, stirring and mashing the beans into the onion mixture.

4. *Serving:* Slice the warm tongue and arrange on the center of a large serving platter. Remove the salted beef, chorizo, linguiça, bacon, pork loin, pig's foot and ears from the bean pot. Arrange the meats and sausages around the tongue. Garnish the platter with pineapple and orange slices. Stir the thickened feijoada bean sauce into the pot of black beans. Adjust seasoning if necessary. Transfer the bean mixture to a large tureen. Serve the feijoada with braised collard greens and fluffy white rice. Ladle the ebony beans and their rich sauce over the meats and rice as desired. The finishing touch is a sprinkling or more of toasted cassava meal (farofa) over the feijoada. Pass the Hot Pepper-Lime Sauce for your guests to add individually.

NOTE: Manioc or cassava flour, available in specialty markets, can be toasted in a heavy skillet over medium heat, stirring often until golden. If unavailable, toast dry cream of wheat until golden.

MAKES 12 TO 15 SERVINGS

Môlho de Pimento com Limao

HOT PEPPER-LIME SAUCE

8 fresh malagueta chiles, or substitute tabasco, piquín, or red serrano chiles, stemmed, seeded, and minced (about ¼ cup)

2 cloves garlic, minced

½ teaspoon salt

1 small white onion, minced (about ¾ cup)

4 green onion stalks, chopped fine (about ¼ cup)

1 cup fresh-squeezed lime or sour orange juice (about 6 limes)

In a mortar or blender, make a paste by grinding the chiles, garlic, and salt. Stir in the onions and lime juice. Let stand 2 hours at room temperature before serving.

VARIATION: To prepare a Hot Pepper-Ginger-Lime Sauce, add 3 to 4 tablespoons of fresh grated ginger. Serve this sauce with fried or grilled fish or Vatapá (Shrimp Coconut Stew, page 89).

MAKES ABOUT 2 CUPS

Feijoada, a hearty combination of meats, beans, vegetables, and fruits, is the best bean dish of all time, served traditionally at midday on Saturday. A plain feijoada may have but one or two kinds of meat, but a feijoada completa (complete) has everything.

CARNE ASADA EN SU JUGO

SAINT'S DAY & BIRTHDAY / MEXICO

BEEF STEAK IN ITS OWN JUICE

Whenever I prepare this dish, we always manage to have a party. Everyone is able to sit at the table and add their favorite condiment. It's a great way for our family to share our thoughts and the day's happenings.

MARIA G. VILLA

1 pound bacon, cut in ½-inch pieces
3 dried red árbol chiles, stemmed
2 pounds beef sirloin or top round, cut into 2-inch strips
4 cloves garlic, crushed
¼ cup lemon or lime juice
9 cups cooked pinto beans (about 4 cups beans and 5 cups broth) (see Frijoles de la Olla recipe, page 154)

Salt
2 ripe tomatoes, diced
1 large onion, minced
1 bunch cilantro, cleaned and chopped
5 jalapeño peppers, minced (optional)
Flour tortillas
Lime wedges

1. *Frying and toasting ingredients:* In a heavy skillet, fry the bacon over medium heat until crisp. Drain on absorbent towels. Pour the bacon grease out of the skillet; reserve. In the same skillet, toast the whole árbol chiles over medium heat until the chiles release their aroma and just blacken. Remove the chiles; set aside.

2. *Searing meat:* Heat 2 tablespoons of the reserved drippings in the same skillet. Quickly pan-fry the beef strips with the garlic until seared. Remove the meat and garlic from the skillet and place in a bowl. Add the lemon juice to the hot skillet. Stir and scrape with a wooden spoon to loosen the meat particles. Pour the juice over the meat strips.

3. *Simmering and serving:* In a small stockpot, heat the beans, bean broth, and 1 to 3 toasted árbol chiles to boiling. Stir in the meat strips with their juices and the fried bacon pieces. Season to taste with salt. Serve with bowls of diced tomatoes, minced onion, cilantro leaves, and minced jalapeños for garnishing. Offer each guest warm flour tortillas and lime wedges.

MAKES 6 SERVINGS (PORTION SIZE: 1½ CUPS)

Sancocho

CHICKEN AND SEAFOOD STEW

Outings to the countryside were commonplace in our family. We would drive out to the river early in the morning, set up camp, and enjoy lots of outdoor activities while a pot of Sancocho would simmer over an open fire.

TITI YEPES

CHICKEN STOCK

2 chickens, about 3½ pounds each, cut into serving pieces

1 leek, halved lengthwise and well washed

1 large onion, chopped

1 head garlic, cloves separated and peeled

4 stalks celery, cut into 1½-inch pieces

3 carrots, scraped, each cut into 4 pieces

1 large tomato, peeled, seeded, and chopped

2 or 3 sprigs fresh cilantro

Salt and ground black pepper ·

ROOT VEGETABLES

2 coconuts or 4 cups coconut milk (see page 90)

1 tablespoon achiote (annatto paste) or bijol (yellow coloring)

1 pound yuca (cassava or yucca root), peeled and cut into 1½-inch slices

1 pound calabaza (West Indian pumpkin) or any yellow winter squash, peeled and cut into ½-inch slices

1 pound ñame (yam, not orange sweet potatoes), peeled and cut into 1½-inch slices

1 pound boniato (white sweet potato), peeled and cut into 1½-inch slices

1 pound potatoes, peeled and cut into 1½-inch slices

FISH AND VEGETABLES

2 pounds any combination of firm-fleshed fish such as cod, bass, halibut, catfish, or snapper, boned and cut into 2-inch pieces

1 small cabbage, blanched and cut into 8 wedges

3 ears corn, each cut into 4 pieces

3 green or yellow plantains, peeled and cut into 1½-inch slices

2 bunches cilantro, cleaned, stemmed, and chopped

1. *Simmering chicken stock:* In a large stockpot, place the chicken with water to cover (about 3 quarts). Add the leek, onion, garlic, celery, carrots, tomato, cilantro, salt, and pepper. Bring to a boil, reduce heat to a brisk simmer, and cook covered for 30 minutes. Remove the chicken and let cool. Shred the meat, discarding skin and bones.

2. *Cooking root vegetables:* Add the coconut milk, achiote, yuca, calabaza, yam, sweet potatoes, and potatoes to the stockpot. Continue cooking 20 to 30 minutes uncovered, or until the vegetables are tender when pierced with a fork.

3. *Finishing:* Add the fish, cabbage, corn, plantains, and chicken meat to the stockpot. Cook over medium high heat just long enough to heat through. Before serving, season to taste, adding additional coconut milk, salt, or pepper. Ladle the sancocho into soup bowls and garnish with a generous portion of cilantro leaves. Serve in soup plates with Salsa de Pebre (Chilean Condiment Sauce, recipe follows) and French bread.

MAKES 12 SERVINGS (PORTION SIZE: 1 CUP VEGETABLES AND 1 CUP MEAT AND BROTH)

SALSA DE PEBRE
TABLE CONDIMENT / CHILE

CHILEAN CONDIMENT SAUCE

⅓ cup olive oil
2 tablespoons red wine vinegar
⅓ cup water
2 tablespoons lemon juice
4 fresh ají peppers, stemmed, seeded, and minced, or substitute 2 orange serrano chiles or 1 red jalapeño chile

4 cloves garlic, minced
¾ cup minced white onion
½ cup chopped parsley or cilantro leaves
1 tablespoon minced fresh oregano (optional)
Salt and black pepper

In a glass bowl, combine the olive oil, vinegar, water, lemon juice, chiles, garlic, onion, parsley, and oregano. Mix well and season to taste with salt and pepper. Let stand 2 hours at room temperature or refrigerate overnight before serving.

MAKES 3 CUPS

PUCHERO

BEEF POT

In Argentina, there is a Puchero for every season of the year. Although Pucheros contain a great many vegetables, you will never find greens such as spinach or strong spices and herbs. If pucheros are to be seasoned, the condiment is offered on the side.

1 pound marrow bones with some meat (ask butcher for lower beef shank bones)

1 large beef or veal knuckle bone, sawed into pieces (about 3 pounds)

3 pounds chamorro (beef shank), cut into 2-inch-thick pieces

3 bay leaves

Juice of 1 lemon

2 pounds beef stewing meat

2 large leeks, white part only, cleaned and chopped

4 sprigs fresh parsley

3 large cloves garlic, passed through a press

1 teaspoon salt

½ teaspoon ground black pepper

2 potatoes, peeled and quartered

2 sweet potatoes, peeled and quartered

3 carrots, peeled and cut into 1-inch pieces

1 large piece yellow winter squash, such as pumpkin, acorn, or banana squash, cut into 1-inch cubes (about 1½ cups)

2 ears corn, husked and cut into 4 pieces

1. *Preparing rich beef stock:* In a large pot, combine marrow bones, knuckle, beef shank, bay leaves, and lemon juice with enough cold water to cover, about 4 quarts. Bring to a slow boil (this will prevent scum from forming). Lower the heat and gently simmer uncovered about 1 hour.

2. *Stewing meat:* Add the stewing meat, leeks, parsley, garlic, salt, and pepper to the pot. Continue simmering uncovered for 1 hour. Remove part of the broth (a rich beef consommé) and reserve for another use (about 4 cups).

3. *Cooking vegetables:* Add the potatoes, sweet potatoes, carrots, pumpkin, and corn to the pot. If the vegetables are not covered by broth, add

additional broth to cover. Bring to a gentle boil, reduce the heat, and cook for 30 minutes, or until vegetables are tender. Season to taste with additional salt and pepper.

SERVING SUGGESTION: There are many ways to serve this soup. One of the most popular is serving the beef and vegetables on a platter separate from the consommé. This allows each guest to place the beef or vegetables in the consommé to be eaten as a soup or to enjoy the beef and vegetables with a condiment sauce such as Salsa Para Asados (Roasted Meat Sauce, recipe follows).

MAKES 8 SERVINGS (PORTION SIZE: 1 CUP VEGETABLES WITH MEAT AND 1 CUP BROTH)

SALSA PARA ASADOS
CONDIMENT SAUCE AND MARINADE / URUGUAY

ROASTED MEAT SAUCE

A fresh (uncooked) sauce, an aliño such as this salsa, is commonly used as a condiment for roasted meats and chicken. You can also use this sauce as a wonderful marinade.

1 cup olive oil
½ cup red wine vinegar
12 cloves garlic, minced or passed
    through a press
1 cup finely chopped parsley
1 teaspoon dried oregano leaves
1 teaspoon crushed dried thyme

2 teaspoons pimentón (ground red pepper), or substitute ½ teaspoon
    ground cayenne pepper mixed with
    1½ teaspoons sweet paprika
Salt
Freshly ground black pepper

Combine the olive oil, vinegar, garlic, parsley, oregano, thyme, and pimentón in a medium bowl. Whisk until smooth and season with salt and pepper. Allow to stand a minimum of 2 hours or refrigerate overnight.

MAKES 2½ CUPS

T̲hroughout the Americas you'll find many variations of paella, a Spanish saffron rice dish with seafood, usually some chicken, and oftentimes pork. Arroz con pollo, chicken with rice, a simplified version of paella, evolved over the centuries to become Latin comfort food.

Arroz con Bacalao

LENT / CUBA

RICE WITH SALT COD

Perhaps it is a coincidence, but as a child I remember my mom preparing Arroz con Bacalao whenever the sky became stormy and the rain would fall. Today, this dish takes me back to those carefree days.

MARGARITA DUTOC

¼ cup Spanish olive oil

2 cloves garlic, minced

2 medium onions, chopped (about 1 cup)

½ green bell pepper, chopped (about 1 cup)

½ teaspoon bijol (yellow coloring) or ¼ teaspoon powdered saffron

2 cups raw long-grain white rice

¼ cup dry sherry

1 pound (2 cups) dried salt cod, soaked and shredded following directions on page 6

¼ teaspoon salt

Minced fresh parsley to garnish

1. *Sautéing ingredients:* In a medium skillet or saucepan, warm the oil over medium heat. Sauté the garlic, onions, and green pepper, stirring until tender, about 5 minutes. Add the bijol and rice. Continue stirring and cooking until the rice is evenly colored and oiled, about 2 minutes.

2. *Cooking and serving:* Stir in 4½ cups of water, the sherry, salt cod, and salt. Bring to a boil, lower the heat, and simmer covered for 25 minutes. Uncover and continue cooking undisturbed until the rice appears dry. Garnish with parsley before serving.

SERVING SUGGESTION: To complement this colorful and satisfying meal, all that is needed is Plátanos Maduros Fritos (Fried Sweet Plantains, page 168) for those family members with voracious appetites!

MAKES 6 SERVINGS (PORTION SIZE: 1 CUP)

Arroz con Pollo (Cubano)

CUBAN RICE WITH CHICKEN

What would life be without memories? An empty bowl. Fortunately, mine overflows with countless cups of love, plenty of heaping tablespoons of laughter, a big pinch of spiritual magic, a sprinkle of good friends, a provocative glance from the man I love, Papi's smile, and Mami's arroz con pollo. ¡Que rico, la vida!

RODRI J. RODRIGUEZ

Olive oil for frying (about ⅓ cup)
10 skinless and boneless chicken
    breast fillets or chicken pieces
1 medium white onion, chopped
1 green bell pepper, chopped
1 red bell pepper, chopped
8 large cloves garlic, crushed
¼ teaspoon ground cumin
½ bunch fresh cilantro leaves

1 (14½-ounce) can tomato purée
6 cups water or chicken broth
2 pounds (4 cups) medium-grain rice
2 teaspoons salt
¼ teaspoon bijol (yellow coloring)
1 (12-ounce) can beer
1 (28-ounce) can peas, drained
1 (4-ounce) can pimientos, drained
    and sliced

1. *Frying and seasoning:* In a large skillet, warm the oil over medium high heat. Add the chicken and fry until lightly browned. Stir in the onion, bell peppers, garlic, and cumin. Continue cooking, stirring frequently, until the onion is tender. Stir in the cilantro and cook 1 minute.

2. *Simmering:* Add the tomato purée to the skillet. Reduce the heat to medium low and simmer uncovered for 5 minutes. Add 6 cups of water, the rice, salt, and bijol, stirring to mix thoroughly. Bring to a boil; reduce the heat to very low. Cover and simmer **undisturbed** for 30 minutes. Do not remove lid or stir while rice is simmering.

3. *Finishing and serving:* Remove lid from skillet. Slowly pour beer over cooked rice until it is completely absorbed. When the beer foam subsides, stir to mix lightly and continue cooking uncovered for 2 to 3 minutes. Transfer the arroz con pollo to a platter (or leave in the skillet) and garnish with peas and pimientos. Serve immediately.

MAKES 8 SERVINGS (PORTION SIZE: ABOUT ½ BREAST AND 1 CUP RICE)

Paella Valenciana

PAELLA FROM VALENCIA

I love making paella! Whenever I make it I think of Ponce, where I grew up, and the regular get-togethers with family and friends. I remember how I loved to watch my father's friend Pachín make the best paella right in the middle of a party. This recipe is his, although I have since modified it and have added my own special touch. Like Pachín, I make paella with lots of people around me and get them involved in the preparation. It makes for great conversation!

MARI RODRIGUEZ BELLAS

SOFRITO (SEASONING)
2 white onions, quartered
1 bunch green onions, chopped
1 large red bell pepper, cut up
1 head garlic (about 15 cloves), peeled
1 bunch cilantro, washed

SEAFOOD AND BROTH
1 (12-ounce) bottle beer
3 pounds green New Zealand mussels, scrubbed
3 pounds small clams, scrubbed
2 bay leaves
½ bunch parsley, cleaned
5 pounds medium shrimp, in the shell
1 bottle (about ⅛ ounce) saffron threads or bijol (yellow coloring)
2 extra-large seafood, shrimp, or chicken-flavored bouillon cubes

MEATS
1 cup olive oil
6 pounds chicken legs and thighs, seasoned with salt
3 pounds thick pork chops, diced
3 pounds bulk Mexican chorizo (sausage) or 1½ pounds sliced Spanish chorizo (hard sausage)
1 (32-ounce) can crushed tomatoes
1 (16-ounce) can tomato sauce
12 cups long-grain white rice
15 cups hot water (plus additional 15 cups seafood broth—see step 2, page 117)
1 (15-ounce) can pitted black olives
2 (7-ounce) cans sweet red pimientos, sliced
1 (16-ounce) package frozen baby peas
2 bunches asparagus, sliced and steamed
Lemon wedges to garnish

1. *Pureéing sofrito:* In a blender container, purée the onions, red bell pepper, garlic, and cilantro, using up to 2 cups of water. Set aside.

2. *Preparing seafood broth:* In a large pot, combine the beer, mussels, clams, bay leaves, and parsley with enough water to cover. Bring to a boil, lower the heat, and simmer vigorously, uncovered, for 5 minutes, or until the shells open. Immediately remove the clams and mussels, discarding any that have not opened; set aside to cool. In the same pot, cook the shrimp until just pink (do not overcook). Strain the broth into a large bowl or pot and set the shrimp aside to cool. Add the saffron and bouillon cubes to the broth, stirring until dissolved. Add enough hot water, about 15 cups, to make 30 cups of seafood broth.

3. *Frying meat:* In a large paellera (a paella cooking pan) or wok, heat the olive oil. Add the chicken and fry over medium high heat until golden, about 10 minutes, turning occasionally; remove from the pan. Add the pork and sausage pieces and continue cooking until browned.

4. *Seasoning meat:* Stir in the sofrito (puréed onion mixture) and fry 5 minutes, stirring to loosen browned bits of meat. Mix in the tomatoes and tomato sauce. Return the chicken to the pan. Bring to a boil, lower the heat, and cook uncovered for 15 minutes, basting the meat often.

5. *Adding rice:* Pour the rice into the pan in a cross, spreading out slowly to fill the pan. Make a hole in the center and slowly pour the warm seafood broth in a steady stream to keep the temperature constant. Tightly cover the pan and vigorously simmer for 20 minutes undisturbed.

6. *Finishing:* Remove the cover. Arrange the clams, shrimp, and mussels around the edge of the pan. Sprinkle the rice with olives, pimientos, peas, and asparagus. Cook covered for an additional 5 to 10 minutes, until the rice is completely tender, adding additional broth if necessary. Decorate with lemon wedges before serving.

MAKES 50 SERVINGS (PORTION SIZE: 2 CUPS)

T hroughout Latin America, the word tamal is recognized as a wrapped, steamed dough which, based on the country, can be made with fresh corn, nixtamal (cured corn), hominy, corn flour, plantains, yaútia, or other starchy vegetables. Tamales can be savory or sweet, and are wrapped in corn husks or tropical leaves which impart a lovely scent and distinctive flavor. These steamed bundles are Latin America's famed celebration food— a Christmas specialty known as hallacas in Venezuela, bollos in Colombia and Ecuador and some parts of Central America, pasteles in Puerto Rico and Central America, humitas en chala in Argentina, Uruguay, and Paraguay, paches in Guatemala, and tamales throughout Mexico, our own Southwest, and Central America.

HUMITAS EN CHALA
OUTDOOR ASADO / ARGENTINA

STEAMED FRESH CORN AND BASIL HUMITAS

16 ears fresh-picked corn (see Note)
4 tablespoons (½ stick) butter
⅓ cup minced green onion
1 teaspoon salt
Sugar to taste
12 large leaves sweet basil, minced

½ cup harina Pan (see page 3) or masa harina (corn flour)
8 ounces soft white cheese (Sonoma Jack, manchego, or teleme), cut into 12 (2 ×⅜-inch) strips

1. *Scraping corn:* Remove husks and silk from the corn. Select about 30 of the delicate inner husks with the best size to use as wrappings. Refrigerate the selected husks; set aside the remaining husks to use when steaming. Grate the corn from the cobs into a bowl; set aside the cobs. Makes about 3 cups.

2. *Cooking humitas:* In a large skillet, melt the butter over medium heat. Sauté onions until soft. Add the scraped corn. Season to taste with salt and a little sugar (amounts will depend on the maturity of the corn; the younger corn will be sweeter). Cook uncovered over medium heat, stirring occasionally, until the mixture is reduced and resembles thick cream of

wheat. Remove from the heat. Add the basil and corn flour to corn mixture, mixing well.

3. *Wrapping humitas:* Place a green corn husk rough side down on a cutting board. Evenly spread 2 to 3 tablespoons of corn mixture on the lower half of the husk. Place 1 slice of cheese lengthwise in the center of the mixture. Fold the edges of the husk over the cheese to make an oblong package. If necessary, use an additional husk and cement them with a bit of filling. Fold the ends of husks (the nonfilled section) down over the lower half. Secure the open end with a strip of corn husk.

4. *Steaming the humitas:* In a pot with a tight-fitting lid, place a thick layer of scraped corncobs covered with a layer of unused husks; add boiling salted water to nearly cover the cobs and husks. Arrange the humitas on husks, tied side upright, side by side. Cover with a second layer of unused husks. Cover tightly and steam 30 to 40 minutes over medium high heat. Check after 20 minutes, adding boiling water if needed. (If the steamer is not tightly covered, humitas can take up to 1 hour to cook.) Let cool and serve warm.

NOTE: Select corn that is tender yet firm. To check, push a fingernail into the kernels; they should be juicy, not dry. If you have to press too hard, the corn is too starchy.

SERVING SUGGESTION: Serve Humitas en Chala with grilled chicken on a bed of watercress sprinkled with fresh lime juice along with a white bean salad (seasoned with olive oil, garlic, tomatoes, and onion).

MAKES 12 SERVINGS (PORTION SIZE: 1 HUMITA)

Humitas en Chala, fresh corn cakes steamed in their own husks, are traditionally served as a side dish with Argentinian or Uruguayan asado, or meats barbecued outdoors. The famous Argentinian asado is far more elaborate than the American outdoor barbecue. Several kinds of meat—chicken, lamb, and beef—are carefully grilled over the open fire along with a variety of sausages and organ meats.

HALLACAS

CHRISTMAS / VENEZUELA

VENEZUELAN STEAMED HALLACAS

The communal preparation of Hallacas among all my Venezuelan friends who had lived abroad for many years would somehow transport us back to our country, our homes, and our childhood. The sharing of memories, the laughter, and the music gave me a sense of family even in the absence of my own. Although I never learned how to make Hallacas as a young adult, after I left my country I had a yearning for this dish. So I made an effort to make this part of my holiday tradition.

VIVIANNE SCHAEL

1 DAY PRIOR TO PREPARATION
CHICKEN FILLING

2 (3-pound) broiler/fryer chickens, cut up

1 large white onion, halved

2 bay leaves

1 whole head garlic, outer skin rubbed clean, top third sliced off

2 large chicken-flavored bouillon cubes

Salt and ground black pepper

CORN FOR FILLING

½ cup dried white corn or ⅔ cup harina Pan (precooked white cornmeal) or 1 cup canned whole hominy

MASA (CORN DOUGH)

3 pounds bacon, chopped

5 cups lard

6 large cloves garlic, minced

5 tablespoons salt

6 tablespoons achiote (annatto seeds)

5 pounds dried white corn or 30 cups cooked white corn or canned whole hominy

DAY OF PREPARATION
HALLACA FILLING

12 ripe tomatoes

1 red bell pepper, cored and seeded

25 large cloves garlic

2 large white onions, cut into chunks

2 large green bell peppers, cored and seeded

1 large red bell pepper or 4 ajíes dulces (sweet red chile peppers), cored and seeded

1 to 2 chile peppers, cored and seeded

5 pounds boneless trimmed pork shoulder, cut into 1-inch pieces
Salt and ground black pepper
4 strips bacon, cut up
1 cup olive oil
2 cups sliced green onions (including green and white portions)
2 cups leeks, chopped (white portion)
½ cup large capers
½ cup pickled vegetables packed in mustard, chopped

Banana leaves, parchment paper, or aluminum foil for wrapping

1 cup grated papelón (Venezuelan raw sugar) or 1 cup brown sugar plus 1 tablespoon molasses
1½ tablespoons pimentón (ground sweet red pepper or paprika)
2 tablespoons mild chile powder
1 tablespoon ground black pepper
¾ cup prepared mustard
2 cups sweet wine, such as sherry
1 cup vinegar

GARNISHES

2 cups large capers
2 cups raisins
5 red bell peppers, cut into long strips (about 100 strips)
4 cups blanched whole almonds

4 cups pimiento-stuffed olives
5 white onions, sliced into rings (about 100 rings)
1½ dozen hard-cooked eggs, sliced into 6 wedges each

ONE DAY PRIOR TO PREPARATION

1. *Preparing chicken:* In a large pot, combine the chicken, onion, bay leaves, garlic, and bouillon cubes with 12 cups of water. Season with salt and pepper. Bring to a boil, lower the heat, and cook, partially covered, for 25 minutes. Remove from the heat and let the chicken cool in its own broth. Strain, reserving chicken and broth. Pull off and shred the chicken meat, discarding the skin and bones. Cover and refrigerate.

2. *Soaking and grinding corn for filling:* In a small saucepan, combine the dried white corn with water to cover by 3 inches. Bring to a boil and cook covered over medium low heat for 35 minutes. Remove from the heat and let cool. Drain the corn, reserving the liquid. Place the corn in a grinder or food processor bowl and grind with just enough cooking liquid to process. Cover and refrigerate.

3. *Flavoring lard for masa:* In a pot, combine the bacon, lard, garlic, and salt. Cook for 30 minutes over medium heat until the bacon browns. Remove from the heat, strain, and let cool. Pour half the melted lard

(continued on next page)

mixture into a bowl with the annatto seeds. When the fat has colored, strain. Refrigerate the colored and uncolored lard.

4. *Cooking and grinding corn for masa:* Place the dried corn with water to cover in a large pot. Bring to a boil, reduce the heat, and simmer, partially covered, for 1 hour. Remove from the heat and let stand in the cooking liquid overnight to soften. Grind the corn in a food processor or a meat grinder to the consistency of Grape-Nuts cereal. Refrigerate.

DAY OF PREPARATION

1. *Puréeing and chopping ingredients for meat filling:* In a workbowl of a food processor, purée the tomatoes and red bell pepper in batches until smooth. You will have about 6 cups of purée. Pour into a bowl and set aside. In the same workbowl, separately chop the garlic, white onions, bell peppers, and chile peppers; set aside and keep separate.

2. *Braising ingredients for meat filling:* Generously sprinkle the pork with salt and pepper. In a large pot, fry the pork pieces and bacon over medium high heat until browned. Remove the pork from the pot; cover and set aside. In the same pot used to fry the pork, heat the olive oil. Stir in the chopped garlic and chopped white onion. Add the green onions and leeks. Sauté until soft, stirring and scraping the bottom of the pan to release browned bits of meat. Add the chopped green and red bell peppers and chile peppers. Sauté 2 to 3 minutes, or until tender. Stir in the capers and ½ cup of the reserved chicken broth. Continue cooking uncovered for 15 minutes, or until the broth has almost evaporated. Stir in the toma-to–bell pepper purée, pickled vegetables, brown sugar, ground red pepper (or paprika), chile powder, black pepper, mustard, sweet wine, and vinegar until thoroughly blended. Cook 5 minutes over medium heat. Add the cooked pork, cooked chicken, and 2 cups of the reserved chicken broth. Mix well and season with black pepper and salt to taste. Lower the heat and simmer covered for 40 minutes, stirring occasionally.

3. *Finishing masa (dough):* In a bowl, combine the ground corn, 2 cups of the uncolored lard, and 2 cups of the colored lard, or enough to tint the dough the desired orange color. (If desired, add in 2 whole eggs.) Mix until the dough is smooth. Slowly mix in 3 cups of reserved broth and salt to taste. The masa should be smooth and orange colored.

4. *Finishing and thickening meat filling:* In a small bowl, combine the ground corn with 1½ cups of reserved warm chicken broth until blended. Pour into the meat mixture and mix thoroughly. Continue cooking covered for 30 minutes, or until the preparation has thickened. Makes 12 cups.

5. *Preparing banana leaves:* Using a knife, remove the central ridge from the banana leaves. Divide the leaves into sections about 10 by 10 inches or 8 by 8 inches, depending on the size of the leaves.

6. *Forming hallacas:* Lay one banana leaf on a counter. Lightly oil the smooth side of the leaf. Evenly spread ⅓ cup of masa on the oiled side of the banana leaf ¼ inch thick, using a spatula. Place 3 to 4 tablespoons of the meat mixture over the center of the masa. Arrange a few capers, 8 raisins, 2 pimiento strips, 1 almond and 1 olive, 1 onion ring and 1 egg wedge on top of the filling. Lay a corn dough–covered banana leaf over each meat-filled one, with the corn side down. Tuck in all the edges to make a flat, square package about 1 inch thick. Cover with another wrapping of banana leaves and securely tie with several strands of heavy thread. (Packages should be about 1 inch thick and 6 to 8 inches square.)

7. *Steaming:* Fill the bottom of a steamer with 5 inches of salted water. Insert a rack and add banana leaves up to the water level. Loosely layer the hallacas over the leaves. Cover the pot and bring to a rpaid boil. Lower the heat and simmer covered for 45 minutes. Midway through the cooking process, turn and reverse the position of the pasteles. Remove the lid and let pasteles cool and set before serving.

NOTE: Yellow corn is preferred, but North American white hominy that comes in a package will do (even cornmeal serves for dough when scalded with boiling salted water to form a thick mush). In Venezuela, as in Mexico, this corn dough, or masa, ground to a fine consistency, can be purchased ready-made in the markets. If banana leaves are unavailable, well-oiled heavy paper can be used, but the fresh leafy flavor will be missing.

MAKES 6 DOZEN (PORTION SIZE: 1 LARGE HALLACA)

Pasteles de Masa

PUERTO RICAN STEAMED PASTELES

The preparation of pasteles marked the beginning of the Christmas season's festivities in my childhood home. Each female member of the family would be given a task in the production of this intricate recipe. We would all form an assembly line of sorts, make dozens of pasteles, laugh, and learn family folklore.

ANA JIMÉNEZ-INMAN

MEAT FILLING

4 large cloves garlic
1 teaspoon salt
1 teaspoon ground black pepper
1½ teaspoons oregano
4 red ajíes (sweet red chile peppers) or 1 red bell pepper and 1 red jalapeño pepper, chopped
1 cup chopped cilantro leaves or 8 culantro leaves
⅓ cup lard or olive oil
1 tablespoon achiote (annatto seeds)
4 pounds boneless pork shoulder, trimmed and cut into small pieces (about 6 cups)

2 teaspoons adobo seasoning
1 medium white onion, chopped
1 green bell pepper, chopped
1 (8-ounce) can tomato sauce
1 cup cubed cured ham
1 (5-ounce) jar pimiento-stuffed olives, drained
1 (7-ounce) can pimientos with liquid, chopped
1 (15-ounce) can garbanzo beans, drained
¾ cup raisins

MASA (DOUGH)

4 pounds yautía blanca (taro)
3 pounds yautía amarilla (malanga)
2 pounds unripe green bananas (about 8)
1 large green plantain
1 pound colored lard (see Note), or 2 cups oil heated with 1 cup achiote (annatto seeds)

1 cup warm milk
Salt to taste
Plantain leaves (about 20 large), parchment paper, or aluminum foil for wrapping

1. *Grinding recaíto (seasoning paste):* In a pilón or mortar, grind the garlic into the salt, pepper, and oregano to form a paste. Add ajíes and cilantro and continue mashing until blended. Set aside.

2. *Frying and seasoning meat:* In a pot, melt the lard over medium heat. Add the achiote seeds and cook, stirring occasionally, until the achiote colors the lard. Remove the seeds. Add the diced pork to the pot. Sprinkle adobo seasoning over the pork and fry, stirring occasionally, until the meat has browned. Add the onion and green bell pepper and continue frying for 2 minutes. Stir the racaíto seasoning paste into the meat. Continue cooking for 5 minutes, stirring and scraping the bottom of the pot to gather up any browned bits of meat.

3. *Simmering and finishing meat filling:* Add the tomato sauce and 1 1/2 cups of water. Bring to a boil, lower the heat, and cook covered for 25 minutes, or until the meat is very tender. To finish, stir the ham, olives, pimientos and their liquid, garbanzo beans, and raisins into the meat mixture. Continue cooking for 20 minutes, or until the flavors are fully developed. Season to taste. Remove the pot from the heat and set aside 3/4 cup of the liquid to use in the masa (dough). Makes 10 cups.

4. *Preparing masa:* Peel the yautías, green bananas, and plantain; soak in salted water for 10 minutes to prevent discoloration. Using the finest grating blade of a food processor, grate the yautías, green bananas, and plantain in small batches. Empty into a bowl. Add the grated yautía mixture, colored lard, warm milk, the reserved liquid from the meat, and salt to taste. Insert the steel blade into the food processor bowl. Process the mixture in small batches to make a smooth, even-colored paste. Do not overmix.

5. *Preparing plantain leaves:* Using a knife, remove the central ridge from the plantain leaves. Divide the leaves into sections about 10 by 10 inches or 8 by 8 inches, depending on the size of the leaves. Clean each section with a damp cloth. Using tongs, pass each section over a medium flame or electric burner to toast lightly, being careful not to burn or dry out the leaf. Arrange the warmed leaves in a pile and cover with foil to keep warm.

6. *Shaping pasteles:* Lay 1 warm plantain leaf on a counter. Lightly oil the smooth side of the leaf. Evenly spread 4 tablespoons of masa on the oiled side of the plantain leaf. Place 2 heaping tablespoons of meat filling in the center of the masa. Fold 2 edges over the filling. Fold the open

(continued on next page)

ends over. Repeat the process to make an additional pastel. Place 2 pasteles facing each other, seam sides together. Tie securely with string. Repeat the process with the remaining ingredients.

7. *Steaming:* Fill the bottom of a steamer with 5 inches of salted water. Insert a rack and add enough plantain leaves to come up to the water level. Loosely layer the pasteles over the leaves. Cover the pot and bring to a rapid boil. Lower the heat and simmer covered for 45 minutes. Midway through the cooking process, turn and reverse the position of the pasteles. Remove the lid and let the pasteles cool and set before serving.

NOTE: To prepare colored lard, follow the directions in step 2, using 6 to 8 tablespoons of annato seeds to 1 pound of lard.

SERVING SUGGESTION: Your Puerto Rican Christmas buffet can include pasteles, Arroz con Gandules (Puerto Rican Rice with Pigeon Peas, page 144) and habichuelas rosadas (red bean stew). Serve with your favorite salad and vegetables. For appetizers, select either Tostones con Salsa de Tomate de Ajo (Fried Plantains with a Tomato-Garlic Sauce, page 167) or guineos verdes en escabeche (pickled green bananas).

MAKES ABOUT 5 DOZEN (PORTION SIZE: 1 PASTEL)

Throughout the Latin continent, forty or more varieties of root vegetables have the status of staple foods. These coarse brown tubers vary not only in shape and flavor but in names as well. The Cuban malanga and malanga isleña are known respectively as yautía amarilla and yautía blanca (or taro) by the Puerto Ricans. Yuca or cassava, perhaps the most popular of all tubers, is used in every country where cooks appreciate the buttery, delicate flavor and the dense texture that is so quick to absorb the flavors of sauces and stews.

Boniato, the Cuban sweet potato, has a lovely chestnut flavor and is also known as batata or camote in other countries. To confuse matters more, the orange-fleshed yam found in North American stores is actually a sweet potato, called camote in Latin America, and the true yam generally is called ñame. Potatoes, another South American tuber, come in every color and size imaginable. Another important staple, plátanos, plaintains or cooking bananas, should not be confused with guineos or unripe green bananas.

Bollos Dulces con Anís

CHRISTMAS / PANAMA

SWEET ANISE STEAMED BOLLOS

In Panama, Venezuela, and Colombia, bollos are steamed corn dough wrapped in their own husks (or leaves) with or without a filling. In this version, the dough is sweetened with honey and flavored with anise to create a special feast day bollo, which can be served with vanilla atole!

2 pounds prepared masa (corn dough)
2 teaspoons ground anise seeds
½ teaspoon anise extract (optional)
1 cup honey or raspadura (Central American grated or melted raw sugar)

1 teaspoon salt
Large dried corn husks, soaked in hot water for 30 minutes
1 pound fresh cheese, cut into thick slices

1. *Preparing masa:* In a bowl, combine the prepared masa, anise seeds, anise extract, honey, and salt. Beat until mixed. Cover and refrigerate.

2. *Forming bollos:* Drain the corn husks and pat them dry. Thickly spread 2 to 3 tablespoons of dough evenly onto the smooth side of the husk. Place a cheese slice in the center of the dough and fold the edges over to cover cheese. Secure with string or strips of corn husks.

3. *Steaming:* Fill the bottom of a large steamer with 3 inches of water; insert a rack. Arrange the bollos on the rack, open end up, side by side. Cover with a damp kitchen towel and top with a dry towel. Place the lid securely on the steamer. Bring to a boil; steam 40 minutes. Remove 1 bollo and unwrap it. The husk should easily release from the dough. (The cooked dough will not be firm until partially cooled.) Remove the pot from the heat and let stand 20 minutes. Remove husks before serving.

PREPARED MASA
Prepared corn masa (dough) is premixed with lard or oil, water or broth, and salt that can be purchased in a tortillería (Mexican deli).

MAKES 20 BOLLOS (PORTION SIZE: 1 BOLLO)

TAMALES ROJOS

RED CHILE AND PORK TAMALES

Tamales played an important role in my family life. At Christmastime, I remember accompanying my mother to purchase all the ingredients. Our family would stand around the kitchen table for what seemed like hours preparing tamales for our Christmas Day feast. Laughter, stories, and just catching up on the year's activities were shared at our meal table. Tamales were made not only at Christmas but also for funerals and baptisms, signifying the passage of time and a gift of love.

REGINA BOUBION CORDOVA

PORK AND RED CHILE FILLING
5 pounds bone-in pork shoulder butt
8 large cloves garlic, peeled
Salt
1 package (about 18) dried New Mexico red chiles

1 small white onion, halved
¼ cup lard or pork fat (see step 1)
2 tablespoons flour

MASA (DOUGH)
1½ pounds fresh lard, refrigerated
2 teaspoons baking powder
2 to 2½ tablespoons salt
5 pounds fresh masa (corn dough), ground for tamales

2 (8-ounce) packages hojas (dried corn husks), silk removed and soaked 1 hour in warm water

1. *Cooking pork:* (Do this at least a day before you assemble the tamales.) Score the pork with 2-inch-deep cuts 2 inches apart. In a stockpot, combine the pork, 6 cloves garlic, 2 tablespoons salt, and enough water to cover by 2 inches. Bring to a boil; lower the heat and cook covered until tender, about 1 to 1½ hours. Let cool. Strain, reserving the broth. Shred the pork and discard the bones. Refrigerate the pork and broth overnight. (The next day, lift off the hardened fat from the broth; reserve for the dough.)

2. *Preparing chile purée:* Lightly rinse the chiles under cold running water. Remove the seeds, stems, and veins. Place the chile pods in a large kettle;

cover with boiling water and soak covered until plump (about 20 minutes). Drain the chiles, reserving about 2 cups of soaking liquid. In small batches, blend the softened chiles with 2 garlic cloves, the small white onion, and salt to taste. Add $1/2$ to 1 cup of the reserved liquid and purée until the mixture has the consistency of pourable cream. Strain the chile purée through a fine sieve.

3. *Pork–red chile filling:* In a 3-quart stockpot, fry the lard and flour over medium heat, stirring constantly, until the flour turns light brown. Pour in the chile purée and mix briskly. Heat to boiling and add the shredded pork and $1/2$ cup of the reserved pork broth. Lower the heat and simmer covered for 30 minutes, or until flavors combine. Season to taste, adding salt and/or additional garlic. If the meat filling is dry, add more broth to make a chile sauce the consistency of gravy. Set aside. Makes 2 quarts.

4. *Masa (dough):* In a large mixing bowl, beat the lard and 1 cup of reserved pork fat (from cooking the pork) until light and fluffy. Beat in the baking powder and salt. Add 3 pounds (about half) masa to the whipped lard, 1 cup at a time, beating after each addition until the mixture returns to a fluffy consistency. Add the remaining masa and broth, alternating each, $1/2$ cup at a time, beating well after each addition. The dough will be creamy and light. To test dough, place $1/2$ teaspoon in 1 cup of cold water. It will float to the surface; if not, continue beating to incorporate more air into dough.

5. *Assembly:* Place a soaked husk in your palm, smooth side up and wide end at your fingertips. Add a generous spoonful of masa (about $1/3$ cup) in the center of the wide end of the husk. Spread evenly (about $1/4$ to $3/8$ inch thick) to completely cover the wide end within $1/2$ inch of the edges. Spread halfway toward the pointed end. Place a heaping spoonful of filling in the center of the dough. Loosely fold the sides of the husks to overlap. Fold the pointed end upward to enclose.

6. *Steaming:* Fill the bottom of a large steamer with 3 inches of water. Arrange the tamales on the rack, open end up, side by side. Cover with a damp kitchen towel; top with a dry towel and cover. Bring to a boil; steam 45 minutes. Remove 1 tamale and unwrap. Let cool 5 minutes. The cooked dough should easily release from the husk and be firm to touch when partially cooled.

MAKES 5 DOZEN TAMALES (PORTION SIZE: 2 TAMALES)

Harina de Camarón

CUBAN SHRIMP ''POLENTA''

My grandmother used to say, "La persona pobre sabe comer mejor que la gente rica!"—the poor know how to eat better than the rich!—because even the simplest ingredients, given their proper place in the pot and cooked with patience and skill, create fabulous dishes that money can't buy. This simple dish was always my favorite and is what I would request for my birthday.

OLGA BETANCOURT

⅔ cup Spanish olive oil

12 large cloves garlic, minced

1 cup chopped onion

1 cup sliced green onions

1½ cups finely chopped green bell pepper

1 (½-pound) package dry Spanish chorizo, cut into slices and halved (about 4 links)

1 (12-ounce) can tomato sauce

1 tablespoon white wine vinegar

3 large shrimp bouillon (optional)

1½ tablespoons salt

1 teaspoon ground black pepper

4 cups harina de maíz (coarse yellow cornmeal)

4 pounds peeled medium shrimp

1 (12-ounce) bottle beer

Avocado and white onion slices

Extra-virgin olive oil (optional)

1. *Sautéing:* In a stockpot, warm the olive oil over medium high heat. Fry the garlic, onion, green onions, and bell pepper, stirring occasionally, about 5 minutes. Stir in the chorizo, tomato sauce, and vinegar. Cook for an additional 5 minutes.

2. *Simmering:* Add 15 cups of cold water, bouillon, salt, and pepper. Briskly whisk in the cornmeal. Bring to a boil, stirring constantly to prevent lumps from forming. When the cornmeal begins to thicken, lower the heat and cook for ½ hour covered, stirring occasionally. Stir in the shrimp and beer. Tightly cover and simmer over very low heat for 1 hour, stirring every 10 minutes, until the mixture is very thick. Garnish the harina with avocado and white onion slices; sprinkle with extra virgin olive oil, if desired.

MAKES 12 SERVINGS (PORTION SIZE: 1½ CUPS AND 8 TO 10 SHRIMP)

*E*nchiladas are another celebration food with a tremendous number of regional variations throughout Mexico. In this section you'll find several unique and exquisite enchilada and casserole dishes that make beautiful main courses or a light supper antojito.

PENEQUES

FAMILY GET-TOGETHERS / MEXICO

CHEESE-FILLED CORN TORTILLAS IN A CHIPOTLE TOMATO SAUCE

This recipe reminds me of my life in Mexico City, when family and friends would just drop in to say hello and visit. In Mexico you do not need the formality of a phone call or an appointment to visit a close friend. In fact, when a friend comes by for a visit, it's an excuse to cook up a quick dish. This is one of those dishes that can be prepared in the kitchen while you are visiting. Remember that the concept of family is very different in Mexico. For example, when our tíos (aunt, uncle, and cousins) dropped in, a family of six or eight would double to twelve or sixteen. So naturally you would need a recipe that was quick, easy, and could feed a large number of hungry appetites. Peneques is the perfect recipe.

PATRICIA PEREZ

QUESADILLAS
3 dozen corn tortillas
2 pounds asadero, manchego, provolone, or Jack cheese, sliced (see Note)

Oil for frying
12 whole eggs, separated
Flour for dusting

CALDILLO (TOMATO BROTH)
6 (14½-ounce) cans whole peeled tomatoes and juice
1½ medium onions, cut up
6 large cloves garlic
½ cup canned chipotle chiles in adobo sauce (optional)

⅓ cup vegetable oil
2 cups chicken broth
Salt and ground black pepper

(continued on next page)

1. *Forming quesadillas:* On a heated comal (griddle), warm the tortillas, turning each of them once, until softened and lightly speckled. Place 1 slice of cheese on each tortilla and fold over. Remove and stack on a plate; cover to keep warm. Continue the process with the remaining tortillas and cheese.

2. *Coating and frying quesadillas:* In a large skillet, heat ⅓ inch of oil for frying. In a bowl, beat the egg yolks to a lemon yellow color. In a separate bowl, beat the whites until just stiff. Gently stir the yolks into the whites until combined. Dust each quesadilla with flour. Dip each quesadilla into batter and immediately place in the hot oil. Fry a few at a time, turning once, until golden. Set aside and keep warm in a 200°F oven.

3. *Preparing caldillo (broth):* Purée the tomatoes and juice in a blender container with the onions, garlic, and chipotle chiles, if desired. In a large skillet, warm the oil over medium high heat. Pour in the tomato purée and chicken broth. Heat to boiling and cook uncovered until the sauce reduces to the desired consistency. Season to taste. The caldillo should be the consistency of a thickened tomato juice.

4. *Simmering and serving:* Remove the quesadillas from the oven and place in the heated caldillo. Simmer 1 minute. Arrange 2 quesadillas on each plate with additional broth.

NOTE: Any white melting cheese will work fine in this recipe. The advantage in using asadero or provolone cheese, besides flavor, is that it's presliced.

SERVING SUGGESTION: Serve Peneques with Frijoles Negros (Cuban Black Beans, page 152) and Sopa de Arroz (Mexican Rice, page 145).

MAKES 16 SERVINGS (PORTION SIZE: 2 PENEQUES)

ENCHILADAS POTOSINAS

FIESTAS PÁTRIAS (PATRIOTIC PARTIES) / MEXICO

SAN LUIS POTOSÍ–STYLE ENCHILADAS

As a child, I was raised to be proud of my Mexican heritage. Our family gatherings were an opportunity to prepare and enjoy the wonderful meals my mother would make from scratch with lots of love; to learn about Mexican history and where our ancestors came from; to observe El Viernes Santo (Good Friday) with this meatless dish. My mother passed away in May of 1978, and I remember and praise the Lord for the wonderful background she instilled in us.

ALICIA BONILLA-CULLEN

TOMATILLO SAUCE
½ pound (about 12 small) tomatillos
½ pound (about 2) ripe tomatoes, roasted (see page 134)
3 tablespoons vegetable oil
2 cloves garlic, minced

1 small white onion, minced (about ¾ cup)
½ cup sliced roasted poblano or pasilla chiles

ENCHILADAS
3 dried anchos
4 cups masa harina (corn flour)
1 teaspoon salt

2 cups (8 ounces) crumbled fresco or feta cheese
Oil for frying (optional)

GARNISH
Finely shredded lettuce
Avocado slices

Chopped green onion

1. *Puréeing tomatillos and tomatoes:* Remove husks and rinse the tomatillos under warm running water. Place them in a small pot with water to cover. Cook covered over medium high heat until tender, about 10 minutes. Purée the cooked tomatillos with about ½ cup of their cooking liquid and the roasted tomatoes in a blender container until smooth. Makes 3 cups.

2. *Simmering sauce:* Warm the oil in a skillet over medium high heat. Sauté the garlic and onion until soft; stir in the chile strips and cook 1 minute. Pour the blended tomatillo purée into the hot oil, stirring con-

(continued on next page)

stantly for 4 minutes, until the purée darkens. Stir in ½ cup of water; heat to boiling. Reduce the heat to medium and simmer until thickened. The sauce should be the consistency of a thin tomato sauce. Set aside.

3. *Puréeing chiles for enchiladas:* Rinse the chiles anchos under cold running water. Remove the stems and seeds. Pat dry. Place on a heated comal (griddle) and toast over medium heat until the chiles change color and release their aroma. Do not burn or blacken. Soak the chiles in hot water to cover for 30 minutes. When they have swollen, place them in a blender container with ½ cup of the soaking liquid. Purée the chiles until smooth.

4. *Preparing corn dough:* In a bowl, combine the masa harina with the blended chile purée and salt. Add 2 cups of water and with the hands combine thoroughly to make a pliable dough. Mix in an additional ½ cup water if necessary. Cover with a damp cloth and let stand 20 minutes.

5. *Forming enchiladas:* Divide the dough into 18 equal-sized balls about 1½ inches in diameter. In a tortilla press or between 2 pieces of plastic wrap, press 1 ball of dough into a 5-inch tortilla. Spoon a tablespoon of crumbled cheese and a tablespoon of sauce in the center of the tortilla; fold over and pinch the edges to seal. Repeat with the remaining dough balls, covering the sealed enchiladas with a damp cloth until ready to cook. At this point, you can cook the enchiladas on a greased griddle over medium heat, turning until golden (but not toasted), or the enchiladas can be fried in ½ inch of oil over medium heat, turning once until golden. *These enchiladas should never be crisp but rather golden and soft enough to be cut with a fork.*

6. *Finishing and serving:* Place the remaining 1 cup of sauce in a skillet; stir in 1 to 2 cups of water. Heat to boiling; lower the heat and simmer covered 10 minutes. Place the fried enchilada in the sauce for a minute or two to heat through. Arrange enchiladas on a serving plate; ladle sauce over them. Garnish the plate with shredded lettuce, avocado slices, and chopped green onions.

ROASTED TOMATOES
Put whole tomatoes in a shallow foil-lined pan and place under a hot broiler. Cook, turning occasionally, until the skin is charred.

MAKES 9 SERVINGS (PORTION SIZE: 2 ENCHILADAS)

@@@@@@@@@@@@@@@@@@@@@@@

ENCHILADAS ESTILO MICHOACÁN

FAMILY GATHERING / MEXICO

ENCHILADAS MICHOACÁN-STYLE

My mother, who is from the State of Michoacán, Mexico, prepares these enchiladas whenever all of her children arrive home for the holidays or for a family gathering. We love being together as much as we love Mom's enchiladas!

MARICELA C. RAMIREZ

ANCHO CHILE SAUCE
6 dried red ancho chiles
1 dried guajillo chile (cascabel)
3 large cloves garlic, peeled
1 teaspoon salt

½ white onion, quartered
½ teaspoon dried oregano leaves
1 tablespoon white vinegar

PICKLED VEGETABLES
3 russet potatoes
4 carrots

½ cup rich chicken broth
2 tablespoons vinegar

ENCHILADAS
Oil for frying
12 corn tortillas
3 cups shredded cooked chicken (see page 33)

1 cup crumbled cotija, enchilado, or feta cheese
1 small white onion, minced

GARNISH
12 romaine leaves
12 saltine crackers

12 pickled jalapeño slices
White onion rings

1. *Preparing ancho chile sauce:* In a small saucepan, combine the ancho chiles, guajillo chile, garlic, and salt; add water to barely cover. Bring to a boil, lower the heat, and simmer covered until soft, about 10 minutes. Remove from the heat and strain, reserving the cooking liquid. Place the chiles and garlic in a blender container with the onion, oregano, and the tablespoon of vinegar. Blend until smooth, adding ³/₄ to 1 cup of the reserved chile cooking liquid. The purée should be the consistency of a thick pourable cream. Pour the purée through a fine wire mesh strainer

(continued on next page)

MAIN DISHES • 135

into a medium skillet, using a wooden spoon to press the solids. Discard the chile seeds and skin. Season the purée with salt to taste. Set aside.

2. *Preparing pickled vegetables:* Peel and dice the potatoes and carrots. Place in a small saucepan with water to cover. Cook, covered, over medium high heat until soft. Drain and return to the saucepan. Add the chicken broth and the 2 tablespoons of vinegar. Let stand 30 minutes, or until the flavor of the vinegar has been absorbed. Drain and allow the vegetables to air dry.

3. *Frying:* In a medium skillet, fry the pickled potatoes and carrots in oil over medium high heat. Remove with a slotted spoon and place on absorbent towels to remove excess oil. In the same skillet, lightly fry the tortillas one at a time until just softened (using tongs, pass each tortilla through the oil until coated on each side). Stack the fried tortillas; cover and keep warm. Add additional oil to skillet if necessary and fry the cooked chicken pieces until heated through. Remove and keep warm.

4. *Assembling enchiladas:* Heat the chile purée to a rapid simmer over medium high heat; lower the heat. Assemble all ingredients around the stovetop. In the same skillet used for frying the chicken, heat additional oil. Using tongs, pass 1 tortilla through the heated chile sauce to completely coat it and carefully place it in the hot oil. Fry the tortilla quickly, turning once. Immediately remove it from the oil and place it on an individual serving plate. Top with a generous spoonful of chicken and cheese. Sprinkle with minced onion. Fold the tortilla over the filling. Repeat the process, placing 2 enchiladas on each serving plate.

5. *Serving:* Arrange 2 romaine leaves and 2 crackers on each side of the enchiladas. Place jalapeño slices on top of each cracker. Cover each enchilada serving with about 1/4 cup of the fried potato and carrot mixture. Sprinkle with the remaining cheese and garnish with onion rings.

SERVING SUGGESTION: The topping of vegetables, the crisp lettuce garnish, and the chicken filling make a complete and well-balanced meal. Sopa de Arroz (Mexican Rice, page 145) complements this visually appealing and absolutely delicious regional enchilada dish.

MAKES 6 SERVINGS (PORTION SIZE: 2 ENCHILADAS)

ENCHILADAS ESTILO DE SONORA

HOLIDAY / MEXICO

SONORAN-STYLE ENCHILADAS

I remember Mom beginning our dinner meal early in the morning by placing the pot of beans to cook. With nine children to feed and care for, quite a bit of Mom's time was spent in the kitchen. Every day she would prepare Sonoran-style tortillas, gigantic, thin, and delicate tortillas large enough to cover the kitchen table. We had a special large comal (griddle) just to cook these Sonoran specialties. I remember my mother preparing Sonoran enchiladas with a precision only years of practice could bring. All our family looked forward to our Holy Friday meal of enchiladas, prepared without meat and with a tomato-based sauce instead of a chili sauce so all the children could enjoy this special treat.

ADELINA BOUBION CRANE

GORDAS (THICK TORTILLAS)

¼ cup vegetable shortening or lard   2 cups masa harina (corn flour)

ENTOMATADO (TOMATO SAUCE)

3 cups (28-ounce can) crushed   1½ teaspoons oregano, crushed
  tomatoes   ¼ teaspoon ground allspice
1 medium onion, quartered   ½ teaspoon salt
4 cloves garlic   3 tablespoons vegetable oil
3 to 5 serrano chiles, trimmed

TOPPING

3 roasted poblano, pasilla, or Anaheim   Finely shredded lettuce
  green chiles, peeled, seeded, and   ½ cup sour cream or Mexican cream
  diced   Crumbled enchilado or feta cheese
⅓ cup minced white onion   Cilantro leaves

1. *Preparing gordas:* Heat a greased griddle to 375–400°F. In a bowl, mix the shortening into the corn flour with your hands until it is evenly distributed. Gradually add 1¼ cups of warm water; knead until smooth. Divide into 10 balls; cover with a damp cloth to prevent drying. Flatten each ball between your palms to form a 3 × ⅜-inch-thick gorda (thick corn tortilla). Place on the heated griddle and cook 3 minutes, or until

(continued on next page)

speckled golden brown. Turn; cook an additional 3 minutes. Cover and keep warm. Makes 10.

2. *Entomatado sauce:* In 2 batches, purée the tomatoes with 1½ cups of water, the onion, garlic, serrano chiles, oregano, allspice, and salt until smooth. In a large skillet, heat the oil. Add the blended tomato mixture and fry over medium high heat for 15 minutes until thickened, stirring occasionally. Makes 5 cups.

3. *Assembly:* Place gordas in the sauce and simmer for 10 minutes, or until softened. When ready to serve, pour sauce with gordas onto a shallow serving platter or baking dish. Top each gorda with chile, minced onion, lettuce, sour cream, cheese, and cilantro. Serve hot.

SERVING SUGGESTION: Serve these delicious enchiladas with a generous helping of Sopa de Arroz (Mexican Rice, page 145). A cool and creamy flan (see recipes on pages 188 to 191) or Natilla (Vanilla Custard, page 196) would make a light ending to a simple meal.

MAKES 5 SERVINGS (PORTION SIZE: 2 ENCHILADAS)

Enchiladas are prepared in this way only in the State of Sonora, Mexico. Instead of wrapping the filling in corn tortillas, the cheese sauce and garnishes are placed on top of a thick homemade tortilla that simmers in the sauce. Freshly made corn tortillas and sharp cheese are accented by spicy tomato sauce in this simple dish from Oaxaca. Often found on the brunch table, it is generally served alone as a pasta or as an excellent and interesting accompaniment to plainly cooked meats, chicken, or fish.

PIÑON

SUNDAY GATHERINGS / PUERTO RICO

SAVORY PLANTAIN AND BEEF CASSEROLE

Looking back, I believe that I got my love of cooking from my childhood, particularly from our delicious Sunday brunches. My mother would always surprise us with new recipes or new variations of old family recipes handed down from generation to generation. One such dish was Piñon. I remember fondly how, after sharing the chores in the kitchen, we would sit at the dining table to enjoy each other's company, young and old, while we ate this wonderful dish. I hope to pass on to my children the lesson learned by this tradition: that the backbone of a child's upbringing is a loving and close-knit family.

DENISE OLLER

MEAT SAUCE

2 tablespoons vegetable oil
1 medium onion, chopped
1 green bell pepper, diced
3 cloves garlic, minced
1 pound lean ground beef
1 teaspoon salt
½ teaspoon ground black pepper
1 (8-ounce) can tomato sauce

1 tablespoon raisins
1 tablespoon capers
3 tablespoons pimiento-stuffed green
olives, drained
1 tablespoon wine vinegar
1 tablespoon sweet wine or sherry
1 tablespoon crushed oregano

BATTER

10 large eggs

Salt and pepper to taste

PLANTAINS

8 large ripe plátanos maduros (sweet
blackened plantains) (see Note)
Oil for frying

1 (9-ounce) package frozen french-cut
green beans, thawed
Grated Parmesan cheese (optional)

1. *Meat sauce:* In a heavy skillet, warm the oil over medium heat. Sauté the onion until soft; stir in the green pepper and garlic, cooking an additional 5 minutes. Add the meat, salt, and pepper. Cook over medium high heat, stirring occasionally, until the meat is browned. Stir in the tomato sauce, raisins, capers, olives, vinegar, wine, and oregano. Lower

(continued on next page)

MAIN DISHES • 139

the heat and simmer covered for 20 minutes. Adjust seasoning to taste. Cover to keep warm

2. *Batter:* In a small bowl, beat the eggs with the salt and pepper. Set aside.

3. *Peeling and frying plantains:* To remove the skin, slice off the tips of the plantains at both ends. Make a lengthwise slit through the peel. Pry off the skin by inserting your fingers between peel and plantain. Cut each plantain into 3 lengthwise slices. In a large skillet, heat 1 inch of oil over medium heat. Fry the plantains in the hot oil, turning once, until golden on the outside and tender on the inside (check tenderness by inserting a toothpick). Carefully remove with tongs and place on absorbent towels to drain.

4. *Preparing casserole:* Preheat the oven to 350°F. Generously grease a 13 × 9 × 2½-inch baking dish. Evenly spread half the egg batter over the bottom of the baking dish. Top with half the plantain slices (about 12). Spoon the meat mixture over the plantains to cover; top with an even layer of green beans. Arrange the remaining plantain slices over the green beans and pour in the remaining egg batter to evenly cover the plantains. Bake uncovered for about 40 minutes. Before removing from the oven, sprinkle with Parmesan cheese, if desired, and broil until golden brown, being careful not to burn.

5. *Serving:* Remove from the oven and let cool partially. Slice into 2 × 3-inch pieces. Using a spatula, lift and place on individual plates. If the layers start to separate, let cool an additional 5 minutes before serving.

PLÁTANOS (PLANTAINS)
Plantains can be purchased in varying degrees of ripeness at markets specializing in Latin produce. Plátanos maduros are ripe or sweet plantains that have turned from green to yellow-black. Oftentimes, the plantains are completely black due to refrigeration. Select yellow-black or blackened plantains that are firm to touch without any soft (overripe) spots.

SERVING SUGGESTION: This dish is a meal in itself. All you need is an Ensalada de Aguacate y Tomate (Avocado and Tomato Salad, page 16) and hot garlic bread. Enjoy!

MAKES 8 SERVINGS (PORTION SIZE: ONE 2 × 3-INCH PIECE)

CHAPTER FOUR

Acompañamientos:
Arroces, Pastas,
Legumbres, Y Verduras

Side Dishes:
Rice, Pasta,
Beans, and Vegetables

R*ice and pasta (namely fideo or capel-lini) were first introduced by the Spanish and Portuguese in the sixteenth century. Later, the wave of Italian immigrants to South America brought with them an assortment of pastas which were enthusiastically embraced by those countries adopted by the Italians such as Argentina and Chile. Today, rice and pasta are used all over Latin America and are the popular mainstay of countries such as Brazil, Mexico, Costa Rica, Puerto Rico, and Cuba.*

ARROZ CON COCO Y PASAS
(FRITO O TITOTÉ)

WEEKEND OUTING / COLOMBIA

FRIED COCONUT RICE WITH RAISINS

Our family is from Medellín, which sits in the middle of Colombia's fertile coffee-growing region. Several times a year we would travel to the coastal city of Playa Blanca to relax and enjoy the carefree lifestyle of the Caribbean. The last trip back to my native Colombia was very special. As I was introducing my country and culture to my new husband we found ourselves in Playa Blanca preparing ourselves for a feast of arroz con coco. My husband was so intrigued by the care taken with our meal that he conversed (through sign language and laughter) with the tavern caretaker and cook all morning! Seated at the benches of the thick-boarded tables, the air perfumed by the sea breeze, vendors strolling with tropical fruit platters on their heads, I couldn't help but feel "como que el tiempo se para en un instante!"—"as if life was standing still!"

CLAUDIA YEPES

2 medium coconuts
3 tablespoons light brown sugar
1 cup raisins

2 cups long-grain rice
2 teaspoons salt
2 tablespoons butter

1. Extract the milk from the coconuts following the directions on page 90. You will need 1 to 1⅓ cups thick coconut milk and about 3 cups of thin. Set aside until ready to use.

2. *Extracting titoté (coconut oil):* In a heavy 2-quart saucepan, heat about 1 to 1⅓ cups of thick coconut milk over medium high heat, stirring occasionally, until the titoté separates, forming milk particles. Lower the

heat to medium, add the sugar, and cook, stirring, until the titoté caramelizes to a golden brown color.

3. *Cooking rice:* To the same saucepan, add about 3 cups of thin coconut milk (from the second pressing) and the raisins. Heat to a rapid simmer and cook uncovered about 10 minutes. Stir in the rice and salt. Continue cooking uncovered, stirring frequently, until the milk has almost evaporated. Mix in the butter, cover tightly, and simmer over very low heat for about 35 minutes, being careful not to burn. (This rice needs to cook longer because of the addition of sugar.) Remove from the heat when the rice grains have opened.

NOTE: To shorten cooking time by 15 minutes, cook rice covered in step 3. The flavor will be similar; the texture will be much softer. Ideally, the grains should separate easily and have a soft, yet "al dendê" texture. Use a heat diffuser under the saucepan to disperse heat if possible.

SERVING SUGGESTION: Arroz con coco (titoté) is customarily served for special occasions and holidays with roasted or grilled fish or meats, such as stuffed turkey, baked and glazed ham, or fried fish. Begin your Colombian meal with a refreshing coleslaw salad; serve your favorite grilled fish or pescado frito (fried fish) accompanied by arroz con coco and Patacones (Fried Plantain Slices, page 166). Finish your meal with a tropical fruit sorbet.

MAKES 6 SERVINGS (PORTION SIZE: 1 CUP)

Arroz con coco is one of the great variety of dishes seen throughout the Colombian coast using coconut and attesting to the influence of African culture and cuisine. Extracting the fresh titoté (coconut oil) takes time, so it is not surprising that on Sundays and holidays you will find titoté sizzling at the bottom of the seaside tavern pots, ready to fry the rice for one of the coast's most popular meals. Prepared with care, the rice develops a nutty flavor and absorbs the tropical flavor of coconut, sweetened by the raisins. It is often served with the local fish (swordfish, talápia, catfish, squid, and crab) but also complements meats and poultry.

ARROZ CON GANDULES

CHRISTMAS / PUERTO RICO

PUERTO RICAN RICE WITH PIGEON PEAS

A Puerto Rican Christmas celebration, or for that matter any holiday meal, would not be complete without a large steaming pot of rice with pigeon peas. Served as an essential side dish to complement pernil (roast pork shoulder) or pasteles (Puerto Rican tamales), Arroz con Gandules quiets the Christmas yearning for familiar and comforting foods.

MARTHA MEDINA CARNEY

¼ cup olive oil

3 boneless pork chops, diced

1 tablespoon adobo seasoning

3 tablespoons recaíto seasoning

10 pimiento-stuffed olives, halved

10 capers

3 heaping tablespoons tomato paste

1 (16-ounce) can gandules (green pigeon peas) and liquid or 2 cups cooked dried gandules

2 cups long-grain white rice

1½ teaspoons salt

1. *Frying meat:* Warm the olive oil in a large pot over medium high heat. Sprinkle the pork with adobo seasoning and rub into the meat with your hands. Fry the meat in hot oil, stirring frequently, until golden and crisp, about 5 minutes.

2. *Seasoning rice:* Add recaíto seasoning, olives, capers, and tomato paste to the pot. Lower the heat to medium; stir and cook 1 minute to combine the ingredients. Pour the pigeon peas and liquid into the pot and simmer covered for 5 minutes.

3. *Cooking:* Remove the lid; add the rice, 3 cups of water, and the salt. Bring to a boil; lower the heat and cook covered for 20 minutes without disturbing. Remove the lid and stir gently. Cover and cook an additional 10 minutes over low heat. Remove from the heat and keep covered until ready to serve.

SERVING SUGGESTION: For a hearty meal, serve Arroz con Gandules with Gallina en Fricasé (Chicken Fricassee, page 45) and a green salad.

MAKES 6 SERVINGS (PORTION SIZE: 1 ¼ CUPS)

Sopa de Arroz

MEXICAN RICE

1 medium white onion, chopped coarse
2 large cloves garlic, crushed
2 cups (16-ounce can) whole tomatoes
3½ cups water or chicken broth
3 tablespoons vegetable oil

2 cups long-grain rice, rinsed
2 extra-large chicken bouillon cubes
 (if using water)
½ teaspoon salt
1 cup frozen peas and carrots

In a blender container, purée the onion, garlic, tomatoes and juice, and ½ cup of broth until smooth. Set aside. In a skillet, heat the oil over medium high heat. Sauté the rice, stirring constantly, until golden brown, about 8 minutes. Stir in the blended tomato mixture, remaining broth, bouillon, and salt. Bring to a boil; cover and simmer undisturbed for 25 minutes. Add the vegetables, cover, and remove from the heat. Allow to stand 5 minutes before serving.

MAKES 8 SERVINGS (PORTION SIZE: 1¼ CUPS)

Arroz Blanco Cubano

CUBAN WHITE RICE

2 tablespoons Spanish olive oil
1 large clove garlic, crushed
2 cups long-grain rice, rinsed

3¾ cups water
1 teaspoon salt

Heat the oil in a saucepan over medium heat. Slowly sauté the garlic until golden but not burned; discard the garlic. (If desired, leave clove in the saucepan for additional flavor.) Add the rice, water, and salt. Bring to a boil; lower the heat and simmer undisturbed covered for 25 minutes. Remove from the heat; let set 5 minutes. Fluff rice with a fork before serving. Serve Frijoles Negros (Cuban Black Beans, page 152) spooned over arroz blanco as a delicious side dish.

MAKES 6 SERVINGS (PORTION SIZE: ¾ CUP)

Arroz Amarillo con Almendras

QUINCEÑERA / PANAMA

YELLOW RICE WITH ALMONDS

A quinceñera is a milestone in a young Hispanic girl's life. An elaborate party is staged to present her to the community, after which she officially enters public life. The cost of a quinceñera can rival that of a wedding. To reduce the expense, a variety of dishes such as arroz amarillo are selected for their visual appeal, flavor, and ability to feed large numbers easily.

JACKIE LÁVALOS

⅓ cup vegetable oil
3 cups long-grain rice
2 teaspoons achiote (annatto seed paste) (see Note)
5 cups well-seasoned broth

1 cup dry sherry
⅓ cup raisins
Salt
½ cup slivered blanched almonds, toasted

In a large pot, warm the oil over medium heat. Sauté the rice, stirring, until golden. Add the achiote, stirring until the rice is colored. Add the broth, sherry, raisins, and salt to taste. Bring to a boil; reduce the heat. Cover and simmer undisturbed for 25 minutes, or until almost all the liquid has been absorbed. With a fork, mix in the almonds. Cover, turn off the heat, and set aside for 15 minutes. Serve hot or at room temperature.

NOTE: Achiote, a soft cake made from ground annatto seeds, spices, and liquid, is commonly used in Latin American cooking to add both color and flavor. It is also available in powdered form and can be found in most Hispanic markets.

SERVING SUGGESTION: For an elegant Panamanian dinner, serve turtle soup, followed by Guiso de Cola (Oxtail Stew, page 66), Arroz Amarillo con Almendras, and cooked chochos (chayote) sautéed in butter with a dash of nutmeg. For dessert, serve Dulce de Leche (Milk Caramel, page 191) with dessert cheese and crackers.

MAKES 12 SERVINGS (PORTION SIZE: ¾ CUP)

Arroz de Fideos

FAMILY GET-TOGETHERS / COLOMBIA

GOLDEN VERMICELLI WITH RICE

Each time I think of Arroz de Fideos, I think of my abuelita paterna (paternal grandmother) in the kitchen of our home in Barranquilla, Colombia. I enjoyed nothing more than this rice and vermicelli combination, which is made to accompany a delicious stew or a savory chicken and tomato dish. My friends always asked me to invite them to eat Arroz de Fideos—not only for the flavor of this special dish, but to feel the ambience of my home.

LUZ M. RINCÓN LESZCZYNSKI

1 cup vegetable oil
2 cloves garlic, minced
1½ cups chopped white onion
2 cups fideo (coiled vermicelli) or angel hair pasta
2 cups long-grain white rice

1 extra-large chicken-flavored bouillon cube
1 teaspoon salt
Fresh chopped herbs or grated Parmesan cheese

1. In a large skillet, warm the oil over medium low heat. Add the garlic and onion, stirring until the onion is softened. Crush the coiled fideo in the palm of your hand and add to the skillet. Continue stirring and cooking until the fideo is just turning golden brown and slightly darkened. At this point add the rice and sauté until golden. The fideo should be dark brown but not burnt.

2. Stir in 8 cups of water, the bouillon, and salt; bring to a boil. Lower the heat and cook covered for 20 minutes, or until the rice has swelled and is tender. All the water should be absorbed and the arroz de fideos should be a dark golden brown color.

3. Serve garnished with fresh herbs or Parmesan cheese.

NOTE: Fideos or vermicelli pasta can be purchased in coils or in short, 1-inch strands. Generally, fideos made with durum flour cook up more quickly than brands made with semolina.

MAKES 8 SERVINGS (PORTION SIZE: 1 CUP)

SIDE DISHES • 147

TALLARINES CON NUECES

SUNDAY MEAL / ARGENTINA

THIN NOODLES WITH CHOPPED NUTS

Our family's Sunday meal usually consisted of beef or lamb rather than rabbit, hare, chicken, or partridge. I remember being anxious for our chicken dinner only because our cook always served these homemade tallarines, which in those days were hand cut! Here is the recipe to the best of my recollection.

½ pound (2 sticks) salted butter
⅓ cup finely chopped walnuts
2 tablespoons finely chopped parsley
4 servings (about 6 cups) fresh homemade linguine, cooked al dente

⅓ cup grated Parmesan or Romano
cheese
6 lemon wedges

In a skillet, slowly melt the butter over medium heat. When the butter begins to froth, add the walnuts. Fry until golden brown, stirring constantly. Do not scorch the butter or the walnuts will taste bitter. Stir in the parsley and remove from the heat. Pour the walnut butter over hot cooked pasta; toss, coating well. Generously sprinkle grated cheese and serve with a lemon wedge.

SERVING SUGGESTION: For a lovely Argentine meal, serve these Tallarines con Nueces with roasted Cornish game hens, quail, or partridge accompanied by roasted or braised fennel and carrots. Finish your meal with Frutas en Almíbar de Vino (Fruit in Wine Syrup, page 187) served with cheese.

MAKES 6 SERVINGS (PORTION SIZE: 1 CUP)

In Argentina, fideos are any kind of unfilled pasta—homemade noodles (or tallarines) as well as other types of pasta, such as spaghetti, vermicelli, and rigatoni. They are served hot, covered with some kind of sauce, and topped with an abundance of good grated cheese. In Mexico, fideos is the name given to coiled or cut vermicelli pasta.

Beans, known as granōs, frijoles, or le-gumbres, are found in every color and variety throughout Mexico, the Caribbean, and Central and South America. Each country (or region within a country) has its signature daily fare of rice and beans. Prepared simply and artfully—or presented in elaborate guises—beans and rice, alongside corn and tuber vegetables (potatoes and yucca), are the backbone of the Latin American cuisine.

FRIJOLES CON ESPINACA Y LAS VENAS DE CHILE ROJO

LENT / SOUTHWEST

PINTO BEANS AND SPINACH COOKED WITH RED CHILE VEINS

If there is one childhood impression of my mother's cooking, it's that she didn't waste anything. There was a certain reverence for food, a purpose for every food item we bought, grew, or hunted. Whenever she would prepare chile colorado (red chile), the seeds and venas (veins) from the New Mexico red chile pods would be saved in a jar. This is one of her recipes that use the venas (chile veins) and quelites, a wild green similar to spinach that used to grow around our ranch.

HENRY R. CORDOVA

2 bunches quelites (wild spinach) or fresh spinach, cleaned and cut up, or 2 (10-ounce) packages frozen chopped spinach (see Note)
2 tablespoons vegetable oil
2 tablespoons flour
½ cup chopped onion

3 large cloves garlic, crushed
¼ cup red chile veins or 2 teaspoons crushed red chile flakes
8 cups cooked pinto beans with 1 cup bean broth (see recipe page 154)
1 teaspoon salt
Bolillos (Mexican rolls) (optional)

1. *Cooking spinach:* In a small pot, combine the fresh spinach with 1 quart of water. Heat to boiling; reduce heat to low. Simmer, partially covered, 5 minutes, or until tender. Strain; reserve cooking liquid.

2. *Seasoning beans:* Meanwhile, in a heavy 3-quart skillet or pot, heat the oil and flour over medium heat. Stir constantly until the flour turns light

(continued on next page)

brown. Add the onion, garlic, and chile veins; fry 3 to 5 minutes, stirring frequently, until onion is soft. Add the undrained beans 2 cups at a time, mashing and stirring after each addition. *Do not overmash. The majority of beans should remain whole in a creamy sauce.*

3. *Finishing dish:* Heat the seasoned beans to boiling; stir in the cooked spinach, 1 to 1½ cups of reserved spinach liquid, and salt to season. Reduce the heat. Simmer 10 minutes, stirring, to blend flavors. *Do not boil beans once spinach has been added or the dish will become bitter.* Remove the garlic before serving, if desired.

4. *Serving:* Ladle into shallow bowls and serve with bolillos (Mexican rolls), if desired.

NOTE: You can substitute any green, particularly verdolagas (purslane) or Swiss chard. If using frozen spinach, combine with 1½ cups of water and let soak until thawed; drain, reserving liquid.

MAKES 8 SERVINGS (PORTION SIZE: ABOUT 1½ CUPS)

NEW MEXICAN RED CHILE VEINS

Select New Mexico (or California) dried red chile pods that are soft and pliable when squeezed in your hand. Using gloves, remove the stem and tear open the chile lengthwise with your hands. (The veins of the chile are beige, run down the length of the chile from the stem, and oftentimes have the chile seeds attached to them.) Beginning at the stem end, carefully detach the vein by pulling downward. Store veins and seeds in tightly sealed jar up to 6 months. Before using veins (and seeds) to season dishes, lightly toast in a greased heavy skillet over medium heat, being careful not to burn.

Frijoles Charros

FAMILY DINNERS / SOUTHWEST

COWBOY BEANS

My mother, Beatrice Hernandez, was able to prepare meals very quickly. With twelve children to care for, she was constantly looking for shortcuts. Any meal that took over twenty to thirty minutes was just too elaborate for our busy household. I remember these Frijoles Charros being served alongside enchiladas, chilaquiles, or mole.

HELEN HERNANDEZ

1 pound (2 cups) dried pinto beans
1 small Spanish onion, chopped
6 cloves garlic, chopped
4 strips bacon, chopped
2 fresh jalapeño chiles, stems removed
½ pound chorizo (Mexican sausage)
½ teaspoon dried oregano leaves, crushed

½ teaspoon ground cumin
1 tablespoon fresh cilantro leaves
1 tablespoon salt
Chopped onion, shredded longhorn Cheddar cheese, and cilantro leaves to garnish

1. *Sorting:* Pour the beans onto the countertop. Running the beans through your hands, pick out any small stones, shriveled beans, or debris. Place the sorted beans in a colander and rinse under cold water.

2. *Cooking:* In a stockpot, combine the beans with 12 cups of water, the onion, garlic, bacon, chiles, and chorizo. The water should be about 3 inches above the level of the beans. Bring to a boil. Reduce the heat and simmer covered for 2 hours, or until the beans are almost soft. Check the water level occasionally and add boiling water if necessary.

3. *Seasoning and finishing beans:* Add the oregano, cumin, cilantro, and salt to the beans. Continue simmering uncovered for an additional hour, or until the broth is full-flavored. Adjust seasoning to taste. Sprinkle beans with chopped onion, shredded longhorn Cheddar cheese, and cilantro.

MAKES 6 SERVINGS (PORTION SIZE: 1.³/₄ CUPS BEANS AND BROTH)

Frijoles Negros

CUBAN BLACK BEANS

Served over fluffy white rice, this classic dish of savory stewed black beans is a companion to almost every Cuban entree.

BLACK BEANS

1 pound dried black beans
1 green bell pepper, cored and halved
1 medium onion, peeled and halved

2 cloves garlic, peeled and flattened
1 tablespoon brown sugar
2 tablespoons white wine vinegar

SOFRITO (SEASONING)

1/3 cup olive oil, or as needed
6 cloves garlic, minced
1 1/2 cups finely chopped onion
1 cup finely chopped green pepper

1/2 teaspoon oregano leaves, crushed
2 bay leaves
1 1/2 teaspoons salt

1. *Soaking and cooking beans:* Sort the beans, removing any small stones. Rinse and place the beans in a large pot with water to cover by 4 inches. Soak for at least 8 hours; discard the water and rinse the beans. Return them to the same pot; add about 2 1/2 quarts of fresh water, the bell pepper, onion, and garlic. Bring to a boil. Lower the heat to medium low and cook covered until the beans are tender, about 1 hour. Discard bell pepper and onion.

2. *Preparing sofrito:* Warm the olive oil in a skillet over medium high heat. Sauté garlic for 1 minute. Add the onion and green pepper. Continue sautéing 3 minutes. Stir in the oregano, bay leaves, and salt; cook 2 minutes.

3. *Finishing:* Stir the sofrito mixture into the pot with the beans. Return to a boil; lower the heat and simmer 30 minutes uncovered. Stir in the brown sugar and vinegar during the last 10 minutes of cooking. Season to taste with salt. Before serving, drizzle each bowl with olive oil, if desired.

MAKES 8 SERVINGS (PORTION SIZE: ABOUT 1 1/2 CUPS BEANS AND BROTH)

LENTEJAS DE BUENA SUERTE

NEW YEAR'S DAY / CUBA

GOOD-LUCK LENTILS

The first day of January is celebrated in my family by eating these famous good-luck lentils to bring good luck and economic prosperity. This recipe originated in Spain and was handed down to me by my uncle. Family legend had it that the more lentils you were able to eat, the more prosperous the year would be. For this reason, the competition to eat plates of lentils created incredible excitement at our family table.

MARIA REGINA AVILA

SOFRITO (SEASONING)

2 tablespoons olive oil

3 large cloves garlic, minced

1 small onion, chopped fine (about ½ cup)

1 green bell pepper, chopped fine

6 ounces cooked ham, diced (about 1 cup)

1 Spanish chorizo (spicy hard sausage), cut into pieces (about ⅓ cup)

LENTILS AND POTATOES

1 cup peeled cooked potatoes, cut into pieces

1½ cups dried lentils, sorted and rinsed

1 large fresh or dry bay leaf

½ teaspoon salt

¼ teaspoon ground black pepper

1. *Preparing sofrito (seasoning):* Heat the olive oil in a pot over medium high heat. Sauté the garlic for 1 minute. Add the onion and green pepper and cook, stirring, until the onion has softened, about 3 minutes. Add the ham and chorizo to the sofrito mixture and stir for an additional 2 minutes. Lower the heat, stir in the potatoes, and continue cooking until they have absorbed the flavor of the sofrito, about 10 minutes.

2. *Cooking lentils:* Pour about 4 cups of water into the pot with the sofrito, lentils, bay leaf, salt, and pepper. Bring to a boil, lower the heat, and cook covered over medium heat until the lentils have softened and have almost broken their skin, about 40 minutes. If you see that the lentils are too thick, add additional water. Before serving, remove the bay leaf.

MAKES 6 SERVINGS (PORTION SIZE: 1 CUP)

Frijoles de la Olla

PINTO BEANS ''FROM THE POT''

The minute you walk into my kitchen, you know what's important to me. I have a special clay pot just for preparing Frijoles de la Olla, which sits on my professional range. On my kitchen countertop is a large 2½-foot jarra (glass jar) always full of pinto beans. Unlike my mother, who had a potful cooking daily, I wait until I feel the urge to prepare this dish for my family, usually once or twice a week. As the beans cook, I feel such a sense of motherly satisfaction!

ALMA THOMAS

2 pounds (4 cups) dried pinto beans	1 white onion, halved
1 (4-ounce) piece salt pork or bacon (optional)	1 garlic head, halved
	1 tablespoon salt

SALSA FRESCA (FRESH CHOPPED SALSA)

3 large ripe tomatoes, chopped fine	2 to 4 serrano chiles, minced
1 white onion, chopped fine	Juice of 1 lime
1 bunch cilantro, cleaned and chopped	½ teaspoon salt

1. *Sorting and cooking the beans:* Sort the bean through your hands to pick out any small stones. Rinse and place in a 6-quart pot. Add 4 quarts of water, the pork, if desired, the onion halves, and garlic (the water should come at least 3 inches above the level of the beans). Discard any beans that float. Slowly bring to a rapid simmer over medium heat, about 30 minutes. Lower the heat, cover, and continue simmering for about 2 hours, until the skins of the beans are soft. Stir in the salt and continue cooking for ½ hour. (*At this point, the beans when pressed between your fingers should be creamy and the cooking liquid slighlty thickened. The bean broth should be about 2 inches above the cooked bean level.*) During the cooking process, stir the beans occasionally, adding hot water if needed.

2. *Salsa fresca:* Thoroughly mix tomatoes, onion, cilantro, chiles, lime juice, and salt in a small bowl. Season to taste. Makes 4 cups.

3. *Serving:* Ladle the beans and broth into shallow bowls; top with salsa.

MAKES 8 SERVINGS (PORTION SIZE: 1½ CUPS)

Frijoles Cargamantos

FAMILY GET-TOGETHERS / COLOMBIA

CARGAMANTO RED BEANS WITH PORK

Red cargamanto beans prepared in paisa fashion (paisa, meaning paisano, "our fellow countryman") are a typical dish of Antióquia. Larger than pinto beans, they cook up quite nicely, creating a rich orange-red sauce which is thickened by the addition of grated carrot or plantain. They are available in markets specializing in Latin American products.

2 pounds cargamanto red beans
1½ cups hogao (seasoning) (see below)
1 pound pig's feet or ham hocks

4 large carrots or 1 large green plantain, peeled and grated
Salt to taste

1. *Sorting and soaking:* Pour the beans onto the countertop. Running the beans through your hands, pick out any small stones, shriveled beans, or debris. Place the sorted beans in a colander and rinse under cold water. Soak beans overnight in water to cover by 4 inches.

2. *Cooking:* Drain the beans, discarding the soaking water. Place the beans in a large pot or pressure cooker with 3 quarts of fresh water. Add hogao (seasoning), pig's feet, and carrots; cook for about 45 minutes in a pressure cooker. (Or cook 3 hours in a covered pot over medium low heat, stirring occasionally.) When tender, add salt and allow to simmer uncovered over low heat until reaching desired consistency. To serve, remove meat and accompany with hogao.

HOGAO
To prepare hogao, sauté 2 pounds finely chopped red tomatoes and 6 stalks finely chopped green onions in 4 tablespoons oil. Add salt, cumin, and saffron to taste. A criollo seasoning of fried onions and tomatoes, hogao is used in Colombia much as sofrito is used in Puerto Rico and Cuba.

MAKES 8 SERVINGS (PORTION SIZE: 1½ CUPS)

Along with beans and rice, corn and potatoes are the dominant staples in the Latin American diet. They are consumed on a daily basis with pasta, yucca, quinoa, plantains, winter squash, sweet potatoes, chile peppers, and peanuts. With the exception of rice (and pasta), all these foods are indigenous to the New World.

CALABACITAS

FAMILY GET-TOGETHERS / MEXICO

STEWED SQUASH, CORN, AND CHILE

I always know when my mother wants me to drop in for a visit. She calls and simply lets me know she is making calabacitas, a Mexican skillet of fresh summer vegetables: squash, corn, green chile, and tomatoes! When we were growing up we ate this dish at least once a week. Now, as an adult, I prepare it often for my own family, but it doesn't taste quite the same as when I'm sitting in my mom's kitchen being a little girl once again!

ISABEL RODRIGUEZ

4 cups Mexican calabaza (summer squash) or zucchini, cut up (see Note)

Salt

3 tablespoons butter

2 cloves garlic, minced

1 small onion, chopped fine (about ¾ cup)

1⅓ cups sweet white corn, scraped from 3 cobs, or canned corn

3 fresh poblano or pasilla chiles, roasted, peeled, and chopped fine

1 ripe tomato, diced (about ¾ cup)

¼ teaspoon dried oregano leaves

3 mint leaves

⅓ cup Mexican cream or heavy cream

½ cup shredded white or Jack cheese

1. *Cooking squash:* Place the squash in a saucepan with enough water to barely cover and salt. Bring to a boil; lower the heat and simmer covered over medium heat until very soft. Drain; reserve the cooking liquid.

2. *Simmering:* Melt the butter over medium heat in a skillet large enough to hold the squash in a single layer. Add the garlic and onion; cook until softened. Stir in the corn, chiles, and tomato. Continue cooking until the

tomato has softened and released its juices. Add the cooked squash, 1½ cups of the reserved cooking liquid, the oregano, and mint. Bring to a boil and cook 2 minutes. Lower the heat and simmer uncovered for 5 minutes. Adjust the seasoning to taste. At this point, depending on your preference, you can mash the calabacitas slightly to create a thicker sauce.

3. *Serving:* Before serving, stir in the cream and cook uncovered until the sauce has thickened. Sprinkle with cheese and serve.

NOTE: Mexican summer squash, known as calabacitas, is a pale green 4- to 5-inch squash with light striations sold in markets during the summer season. Calabacitas are softer and disintegrate faster than zucchini.

MAKES 6 SERVINGS (PORTION SIZE: 1 CUP)

SALADA DE REPOLHO E ERVILHAS DE SETEMBRO

INDEPENDENCE DAY / BRAZIL

INDEPENDENCE DAY COLESLAW AND PEA SALAD

¾ cup mayonnaise
½ cup Mexican cream or sour cream
¼ cup cider vinegar
1 tablespoon minced onion
1 tablespoon curry powder
⅛ teaspoon bijol or powdered turmeric (for color)

Salt to taste
1 small head cabbage, shredded
1 cup coarsely chopped roasted
peanuts
1 (16-ounce) package frozen peas
⅓ cup raisins
Chopped peanuts to garnish

In a bowl, mix together the mayonnaise, cream, vinegar, onion, curry, bijol, and salt. Stir in the cabbage, peanuts, thawed peas, and raisins. Cover and refrigerate until chilled. Garnish with chopped peanuts.

MAKES 8 SERVINGS (PORTION SIZE: 1 CUP)

Tortitas de Chocho en Caldillo

CHAYOTE FRITTERS IN A SAVORY TOMATO BROTH

Panamanians consider the chayote, with its beautiful light mint-colored flesh, silky texture, and almond flavor, a delicacy. Combined with cheese, battered and fried, each of these fritters simmers in an aromatic tomato broth. Heavenly!

Tortitas (fritters)
2 chochos or chayotes

6 slices (1 ounce each) asadero, Gouda, or provolone cheese

½ cup all-purpose flour

2 eggs, well beaten

Chopped parsley to garnish

Caldillo (broth)
1 tablespoon vegetable oil, plus additional for deep frying

1 (14½-ounce) can stewed tomatoes, cut up, and juice

1 (8-ounce) can tomato sauce

2 chicken-flavored bouillon cubes

1 teaspoon oregano leaves, ground allspice, or anise seeds

1. *Cooking chayotes:* In a pot, combine whole chayotes with water to cover. Bring to a boil; reduce the heat to medium and cook covered for 50 minutes, or until tender. Drain and let cool.

2. *Forming tortitas (fritters):* Peel each chayote and slice lengthwise into 6 portions. Squeeze each slice, extracting as much water as possible to form a patty. Sandwich a cheese slice between 2 patties, pressing to seal cheese; dust with flour. Set aside.

3. *Broth:* In a large skillet, heat oil. Add the tomatoes and juice, tomato sauce, 2 cups water, the bouillon, and oregano. Bring to a boil; reduce the heat and simmer uncovered for 5 minutes. Cover to keep warm.

4. *Frying and serving:* In a medium skillet, heat 1 inch of oil over medium high heat. Dip a tortita into the eggs; carefully place in the hot oil. Fry until golden brown, turning once. Drain, then place in the heated broth and simmer until heated through. Garnish with parsley.

MAKES 6 SERVINGS (PORTION SIZE: 2 FRITTERS)

Espinaca con Anchoas

SAUTÉED SPINACH WITH ANCHOVIES

Spinach is one of Latin America's favorite vegetables, served in salad, creamed in casseroles, used as a filling, or simply and elegantly sautéed as in this preparation.

4 bags (6 ounces each) cleaned spinach leaves
4 tablespoons virgin olive oil
8 cloves garlic, chopped

Freshly ground black pepper
1 (2-ounce) can anchovy fillets,
drained and mashed
Lemon wedges

1. *Cleaning spinach:* Remove the stems from the spinach and rinse the leaves under cold running water until all debris and loose dirt is removed. Trim any coarse stems or leaves. Makes about 4½ cups.

2. *Cooking:* In a stockpot, heat 4 quarts of water to boiling. Drop the spinach leaves into the water, return to a boil, and cook uncovered for 1 minute. Immediately drain and place in a large bowl filled with ice water. Gently squeeze excess moisture out of the spinach leaves and chop.

3. *Sautéing:* Heat the oil in a large skillet. Add the garlic, stirring until the aroma is released. Add the spinach and sauté, stirring frequently, about 3 minutes. Stir in the black pepper and anchovies until thoroughly mixed. Serve immediately, garnished with lemon wedges.

SERVING SUGGESTION: Serve as a vegetable side dish with meat or poultry entrees or top with fried or poached eggs and serve with toast as a light evening meal.

MAKES 4 SERVINGS (PORTION SIZE: 1 CUP)

QUIMBOMBÓ

FAMILY GET-TOGETHERS / CUBA

OKRA SAUTÉ WITH PLANTAIN DUMPLINGS

When my mother calls and tells me she is preparing Quimbombó, I immediately suggest that I come over for a visit. Undeniably, stewed okra served with tostones (fried plantains) and white rice is the meal that reminds me of my mother's kitchen.

ELLIOTT RODRIGUEZ

OKRA SAUTÉ

2 pounds fresh small okra

Juice of 3 limes

⅓ cup olive oil

3 large cloves garlic, minced

1 medium onion, cut into short strips (about 1 cup)

1 green bell pepper, chopped (about 1 cup)

½ teaspoon salt

½ teaspoon ground black pepper

2 packets or 2 teaspoons sazón (bottled seasoning) (see Note)

BOLAS DE PLÁTANO (PLANTAIN DUMPLINGS)

2 large plátanos pintón (semiripe yellow plantains)

Melted butter (optional)

1. *Soaking okra:* Cut off the okra stems and slice the skin into ½-inch-long pieces. Place in a bowl of cold water to cover with the juice of 2 limes. Soak for 30 minutes to remove the viscous okra juices; drain and pat dry with paper towels. Makes 6 cups.

2. *Sautéing:* In a large skillet, warm the oil over medium high heat. Sauté the garlic, onion, bell pepper, and okra for 5 minutes. Sprinkle with salt, pepper, sazón (seasoning), the remaining lime juice, and ⅓ to ½ cup of water. Reduce the heat to low; simmer covered, stirring occasionally, until tender, about 5 to 10 minutes.

3. *Preparing plantain dumplings:* Cut off the tips of the plantains and slice the plantains into 3 or 4 chunks. (Semiripe plantains should be cooked with their skin on to preserve their sweet flavor.) Place plantains (with skins) in a small saucepan with water to barely cover. Bring to a boil and cook 10 minutes, or until tender when pierced with a fork. Drain, reserv-

ing ¼ cup of cooking liquid, and let cool. Slice lengthwise through the plantain skin with a paring knife and peel. Mash the plantains in a small bowl (or food processor workbowl), adding just enough of the cooking liquid and/or melted butter to make a thick yet smooth doughlike mixture. Using your hands, form small balls about 1 inch in diameter. Cover and keep warm. Makes 16 (1-inch) dumplings.

4. *Finishing:* Just before serving, add the plantain dumplings to the quimbombó. Cook 5 minutes, stirring occasionally, until heated through.

SAZÓN

Sazón is used to enhance the flavor of food. Different brands exist and offer different seasoning blends. If sazón is unavailable in the Latin section of your grocery store, add cilantro, oregano powder, and garlic salt to season plus turmeric or achiote paste to color.

SERVING SUGGESTION: Serve Quimbombó with Arroz Blanco Cubano (Cuban White Rice, page 145) and Ensalada de Aguacate y Tomate (Avocado and Tomato Salad, page 16).

MAKES 6 SERVINGS (PORTION SIZE: 1 CUP OKRA SAUTÉ AND 3 DUMPLINGS)

> A quimbombó is any type of savory okra stew served with bolas de plátano (sweet plantain dumplings) or with tostones (savory fried slices of green plantains). Depending on the recipe, tomato sauce, fresh tomatoes, or stewed tomatoes can be used with broth and/or white wine.

BERENJENAS CON AJO Y PEREJIL

SUNDAY DINNER / ARGENTINA

EGGPLANT WITH GARLIC AND PARSLEY

You'll find variations of this recipe at Argentine restaurants—as a simple first course or as a light meal accompanied by a mixed green salad and empanadas.

2 medium eggplants
Salt

Olive oil (for broiling)

DRESSING

6 tablespoons olive oil
8 cloves garlic, minced or passed
   through a press

3 tablespoons finely chopped parsley
Salt
1 tablespoon grated hard cheese

1. *Broiling eggplant:* Stem the eggplants and slice them about ½ inch thick (about 8 slices each). Lightly salt the eggplant and let stand for 30 minutes to draw out liquid. Pat dry with paper towels. Brush the surfaces of the eggplant generously with oil and arrange on a greased broiling rack. Place 3 inches from the heat source and broil until golden. Turn over and continue broiling until the eggplant is golden brown and soft, about 20 minutes. Brush eggplant with additional oil if the surface is dry. Remove from the oven.

2. *Preparing dressing:* Combine the olive oil, garlic, parsley, and salt to taste. Allow to stand at room temperature for flavors to blend.

3. *Serving:* Place the eggplant slices on a serving platter. Evenly sprinkle with the dressing. Let stand a few minutes. Sprinkle with grated cheese and offer additional olive oil, if desired.

MAKES 8 SERVINGS (PORTION SIZE: 2 SLICES)

Causa

POTATOES WITH ONIONS AND LEMON

Peruvians have many creative ways to celebrate the noble potato, as evidenced by this Andean favorite.

LEMON MARINADE
Juice of 3 lemons (about ½ cup)
1 cup finely chopped onion

¼ teaspoon ground black pepper
1 teaspoon ground red chile powder

POTATOES
3½ pounds yellow (Yukon gold) potatoes (see box, page 99)

1 teaspoon salt
4 tablespoons olive oil, or as needed

GARNISH
Salad greens
Cured black Italian olives

Hard-cooked eggs, sliced into wedges
Fresh farmer or feta cheese

1. *Preparing lemon marinade:* In a small bowl, combine the lemon juice, onion, pepper, and chile powder. Set aside and marinate 20 to 30 minutes.

2. *Cooking and seasoning:* In a pot, combine the potatoes with salt and water to cover. Bring to a boil, lower the heat, and cook uncovered until the potatoes are soft; drain. Peel the potatoes and mash coarsely with a fork. Stir the lemon marinade into the potatoes. Slowly add olive oil until the potato mixture is smooth. Taste and adjust seasoning.

3. *Serving and molding potatoes:* Press the potatoes in a bowl; unmold onto a bed of greens and garnish with olives, eggs, and cheese.

SERVING SUGGESTION: The causa (potato mixture) can be made a day ahead and refrigerated. Be creative and offer an assortment of little garnishes: sliced salami, pickles, mustards, and/or anchovies, for example.

MAKES 6 TO 8 SERVINGS

SOUFFLÉ DE YUCA

YUCCA SOUFFLÉ

In the Caribbean, we are blessed with an abundance of tropical fruits and vegetables, including my personal favorite: yucca. My grandmother, a regal woman, would often prepare simple foods such as yucca in elegant ways. This recipe captures her spirit.

OSCAR CURY PANIAGUA

1 pound yuca (cassava or yucca)
(see Note, page 5)
¼ cup star anise (about 15)
Salt

1 teaspoon sugar
8 tablespoons (1 stick) butter, melted
1 cup milk
3 eggs, separated (see Note)

1. *Cooking yucca:* With a sharp knife, slice off the ends of the yucca; cut the yucca into 3-inch sections and slice again lengthwise. Carefully remove the bark with a paring knife. In a pot, combine the peeled yucca and the anise with enough salted cold water to cover by 2 inches. Bring to a boil, lower the heat, and simmer uncovered for about 20 minutes, or until tender when pierced with a fork. Check the yucca often, as each piece will cook at a different rate. Drain in a colander. When cool enough to handle, remove and discard any fibrous cores as well as the star anise.

2. *Making yucca batter:* Combine the yucca, 1 teaspoon of salt, the sugar, butter, and milk in a bowl. In small batches, purée the ingredients in a blender until smooth. Set aside. In a medium bowl, beat the egg yolks; add the blended yucca mixture and continue beating until smooth. In a separate bowl, whip egg whites until stiff and fold into the yucca batter.

3. *Baking:* Pour the batter into a greased 8-inch springform pan or soufflé dish. Bake in a preheated oven at 350°F until the soufflé has risen and is golden brown, about 30 to 40 minutes. Serve immediately.

NOTE: For a light and airy yucca soufflé, use a total of 4 egg whites and 3 egg yolks.

MAKES 4 SERVINGS (PORTION SIZE: ONE 3-INCH WEDGE)

Yuca Frita con Guasacaca

FRIED YUCCA WITH AVOCADO VINAIGRETTE

In this recipe, yucca is fried crisp on the outside, creamy and soft on the inside. In Cuban cuisine, fried yucca is always accompanied by a good mojo, a garlicky olive oil condiment. In Venezuela, guasacaca, an avocado vinaigrette, is the preferred dressing.

AYAN ALONZO

5 pounds fresh yuca (cassava) (about 3 large) (see Note, page 5)
Salt to taste
Oil for deep frying
2 cups minced green bell peppers
3/4 cup minced white onion
6 cloves garlic, minced

1/2 bunch cilantro leaves, chopped
1/2 teaspoon minced serrano chile
1/4 cup boiling water
5 tablespoons red wine vinegar
2 avocados, peeled and minced
1/2 cup olive oil
1 teaspoon salt

1. *Cooking yucca:* Peel and boil the yucca following the directions on page 164, omitting the star anise. Slice the yucca into 3/8-inch-thick sticks.

2. *Frying:* In a heavy-duty pot or deep fryer, heat at least 2 inches of oil to 380°F. Carefully fry until golden brown; remove with a slotted spoon and drain on paper towels. Sprinkle with salt and serve hot with either Mojo Criollo (see page 69) or Guasacaca.

3. *Guasacaca vinaigrette:* Combine the bell peppers, onion, garlic, cilantro, and chile in a medium bowl. Whisk in the water and vinegar until combined. Add the avocados and olive oil. With a fork, lightly mash to the desired consistency. Do not blend. Season to taste with salt and additional vinegar or oil, if needed. Makes 4 cups.

MAKES 8 SERVINGS (PORTION SIZE: ABOUT 1/2 LARGE STICK AND 1/2 CUP SAUCE)

Patacones

FRIED PLANTAIN SLICES

In Colombia, Patacones, squashed golden slices of fried plantain, are an inseparable companion to most meals in the tropical regions where plantains grow in abundance. Taking the name patacón from the gold Spanish coin, these crisp golden plantains serve as a vegetable or as a snack, alongside bean and/or rice dishes, stewed meats, or shredded beef. Based on the skill of the cook, patacones can vary in size from a small, thick silver dollar to a paper-thin 12-inch "platter." These large crisp patacones are topped with the diner's choice of stewed seafood, meats, and condiments.

4 large plátanos verdes (green plantains)

Oil for deep frying
Salt to taste

1. *Peeling and slicing plantains:* To remove the skin, slice off the tips at both ends. Cut a slit along the length of the plantain through the skin. Pry off the skin by slipping your fingers between the peel and the plantain. Once the plantains are peeled, cut them crosswise into 1½-inch chunks.

2. *Frying:* Heat 2 inches of oil to 360°F in a pot or heavy pan. Working in batches, carefully drop plantain slices into the hot oil and fry until golden and tender when pierced with a fork, about 5 minutes. (The oil is too hot if the plantains turn dark brown before becoming tender.) Remove with a slotted spoon and drain on absorbent toweling.

3. *Squashing and seasoning:* Place a fried plantain piece on a cutting board; cover with a paper towel or wax paper. Using your palm, press down firmly to squash the plantain into a 2- to 3-inch round. (Do not oversquash or the slices will be too thin.) Continue the process with the remaining slices. Dip the flattened slices in cold salted water for 1 minute each; blot dry.

4. *Refrying:* Return the plantain slices to the hot oil and fry until golden and crisp on the outside and soft on the inside, about 3 minutes. Sprinkle with salt and serve hot.

MAKES 5 SERVINGS (PORTION SIZE: 3 SLICES)

TOSTONES CON SALSA DE TOMATE Y AJO

FRIED PLANTAINS WITH A TOMATO-GARLIC SAUCE

TOMATO-GARLIC SAUCE
6 cloves garlic, minced
1½ tablespoons olive oil
1 tablespoon white vinegar

⅔ cup (6 ounces) tomato sauce
2 or 3 drops hot sauce
¼ teaspoon salt

TOSTONES
5 large plátanos verdes (green
  plantains)

Vegetable oil for frying
1 teaspoon garlic salt

1. *Tomato-garlic sauce:* Combine the garlic, oil, vinegar, tomato sauce, hot sauce, and salt in a small bowl; mix well and set aside.

2. *Preparing plantains:* Peel and slice plantains following the directions on page 168.

3. *Frying:* Heat 2 inches of oil in a deep skillet to about 380°F. Fry the plantain pieces for about 10 minutes, or until evenly golden on the outside and tender on the inside (check tenderness by inserting a toothpick). Place on absorbent towels; let cool.

4. *Forming tostones:* Place the plantains, one by one, between 2 small wooden boards (3 × 3 inches) or between foil and press until it becomes a round tostón (squashed plantain) about 3/8 inch thick.

5. *Seasoning and refrying:* In a small bowl, combine 1 cup of cold water and the garlic salt. Place the tostones in the garlic water for 1 minute; shake dry before carefully submerging in hot oil. In small batches, fry tostones for 5 to 7 minutes, or until completely golden. Place on paper towels. Serve immediately with sauce.

MAKES 6 SERVINGS (PORTION SIZE: 4 TOSTONES)

PLÁTANOS MADUROS FRITOS

FRIED SWEET PLANTAINS

☼ *If you are not familiar with maduros, their caramelized, blackened (almost burnt) color and wilted appearance might deter you. After one bite, however, you'll understand why Cubans love their plátanos maduros.*

12 medium ripe plátanos maduros (plantains)　　　Vegetable or peanut oil for frying

1. *Peeling plantains:* To remove the skin, slice off the tips of the plantains at both ends. Make a lengthwise slit through the peel. Pry off the skin by inserting your fingers between peel and plantain. Cut each plantain in half lengthwise.

2. *Frying and serving plantains:* In a large skillet over medium heat, heat 1 inch of oil to 375°F, or until a plantain sizzles when it touches the oil. Fry as many as will fit in a single layer until golden brown, 4 to 5 minutes for each side, turning with a slotted spoon. Drain on absorbent towels and serve immediately. (If you are frying a large number of plantains, keep them warm in a 200°F oven until ready to serve.)

SERVING SUGGESTION: Serve Plátanos Maduros Fritos with Arroz con Bacalao (Rice with Salt Cod, page 114) or with the traditional accompaniments of black beans and white rice.

MAKES 6 SERVINGS (PORTION SIZE: 2 SLICES)

The fact that there are various names for the same preparation of ripe plátanos (plantains)—plátanos maduros in Cuba, tajalas in Colombia, tajadas in Nicaragua, and amarillos in Puerto Rico—is an indication of the versatility of this fruit-vegetable. Once fried, the plantain slices turn a brilliant yellow, sweet and succulent on the inside and lightly crisp on the outside. The flavor and texture of sweet fried plantains complement any number of Latin bean and rice dishes served throughout the Americas.

CHAPTER FIVE

POSTRES Y BEBIDAS

DESSERTS AND BEVERAGES

$\mathbf{M}$any *of the desserts and beverages in-
cluded in this chapter represent treasured family recipes from the colonial period.
Rather than modify these valued recipes to suit the modern palate, we chose to
preserve the family's heritage recipe or recapture a family's lost recipe.*

Buñuelos de Viento

SUMMER OUTING / PUERTO RICO

"PUFFS OF WIND" FRITTERS

*One of the most vivid recollections of my childhood in Puerto Rico is when
my father moved to New York to find a job, taking my two older siblings
with him. My mom, to maintain our normal family activities, would take us on
Sunday outings to the beach. Mom didn't have much money, so to provide us a
treat, she used to prepare the dough for buñuelos to fry at the beach. All nine of
us kids would trail after her, each carrying something for our day's outing: the
dough, cooking oil, wood. . . . As we played in the water, Mom would fry up these
delicacies. The smell of the salty ocean air as I bit into these "puffs of wind" gave
me a sense of peace, a taste of childhood freedom, and a good feeling of being
with my family, even in our father's absence.*

EVA JUDITH LOZANO

1 cup orange flower water (see page
    171) or plain water
1 tablespoon granulated sugar
½ teaspoon salt
3 tablespoons butter

1 cup all-purpose flour
2 teaspoons baking powder
3 large eggs
Oil for deep frying
Confectioners' sugar for dusting

1. *Simmering:* Combine the orange flower water, granulated sugar, salt,
and butter in a heavy saucepan large enough to accommodate the other
ingredients. Heat to boiling, stirring until the sugar is dissolved; remove
from heat. Set the pan on a damp cloth on the counter.

2. *Making choux pastry:* Mix together the flour and baking powder; add to
the heated water mixture a portion at a time, beating with a wooden
spoon until smooth. Add the eggs, one at a time, vigorously beating with
a wooden spoon after each addition. *(The mixture will be slippery after the*

addition of an egg. Continue beating until the dough becomes sticky and difficult to beat.) Continue adding the remaining eggs. Then beat the dough for 3 minutes until it is satiny.

3. *Frying fritters:* In a deep fryer or pot, heat 2 inches of oil to 375°F. Using a tablespoon, scoop up a small portion of the dough and drop into the hot oil. Fry uncovered until the dough has puffed and is golden brown. Cover the pot and continue frying until the dough ball cracks and enlarges, being careful not to burn. Uncover the pot and remove the buñuelo with a slotted spoon when it is completely golden brown. Drain on absorbent towels and immediately dust with sifted confectioners' sugar. Serve immediately.

ORANGE FLOWER WATER
Boil 1¼ cups of water. Remove from the heat and add dried orange blossom tea (purchased at a Hispanic market) or the rind of 2 oranges. Cover the pot and let steep for 15 minutes. Strain before using.

SERVING SUGGESTION: Place Buñuelos de Viento on individual plates, allowing 3 per serving. Serve with a copita (cordial glass) of your favorite liqueur, or top with a flavored syrup and ground almonds.

MAKES 6 SERVINGS (PORTION SIZE: 3 SMALL BUÑUELOS)

In certain parts of Latin America as well as in Spain, "puffs of wind" are typically eaten on All Saints Day, November 1, a date when the living pay their respects to the souls of the dead by spending the day at the family burial grounds and preparing sweet and savory foods. These buñuelos should be sprinkled thickly with confectioners' sugar, although the old Spanish method dictated rolling them in a hearty red wine syrup or orange syrup, and then sprinkling them with confectioners' sugar and finely chopped almonds.

EMPANADITAS SANTA FE

CHRISTMAS / SOUTHWEST

SANTA FE MINCEMEAT TURNOVERS

My earliest memories of the kitchen are with my Grandmother Eloisa in Santa Fe. For me the kitchen was a haven of warmth, smells, and of course nourishment. These "little turnovers" are especially popular during Christmastime, when all of Sante Fe is lighted by the luminarias (sandbag candles).

JOHN RODRIGUEZ SEDLAR

FILLING

2 pounds boneless pork butt, cut into
   1-inch cubes and trimmed
1 cup sugar
2/3 cup unsweetened applesauce
2/3 cup pine nuts, toasted
1/2 cup seedless raisins, halved

1 heaping tablespoon coriander seeds,
   ground in a spice mill or mortar
1/2 teaspoon ground allspice
1/2 teaspoon ground cinnamon
1/2 teaspoon powdered cloves
1/2 teaspoon powdered ginger

DOUGH

3/4 cup lard
2 tablespoons sugar
6 cups all-purpose flour

Oil for deep frying
Anise ice cream (optional)

1. *Cooking pork:* In a small pot, combine the pork with enough water to cover. Simmer briskly, covered, until tender, about $1^{1}/_{2}$ to 2 hours. Drain, reserving the cooking liquid. Using 2 forks, finely shred the pork.

2. *Filling:* In a bowl, mix the shredded pork, sugar, applesauce, pine nuts, raisins, coriander, allspice, cinnamon, cloves, and ginger until well blended. Adjust seasonings to taste. Cover and refrigerate until ready to use. Makes 4 cups.

3. *Dough:* In a mixing bowl, cream together the lard and sugar. Gradually cut this mixture into the flour until the mixture resembles coarse meal. Stir in just enough cold water, about $1^{1}/_{2}$ cups, to make a firm, soft dough. Turn out the dough onto a well-floured cutting board. Knead until smooth and pliable. Cover the dough with a damp towel.

4. *Forming empanaditas:* On the floured board, roll out the dough to $1/_{4}$-

inch thickness. With a 3-inch round cutter, stamp out circles. Lift off excess dough and gather the scraps for rerolling. Place 2 teaspoons of filling in the center of each circle. Using your fingers, moisten the edges of the dough with water. Fold the dough over the filling and seal the edges by pressing down with the tines of a fork.

5. *Frying:* Heat 2 inches of oil in a heavy skillet or deep fryer to a temperature of 380°F. Fry the empanaditas, 5 at a time, for 3 minutes, or until golden, turning once. Drain on absorbent toweling. If desired, serve with anise ice cream.

MAKES 5 DOZEN (PORTION SIZE: 3 EMPANADITAS)

ATOLE

ALL SAINTS' DAY/MEXICO

SWEETENED CORN BEVERAGE

Atole is a thick hot beverage made from milk and/or water, thickened with cornstarch, fresh corn, or masa (corn dough). Flavored with spices, fruits, herbs, or nuts, Atole is oftentimes sweetened or served with panocha, small cone-shaped raw sugar. Depending on the community, flavored atoles are prepared for a particular feast day. Vanilla atole is used as an oferta (offering) on All Saints' Day or the Day of the Dead. It is also used to soothe an upset stomach or to nourish young infants.

½ pound fresh corn masa
5 cups milk
2 tablespoons cornstarch dissolved in
   ¼ cup cold water

2 orange leaves (optional)
2 (3-inch) cinnamon sticks
1½ cups packed brown sugar

In a blender, combine the masa with 3 cups of water; blend until smooth. Pour the mixture into a medium saucepan with the milk, dissolved cornstarch, orange leaves, if desired, and cinnamon sticks. Cook over medium heat, stirring occasionally. When the mixture has thickened, add the sugar to taste and stir until dissolved. (The atole should be the thickness of heavy cream. If it is too thick, you can use milk to dilute.) Remove orange leaves and cinnamon sticks and serve hot.

MAKES 8 SERVINGS (PORTION SIZE: 1 CUP)

SOPAIPILLAS
FAMILY GET-TOGETHERS / SOUTHWEST

FRIED ''LITTLE PILLOW'' PUFFS

Twenty-five years ago, my dad, a crash firefighter and retired army major, was very involved in the Community Chest for the Albuquerque area. For that organization's fundraisers, he would make Sopaipillas at the fire station using his great-grandmother Nana Valles' recipe. He had a special feel for the dough; he knew exactly when it was ready so that it would fry and puff into the little golden pillows we all enjoyed to eat with Albuquerque honey.

GLORIA SANDOVAL

2 cups all-purpose flour
2 teaspoons baking powder
1 teaspoon salt
2 tablespoons lard or shortening

Vegetable oil for frying
Honey or cinnamon sugar

1. *Preparing dough:* In a medium bowl, combine the flour, baking powder, and salt. Using your hands or a pastry cutter, blend the lard into the flour mixture 1 teaspoon at a time until the lard is no longer visible. Add ¾ cup of warm water, ¼ cup at a time, mixing quickly with a fork until the dough is soft, moist, and a little sticky.

2. *Kneading and forming:* Place the dough on a floured work surface. Knead it gently by folding it in half, patting it down, and folding again until soft and pliable. Pinch off 12 dough balls; flatten with the palms of your hands. Using a rolling pin, roll out the dough into 5-inch circles approximately ³/₁₆ inch thick. Cut each disk into 4 triangles.

3. *Frying:* Heat 1 inch of shortening to 350°F in a frying pan. Drop the sopaipillas, one at a time, into the oil and hold them under with a slotted spatula or spoon until they puff. At the right temperature it should immediately bubble, sizzle, and puff. Turn after 20 to 30 seconds and fry until golden; place on absorbent towels.

4. *Serving:* Serve with honey or sprinkle while still warm with cinnamon sugar. Serve immediately.

SERVING SUGGESTION: Although they're related to Indian fry bread and cousins to Mexican buñuelos, New Mexico's sopaipillas, fried "little pillow" breads, are unique, serving as both the bread and dessert at the same meal. Break open a sopaipilla and drizzle it with honey—the sweetness is surprisingly compatible with red chile stews and beans. Save the last few bites to savor as dessert with a wedge of longhorn Cheddar cheese.

MAKES 12 SOPAIPILLAS (PORTION SIZE: 2 SOPAIPILLAS)

QUESADILLA DE ARROZ

FAMILY GET-TOGETHERS / GUATEMALA

GUATEMALAN SWEET BREAD

My hometown of Zacapa, Guatemala, is in a beautiful agricultural area that produces wonderful dairy products. These little cakes were made to celebrate special times: family accomplishments, good grades in school, a new birth, or even losing a tooth as a sign of a child moving foward in life.

½ pound (2 sticks) butter, softened
1½ cups sugar
1½ pounds rice flour (about 3¼ cups)

1 tablespoon baking powder
6 ounces crumbled farmer, fresco, or ricotta cheese (about 1¾ cups)
6 eggs

1. *Mixing:* In a mixing bowl, cream together the butter and sugar until smooth. Sift the flour with the baking powder and beat into the creamed mixture. Mix in the cheese until well blended. Continue beating while adding the eggs one at a time, mixing well after each addition.

2. *Baking:* Preheat the oven to 350°F. Pour the batter into 12 lightly greased or paper-lined muffin cups. Bake 40 minutes, or until golden and firm to the touch. Remove from oven; turn out onto a rack and allow to cool 15 minutes before serving.

MAKES 12 SERVINGS (PORTION SIZE: 1 MUFFIN)

BUÑUELOS

CHRISTMAS / MEXICO

MEXICAN FRITTERS

As a result of the Mexican Revolution, my grandmother Vita (Maria Luisa Hernandez) fled Guanajuato to the U.S., bringing with her one of my favorite dishes of our Mexican culture: Buñuelos. Vita, at age ninety-one, is still able to make these scrumptious Christmas treats.

LISA MARIA HERNANDEZ

BUÑUELOS
3 cups all-purpose flour
¼ teaspoon salt
3 tablespoons lard or solid vegetable
  shortening

2 eggs, beaten
1 cup anise water (see page 177) or
  plain water
Oil for deep frying

CINNAMON-ORANGE SYRUP
1 cup sugar
4 (3-inch) cinnamon sticks

Rind of 1 orange

1. *Preparing buñuelo dough:* Mix the flour and salt in a medium bowl. Blend the lard into the flour, using your fingers, until it is no longer visible. Make a well in the center and pour in the eggs and anise water. Work together with your hands or a fork, incorporating small portions of the wet ingredients with the dry ingredients until the mixture begins to form a dough. Knead the dough on a lightly floured board until smooth. Cover dough with a damp cloth and let rest 20 minutes.

2. *Preparing syrup:* In a small saucepan, combine the sugar with 1 cup of water, the cinnamon sticks, and the orange rind. Bring to a vigorous boil and cook 20 minutes, or until reduced to a pourable syrup. Remove from the heat and let cool. (The syrup will thicken more after cooling.) Strain before serving. This syrup can be prepared several weeks ahead and stored at room temperature in a sealed jar. Reheat before using.

3. *Forming buñuelos:* Divide the dough into 16 even pieces and shape into balls. Cover with a damp cloth while working with dough to prevent drying out. Using the palms of your hands, flatten each piece into a 3-inch

disk. On a floured board, roll out each disk into a paper-thin 7- to 8-inch circle.

4. *Frying:* Pour oil into a 10-inch skillet to a depth of about 2½ inches; heat to 380°F. Fry the buñuelos one at a time, turning once, until golden, about 40 seconds per side. Be careful not to overcook buñuelos. Remove immediately and drain on absorbent towels. Serve with syrup.

ANISE WATER
Combine 12 star anise or 2 tablespoons anise seed with 1½ cups of water in a small saucepan. Cook uncovered over medium high heat until reduced to 1 cup of anise water. Let cool completely before using.

SERVING SUGGESTION: For a traditional Christmas Eve confection, serve Buñuelos in a clay pot or shallow platter stacked one on top of the other. Pour about 1 cup of syrup over the pile so that it cascades downward, accumulating in the bottom of the platter. The last few Buñuelos on the bottom of the pile will be ahogados (drowned) in syrup, ready for the lucky guests to enjoy. These pastries are served with frothy mugs of hot Mexican chocolate (see page 198).

MAKES 16 SERVINGS (PORTION SIZE: 1 BUÑUELO)

Mexican buñuelos (fritters) are tortilla-shaped crisp pastries quite different from the puffy sweet balls of dough seen throughout all other Latin American countries. Although Mexican buñuelos are sold by vendors all year-round, they've come to symbolize la epoca Navideña (the Christmastime festivities) between December 15 and January 6, filled with pastries, music, food traditions, and religious rituals. This particular buñuelo recipe is just as scrumptious, much simpler, and quicker to prepare than the more elaborate method seen in most cookbooks.

BUÑUELOS DE YUCA EN MELADO

NEW YEAR'S EVE / VENEZUELA

YUCCA FRITTERS WITH MELADO SYRUP

It was very important to begin the New Year with something new, as your family strolled from house to house wishing each family a "Feliz Año Nuevo," Happy New Year. A holiday beverage like ponche crema (Venezuelan eggnog) or café con leche (coffee with milk) seemed to warm up the occasion, especially when accompanied by these buñuelos de yuca (yucca fritters). Most homes had a sancocho (Venezuelan stew) cooking, just in case your friends needed a nourishing warm meal after a night of joyous celebration.

LOLA CANTELI-HESS

1 pound yuca (yucca or cassava)
Salt
3 egg yolks
1 teaspoon baking soda
1 ½ teaspoons ground cloves
2 teaspoons sugar

Oil for deep frying
1 ¼ cups maple syrup mixed with ¼ cup molasses or melado (Venezuelan syrup)
Confectioners' sugar

1. *Cooking yucca:* Cook and peel yucca according to directions on page 164.

2. *Preparing yucca dough:* Mash the yucca in the workbowl of a food processor until the consistency of thickly mashed potatoes. With the machine running, add the egg yolks, baking soda, 1 teaspoon of salt, the cloves, and sugar. Process until a soft tacky dough forms, about 25 seconds. Turn the dough onto a damp kitchen towel and knead until soft.

3. *Forming and frying buñuelos:* Form the dough into 28 balls, 1 inch in diameter. In a deep fryer, heat 2 inches of oil to 375°F. Fry the buñuelos for 2 minutes, turning once, until golden. Remove with a slotted spoon and drain on absorbent towels.

4. *Serving:* Heat maple syrup and molasses mixture or melado over medium heat until warm. Drop a few buñuelos into the syrup. Using a slotted spoon, remove immediately. Before serving, dust with confectioners' sugar.

MAKES 14 SERVINGS (PORTION SIZE: 2 BUÑUELOS)

BIZCOCHITOS

TÍA MIMI'S WEDDING COOKIES

In small towns when I was a child, baking was an activity shared among family and friends. Every time there was a wedding or baptism, we made these cookies with my Tía Celia, known as Mimi. She shared a lot of love, tenderness, and laughter in the kitchen as we baked these cookies for the families' weddings. To this day I spend quality time with my own young girls in the kitchen.

GLORIA SANDOVAL

1 cup solid vegetable shortening	2 cups sifted all-purpose flour
2 teaspoons vanilla extract	1 cup finely chopped pecans
½ cup confectioners' sugar	1 cup ground pecans (see Note)
1 teaspoon salt	Confectioners' sugar for dusting

1. *Preparing dough:* In a medium bowl, beat the shortening and vanilla with an electric mixer until fluffy. Continue beating while adding sugar, 1 tablespoon at a time, and salt. Sift the flour into the creamed mixture. Add the chopped and ground pecans and mix until evenly distributed.

2. *Forming and baking:* Preheat the oven to 350°F. Pinch off approximately 35 balls ¾ inch in diameter. Roll each ball between the palms of your hands until smooth; place on a greased cookie sheet ½ inch apart. Bake for 12 minutes. Immediately remove the bizcochitos from the cookie sheet and roll in confectioners' sugar; let cool. Store the cookies in an airtight container for up to 1 week.

NOTE: To grind pecans, place them in a cleaned coffee grinder or food processor and pulverize.

MAKES 36 COOKIES (PORTION SIZE: 3 COOKIES)

In Mexico and the North American Southwest, Bizcochitos fall halfway between a sugar cookie and shortbread, generally flavored with anise and rolled in confectioners' sugar. This version uses pecans, which grow abundantly throughout New Mexico and Texas.

Alegrías del Cielo

''HAPPINESS FROM HEAVEN'' BAPTISMAL CAKES

½ pound (2 sticks) unsalted butter, at room temperature
2 cups sugar
8 eggs, at room temperature
¼ cup water

1 teaspoon almond extract
1⅔ cups all-purpose flour
1½ cups blanched almonds, ground
Confectioners' sugar

1. *Preparing batter:* In a mixing bowl, cream the butter and sugar until light and fluffy. Add the eggs, one at a time, beating well after each addition. Slowly pour in the water while beating. Stir the almond extract, the flour, and ground almonds into the creamed mixture until well mixed.

2. *Baking:* Preheat the oven to 350°F. Line muffin tins with fluted baking paper cups; spoon in batter ¾ full. Bake for 20 minutes, or until golden. Dust with sifted confectioners' sugar before serving.

MAKES 24 CUPCAKES

Chocolate Guatamalteco

GUATEMALAN CHOCOLATE

2 (1-ounce) squares unsweetened baking chocolate
2 cups strong black coffee
1 teaspoon ground cinnamon
⅓ cup granulated sugar

¼ cup packed brown sugar
1 tablespoon cornstarch
1½ teaspoons vanilla extract
Pinch salt
3 cups milk

In a double boiler, melt the chocolate with the coffee and cinnamon over medium heat. Mix together the sugars and cornstarch; whisk into the chocolate. Add the vanilla, salt, and milk. Cook over medium high heat, about 20 minutes. If desired, whip until frothy.

MAKES 6 SERVINGS (PORTION SIZE: 1 CUP)

Rabanadas

EASTER / BRAZIL

BRAZILIAN FRENCH TOAST WITH PORT WINE

This traditional Brazilian dessert is typically served during the Christmas or Easter holidays. Known as torrejas in Spain and Portugal, it can be prepared with fruit syrup, sherry, or port wine syrup.

⅓ cup packed brown sugar	5⅓ tablespoons (⅓ cup) butter,
1¾ cups port wine	softened
1 lemon slice	8 eggs, beaten
8 thick slices French bread (about 1½	½ cup confectioners' sugar
inches thick)	1 teaspoon grated nutmeg

1. *Preparing bread:* In a saucepan, combine the brown sugar, port wine, and lemon slice; cook over medium heat about 15 minutes, until thickened to a light syrup. Remove crusts from the bread, if desired, and arrange in a single layer in a baking dish. Pour the wine syrup over the bread slices; let stand for 2 minutes. Turn the bread, continue to soak, then transfer the slices to a dry platter.

2. *Frying:* In a large cast-iron skillet or griddle, melt 2 tablespoons of the butter over medium low heat, being careful not to burn it. Carefully dip each slice of soaked bread into the beaten eggs. Lift the bread with a spatula or slotted spoon and place on the heated griddle. Fry the bread, turning once, until golden on both sides. Repeat the process with the remaining bread, adding additional butter to the pan as needed. Remove rabanadas to a serving dish and keep warm.

3. *Serving:* Sprinkle warm rabanadas with a mixture of the confectioners' sugar and nutmeg. Serve immediately.

SERVING SUGGESTION: Serve as a special holiday dessert or create holiday appetizers by substituting milk for port wine, omitting sugar and nutmeg, and serving sandwich style with a crab and cream filling.

MAKES 4 SERVINGS (PORTION SIZE: 2 SLICES)

Bien Me Sabe

CHRISTMAS / VENEZUELA

LAYERED COCONUT CREAM TORTE

This traditional Venezuelan holiday dessert would require hours of my mother's time in the kitchen. We, of course, would show our appreciation with every bite. Today, I allow myself this indulgence at Christmas.

VIVIANNE SCHAEL

COCONUT CREAM

3½ cups sugar
6 cups coconut milk, made with 3 coconuts (see page 90)

18 egg yolks
¼ teaspoon salt

BIZCOCHO (SPONGECAKE)

7 eggs, separated
¼ cup cornstarch
6 tablespoons sugar

¼ cup all-purpose flour
½ teaspoon baking powder
¼ teaspoon salt

MERINGUE

5 egg whites
⅓ cup sugar

½ cup sweet cream sherry
Ground cinnamon

1. *Preparing sugar syrup for coconut cream:* Place the sugar in a saucepan; cover with 1 cup of water. Cook over medium high heat until the sugar is dissolved. Do not stir the syrup or the sugar will crystallize. Once the sugar is dissolved, bring to a boil and cook for 10 minutes, or until a thread of syrup spins from the spoon when lifted from the saucepan. Remove from the heat and let cool. Makes 2 cups.

2. *Making bizcocho (spongecake):* Preheat the oven to 350°F. In a small bowl, beat the egg whites to the soft peak stage or until just stiff. While beating, add the yolks one at a time; continue beating while adding cornstarch, sugar, and the flour mixed with the baking powder and salt. Turn the batter into a greased and floured 8-inch cake pan. Bake for 30 minutes. The cake will be golden and a toothpick inserted off-center will come out clean. Let cool in the pan 20 minutes; loosen the cake edges

from the pan and invert onto a baking rack. Split the cake lengthwise with a serrated knife and slice into three ¹/₂-inch-thick sheets.

3. *Preparing coconut cream:* In a medium bowl, beat the egg yolks and salt with an electric mixer until creamy. Continue to beat while pouring in 6 cups of coconut milk. Pour into a large saucepan. While beating constantly, pour the cooled sugar syrup into the coconut cream. Cook over low heat, stirring constantly, until the custard starts a rapid simmer and thickens. Immediately remove from the heat and let cool.

4. *Meringue:* Beat the egg whites in a mixing bowl to the soft peak stage. Add the sugar, 1 tablespoon at a time, beating continuously to the stiff peak stage. Set aside.

5. *Assembly:* Place one layer of spongecake onto a serving platter; sprinkle with sherry. Cover with a layer of coconut cream. Repeat the layers using the remaining ingredients. Cover with meringue and sprinkle with cinnamon. Refrigerate at least 4 hours or until completely chilled.

SERVING SUGGESTION: Serve this traditional Venezuelan Christmas dessert with Café Negrito (Demitasse Coffee, page 202).

MAKES 8 SERVINGS

A remarkable dessert—the coconut cream is richer than flan, the bizcocho (spongecake) light and airy, and the meringue a billowy silken cloud. There must be hundreds of versions of this sweet, whose origins have been variously said to be Portugal, France, England, and Spain. The New World ingredient, coconut, makes this heavenly sweet unforgettable.

The family cookbook of Maria Celeste Arraras from the early 1800s says ". . . coconuts should come from the palms of Guanajibo beach in Mayaguez. These are the last coconuts on the island, sweet and full of juice. Be sure to cut them in the morning when they are at their juiciest."

BANANOS ENDULZADOS

BANANAS COOKED IN CARAMELIZED CREAM

Regardless of how much my mother worked as a single parent, when the holidays arrived, she always found time to tell us stories about our grandmother and great-grandmother back in Guatemala. Our food and those memories Mom shared with us kept our heritage alive. I especially remember how, at the end of an evening, we would sit around the table gossiping, laughing, and enjoying each other. It never failed that one family member would say, "Let's make some Bananos Endulzados." Within ten minutes we would all be eating this special treat and sipping our Guatemalan coffee.

MARGARITA GARZON

1 tablespoon butter   ½ cup evaporated milk
½ cup sugar
2 large ripe bananas, sliced lengthwise (see Note)

1. *Melting sugar:* Over medium heat, melt the butter in a 10-inch nonstick skillet. Add the sugar, stirring until just golden; lower heat.

2. *Sautéing bananas:* Carefully place the bananas in the skillet, being careful not to break. Gently spoon the melted sugar over them until completely coated. Fry until golden, turning once.

3. *Finishing:* Pour in the milk and carefully stir, creating a caramel sauce. Bring to a rapid simmer; lower the heat and cook uncovered for 2 minutes. Immediately remove from heat.

NOTE: This recipe calls for ripe yellow eating bananas, not to be confused with yellow plantains.

SERVING SUGGESTION: Serve 2 banana halves in a banana-split bowl or on a dessert plate. Pour sauce over the bananas and serve hot with Guatemalan coffee or Cafezinho (Demitasse Coffee, page 202).

MAKES 2 SERVINGS (PORTION SIZE: 2 BANANA HALVES WITH ¼ CUP SAUCE)

HIGOS AL HORNO CON QUESO DE CABRA

SUMMERTIME PARTIES / MEXICO

BAKED FIGS WITH GOAT'S CHEESE

As a child I fondly remember green figs oozing with their ripe honey. My abuelita used to bottle these figs in a syrup scented with cinnamon, cloves, and bay leaf. I often enjoyed these poached figs and many other fruit compotes prepared by her able hands and served with fresh goat's cheese. This is her great-grandson's version of that recipe.

RICARDO DI CORY CARMONA

24 ripe green figs
8 tablespoons (1 stick) unsalted butter, cut into small cubes
½ cup packed dark brown sugar

⅓ cup currants or cut-up golden muscat raisins
¾ cup crumbled fresh goat's cheese

1. *Preparing figs:* Preheat the oven to 375°F. Wash whole figs, drain, and pat dry. Slice in half lengthwise. Dot the bottom of a 13 × 9 × 2½-inch baking dish with half the butter. Place fig halves, cut side up, in the dish in uniform rows, firmly touching each other, until the baking dish is filled. Evenly sprinkle sugar over the figs; dot with the remaining butter.

2. *Baking:* Bake covered for 20 minutes, or until heated through. Scatter currants over the top of the dish and finally crumble goat's cheese over the currant layer. Broil for a few minutes to lightly toast the cheese. Cool and serve the figs with some of the syrup on individual dishes.

SERVING SUGGESTION: Serve these higos al horno in place of a fresh fruit and cheese plate as the ending to a lovely outdoor meal. A full-bodied California merlot would add a nice finishing touch.

MAKES 8 SERVINGS (PORTION SIZE: ABOUT 3 FIGS)

Figs, an important crop in sunny Southern Spain, were originally brought to America by the Spanish missionaries. Today, there are many varieties, from the original purple-black Mission fig to the green Calimyrna used in the preceding recipe. Once picked, figs can be refrigerated 2 to 3 days.

CALABAZA ENDULZADA
DAY OF THE DEAD / MEXICO

PUMPKIN COOKED IN A SPICED SYRUP

During the Christmas holiday, I have fond memories of my grandmother preparing buñuelos (sweet fritters) and Calabaza Endulzada (sweetened pumpkin). As a fourth-generation Mexican-American, I had no idea that these foods held a special significance. It was not until I traveled throughout Mexico at the age of twenty that I realized the cultural roots of our family's traditions. I took great pride in learning about the significance of celebrations that I had taken for granted as a child. One memory in particular is of an elaborate altar set up in the backyard of one of my relatives. The time and care taken to decorate the altar and the offerings of an incredible array of foods absolutely baffled me (considering that the foods were not meant for the living guests). It was at this altar that I realized our family's favorite dessert of Calabaza Endulzada was actually a ritual food used at the Day of the Dead altars.

SANDY MENDOZA

1 (4-pound) sugar pumpkin or yellow winter squash such as acorn squash
9 (6-ounce) cones piloncillo (Mexican raw sugar) or 6 cups packed brown sugar plus ⅓ cup molasses
1 orange, sliced

6 (2½-inch) cinnamon sticks
6 star anise or 1 tablespoon anise seed
1 teaspoon whole cloves
6 bay leaves
Whipped cream or evaporated milk

1. *Pumpkin:* Slice the top third off a 4-pound pumpkin. With a small sharp knife make several slashes in the interior flesh without cutting through to the exterior. Do not remove the seeds or fiber because they are delicious once cooked and sweetened.

2. *Syrup:* Wrap the piloncillo in a kitchen towel. With a mallet, crush the sugar cones. In a pot large enough to hold the pumpkin, heat 8 cups of water to boiling. Add the crushed piloncillo, the sliced unpeeled orange, cinnamon sticks, star anise, cloves, and bay leaves. Bring to a boil, reduce the heat to medium, and cook uncovered about 20 minutes.

3. *Cooking:* Once a light syrup has formed, place the pumpkin in the pot open side down, so that the syrup will soak into the pumpkin pulp. Cover the pot and cook over a medium low flame for about 45 minutes to 1

hour, depending on the size of pumpkin. When the pumpkin is soft and the syrup is thickened, remove from the heat and let cool. The skin will look glossy and the syrup will have the consistency of honey. Place whole "candied" pumpkin on a shallow serving platter. Ladle sauce and spices over pumpkin. Allow each guest to scoop out the pulp (the skin is inedible) or cut a slice of pumpkin with accompanying syrup. Serve with whipped cream or evaporated milk.

MAKES 8 SERVINGS (PORTION SIZE: ONE 4 × 4-INCH PIECE AND ¹/₃ CUP SYRUP)

One of the many Day of the Dead foods placed on the ceremonial altar as an offering is Calabaza Endulzada. Bright-colored marigolds, candles, atoles, enchiladas en mole, arroz con leche, candies, and personal objects of the deceased grace the home altars during the festivities.

FRUTAS EN ALMÍBAR DE VINO

FEAST DAYS / SOUTH AMERICA

FRUIT IN WINE SYRUP

2 cups high-quality full-bodied red
  wine
1 cup sugar
2 (3-inch) cinnamon sticks
5 whole cloves

Pinch of freshly grated nutmeg
6 whole pears, fresh peaches, or
  quinces, peeled, pitted, and split in
  halves (or quartered or cut into
  wedges)

1. *Preparing wine syrup:* In a saucepan, combine the wine, sugar, cinnamon, cloves, and nutmeg. Bring to a boil and briskly cook uncovered for 20 minutes.

2. *Poaching fruit:* Add the fruit to the wine syrup. Cook over low heat until the fruit is tender.

SERVING SUGGESTION: Serve these fruits on a spongecake slice (see Bizcocho, Sponge Cake recipe, page 182), soaked with wine syrup.

MAKES 3 CUPS

FLAN

FAMILY GATHERINGS / PUERTO RICO

BLANCA'S FLAN

I always knew when someone special was coming over to our house in Puerto Rico when my mom would begin cooking the caramelo (burnt sugar syrup) for her flan. My memories are very vivid, recalling my abuelito's (grandfather's) frequent visits with our family. We would all be sitting around our kitchen table, eating flan, drinking coffee, teasing and conversing, enjoying those special moments in each other's company.

MARIA ALAMO

CARAMELIZED SUGAR
1 cup sugar

FLAN (CUSTARD)
1 (12-ounce) can undiluted evapo-   1 cup sugar
  rated milk   1 teaspoon vanilla extract
3/4 cup whole milk   Pinch salt
4 to 6 eggs

1. *Caramelizing mold:* Place a 1-quart flan mold close to the stovetop. Using a heavy skillet with straight sides and a lid, combine the sugar and 1/2 cup of water, stirring until the sugar is almost dissolved. Bring the sugar water to a boil and stir the water around the edges of the skillet to wash down any undissolved sugar. Cover the skillet and boil 3 minutes. Uncover and continue boiling until the sugar begins to turn golden. Lower the heat to medium high and slowly stir for about 10 minutes, until the caramel is a deep golden brown, being careful not to burn. (Too light a caramel will not have enough flavor.) Quickly and carefully pour caramel into the bottom of the mold, tilting to evenly coat the bottom and 1/2 inch up the sides of the mold. The caramel will continue to darken once removed from the heat, so be careful not to overcook.

2. *Blending custard:* Preheat the oven to 350°F. Combine the evaporated milk, whole milk, eggs, sugar, vanilla, and salt in a blender container; mix until satiny smooth.

188 • POSTRES Y BEBIDAS

3. *Baking:* Place your filled mold in a shallow pan that is larger than and at least ³/₄ the height as your mold; set on a middle oven rack. Pour hot water into the shallow pan, up to half the height of the mold. Bake 1 hour at 350°F. The flan should be firm when removed from the oven. Let the mold completely cool. At this point the flan can be refrigerated.

4. Unmold and serve according to directions on page 191.

MAKES 8 SERVINGS

CHAMPURRADO

CHRISTMAS SEASON / MEXICO

CHOCOLATE ATOLE

Besides being one of the traditional beverages enjoyed during the Christmas festivities, Champurrado (chocolate-flavored atole) is part of a typical break-fast of enchiladas and tamales enjoyed on Viernes de Dolores (Friday of the Seven Sorrows of our Lady).

1 cup masa harina (corn flour mix)

2 tablespoons maizena (cornstarch) dissolved in ¹/₃ cup cold water

2 large (6 ounces each) piloncillo cones (Mexican raw sugar) or 1¹/₂ cups packed brown sugar

5 cups whole or low-fat milk

1 (3-ounce) tablet Mexican chocolate (see Note, page 198)

2 teaspoons almond or vanilla extract

1 teaspoon anise seeds, crushed

Place the masa harina, dissolved cornstarch, and 2 cups of water in a blender; purée until smooth. Pour into a 4-quart saucepan. Bring to a boil over medium heat, stirring constantly with a whisk, and cook for 8 minutes, or until the mixture has thickened. Stir in the piloncillo, milk, chocolate, almond extract, and anise seeds. Continue cooking for 15 to 18 minutes, stirring constantly, until the ingredients have dissolved and the mixture has thickened. Remove from the heat; ladle into mugs.

MAKES 8 CUPS

QUESILLO

VENEZUELAN FLAN

When I lived in Venezuela, this dessert on the Christmas buffet always caught my eye and appetite. It is without doubt one of the best flans I've tasted, a cross between a cheesecake and crème caramel!

MAITE D'AMICO

CARAMELIZED SUGAR
1 cup sugar

QUESILLO (CUSTARD)
8 whole eggs
2 (14½-ounce) cans sweetened condensed milk

3½ cups whipping cream
1 tablespoon vanilla extract

1. *Caramelizing mold:* See directions on page 188 to caramelize mold.

2. *Blending custard:* Combine the whole eggs, sweetened condensed milk, cream, and vanilla in a blender container; mix until satiny smooth. Pour the custard through a fine sieve into the caramel-coated mold. The sieve is not necessary, but it will remove any unblended egg particles, ensuring a velvety smooth custard.

3. Use one of the following two methods to cook your quesillo:
Cooking in pressure cooker: Pour the blender contents into the mold; cover tightly with aluminum foil. Place the mold in a pressure cooker with water halfway up the sides of the mold. Secure the lid and bring to a boil. Lower the heat to medium and cook for 35 minutes. Remove from the heat and let cool. Place under running water to allow steam to escape. Remove the flan and let cool.
Baking method: Preheat the oven to 350°F. Place the filled mold in a shallow pan that is larger and at least ¾ the height of the mold; set on a middle oven rack. Pour hot water into the shallow pan, up to half the height of the mold. Bake for 1 hour 20 minutes. The flan should be firm and not quiver when removed from the oven. Let the mold cool completely on a baker's rack. At this point the flan can be refrigerated.

4. *Unmolding and serving:* If refrigerated, allow the flan to come to room temperature. Run a thin knife around the mold edges to loosen, being careful not to cut into the custard. Holding the edges of the mold, gently shake the mold in a circular motion until the flan has loosened. Place a large serving platter (at least 3 inches larger in diameter than the flan) over the mold and quickly turn the platter and mold over, allowing the caramel to bathe the flan.

SERVING SUGGESTION: Serve this thick and rich Quesillo as you would cheesecake. A small wedge will more than satisfy your guest. Pour the caramel sauce over the Quesillo wedge before serving. Accompany with Café Negrito (Demitasse Coffee, page 202).

MAKES 8 SERVINGS (PORTION SIZE: 1 WEDGE)

DULCE DE LECHE
DINNER PARTIES / SOUTH AMERICA

MILK CARAMEL

This dessert is found throughout Latin America and is considered the most popular of preserves in Argentina, Mexico, and Central America. It is used as a spread on bread, crackers, cakes, and pastries as well as a filling for cakes and other sweets.

1 quart (4 cups) milk
2½ cups sugar

1 vanilla bean, split
¼ teaspoon baking soda

In a heavy pot, combine the milk, sugar, vanilla bean, and baking soda. Rapidly bring to a boil; lower the heat to medium low and cook, stirring occasionally, until the milk begins to turn to a light coffee color, about 40 minutes. Lower the heat and simmer *uncovered,* stirring occasionally with a wooden spoon to avoid scorching. The mixture will take about 1 additional hour to cook and thicken. Remove from the heat when the mixture has caramelized and thickened.

SERVING SUGGESTION: Serve as an after-dinner dessert with water crackers, spongecake, and an assortment of cheeses.

MAKES 2 CUPS

CAZUELA DE TÍA AMPARITO

THANKSGIVING / PUERTO RICO

SWEETENED PUMPKIN AND YAM CASSEROLE

As the end of the year approached in my native Puerto Rico, preparations for Thanksgiving and Christmas would begin. Although some traditional fare was always planned, Tía Amparito's cazuela was always a must, especially for the gorditos—the chubby ones in the family. All the kids call it "low calorie" because of the relatively little sugar the recipe contains!

MARI CARMEN APONTE

1½ cups cooked sweet potatoes
2 cups cooked calabaza (West Indian pumpkin) or cooked acorn squash (see Note)
4 eggs, beaten
8 tablespoons (1 stick) butter, melted
1 cup canned coconut milk

⅓ cup plus 2 tablespoons rice flour
½ to ¾ cup sugar
2 tablespoons ground cinnamon
1 tablespoon ground cloves
1 teaspoon grated nutmeg
Whipped cream (optional)

1. *Pumpkin-potato purée:* In a large bowl, mash together the cooked and peeled sweet potatoes and pumpkin until smooth.

2. *Batter:* Preheat the oven to 350°F. Beat the eggs, melted butter, and coconut milk into the pumpkin purée until smooth. Stir in the flour, sugar, cinnamon, cloves, and nutmeg and mix well.

3. *Baking:* Pour the mixture into a greased 9 × 7½ × 2½-inch baking dish. Bake for 1 hour. Remove and let cool before serving. Top with a dollop of whipped cream, if desired.

NOTE: Calabaza or West Indian pumpkin has a green skin and bright yellow-orange flesh. It can be found in boutique supermarkets. If unavailable, substitute acorn squash. Banana squash is too porous to be used in this recipe (a dense flesh creates desirable heavy texture). This dish can be made either as a sweet side dish complementing a roasted turkey or as a dessert, depending on the amount of sugar.

MAKES 8 SERVINGS (PORTION SIZE: ONE 2 × 3-INCH PIECE)

CAPIROTADA

MEXICAN BREAD PUDDING

My grandmother made Capirotada during Lent. I used to help her prepare it, and I loved smelling its sweet aroma as it filled the entire house with its spicy scent. I would eagerly wait for it to finish baking and loved it best when it was warm out of the oven.

GLORIA ANN MONTEROS

1 loaf French bread (about 21 slices) or white sandwich bread or bolillos (Mexican rolls), sliced
½ pound (2 sticks) butter, melted (1 cup) (optional)
8 piloncillo (Mexican raw sugar) cones or 3 cups packed dark brown sugar
1½ tablespoons whole cloves
5 (3-inch) cinnamon sticks

1½ tablespoons anise seeds
1 cup unsalted shelled peanuts
20 colaciones (candied peanuts), about 2 (⅞-ounce) packages (optional)
1 cup raisins
2 cups shredded white Cheddar or Jack cheese

1. *Preparing bread:* Arrange the bread on 2 greased cookie sheets. Bake at 400°F until golden. Turn and continue baking until both sides are toasted. Using a pastry brush, coat or drizzle the bread with melted butter, if desired.

2. *Making syrup:* In a small pot, combine the sugar, cloves, cinnamon sticks, and anise seeds with 8 cups of water. Bring to a boil and cook uncovered, stirring occasionally, until the sugar is dissolved. Reduce the heat and simmer vigorously uncovered until the liquid reduces to a syrup, about 25 minutes. Makes 6 cups.

3. *Preparing casserole:* Preheat the oven to 350°F. Butter a 13 × 9 × 2½-inch baking dish. Place a layer of the buttered bread on the bottom of the dish. Slowly pour 1 cup of syrup evenly over the bread layer and allow the bread to soak up the syrup. Sprinkle with a third each of the peanuts (both shelled and candied, if using), raisins, and cheese. Repeat the layers twice, ending with cheese. Pour the remaining syrup over casserole.

(continued on next page)

4. *Baking:* Bake covered at 350°F for 30 to 45 minutes, or until the cheese has melted. During the last 10 minutes, uncover and top the casserole with additional colaciones, if desired.

SERVING SUGGESTION: Enjoy this very special bread pudding during Lent (or Christmas) as a sweet dessert served with whipped cream or as an early morning breakfast dish served with heated milk.

MAKES 12 SERVINGS (PORTION SIZE: ONE 2 × 3-INCH PIECE)

During La Semana Santa, Holy Week, capirotada (bread pudding) is perhaps one of the most typical dishes served. Originally, capirotadas were not only sweet but savory combinations of bread and vegetables, such as squash, turnips, and sweet potatoes layered between milk seasoned with spices and cheese. These fast-day dishes were meant to substitute for meat during the Lenten season. The sweet dessert version is now the most popular, varying from family to family, the main ingredients being day-old bread, either bolillos (Mexican "French" bread) or pan de huevo (egg bread), and a syrup mixture of piloncillo (cone-shaped unrefined brown sugar) flavored with spices such as bay leaf, cinnamon, anise, and cloves. You'll find either peanuts, walnuts, pecans, colaciones (candy-coated peanuts), or pine nuts in capirotada, depending on the region. Traditional fruits include raisins, apples, bananas, pineapple, and coconut.

SOPA BORRACHA

CHRISTMAS SEASON / PUERTO RICO

DRUNKEN CAKE

This recipe has been in the family for three generations, starting with my great-aunt in Spain. She always made this on Christmas or New Year's Eve and would have to serve everyone at the same time or else there would be none left for those who arrived at the table late.

MARIA CELESTE ARRARAS

24 egg yolks
2 pounds (4 cups) sugar
1 liter fine dry sherry (about 4 cups)
20 muffin-size spongecakes (see spongecake recipe, page 182)

2 cups anise liqueur
12 egg whites
Zest from 2 lemons (about ¼ cup grated lemon rind)

1. *Sherry custard:* In a double boiler, beat the egg yolks over medium heat until creamy. Continue beating while adding 2 cups of the sugar. Remove from the heat and chill. Once cool, beat in the sherry.

2. *Spongecake:* Sprinkle each spongecake liberally with anise liqueur; dip into the sherry custard until completely soaked. Using a slotted spoon, carefully lift the soaked cake into a large glass serving bowl.

3. *Meringue and assembly:* Beat the egg whites in a large mixing bowl to the stiff peak stage. Add the remaining 2 cups of sugar, ¼ cup at a time, while beating continuously. Spread the meringue over the soaked spongecake. Sprinkle with lemon zest and refrigerate until ready to serve.

MAKES 15 SERVINGS (PORTION SIZE: ³/₄ CUP)

Sopa Borracha is a much loved yet oddly named cake, so called because it is soaked in liqueur—in this case dry sherry and anisette. The dish has its origins in the time when English and Spanish immigrants came to the islands in the middle of the nineteenth century. Sopa Borracha is the Caribbean equivalent of a trifle.

DESSERTS AND BEVERAGES • 195

NATILLA

VANILLA CUSTARD

I remember the food at my great-aunts' house—two widows and a spinster devoted to perpetuating the family food tradition: everything festive and flavorful. My favorites were the puddings and custards, comfort food at its best. It was a luxurious treat for a child, like velvet on the tongue.

DILYS TOSTESON GARCÍA

6 cups milk
1 vanilla bean, split, or 1 tablespoon
 vanilla extract
8 egg yolks

1⅓ cups sugar
⅓ cup cornstarch
Toasted almonds

In a heavy saucepan, combine the milk and vanilla. Bring to a rapid simmer over medium high heat until scalded (milk is scalded when tiny bubbles form and have not yet popped). While the milk is heating, beat the egg yolks and sugar together until thick. Add cornstarch to the yolk mixture, beating until completely combined. Slowly pour the beaten yolks into the heated milk while beating with a whisk or fork. Lower the heat and cook, stirring constantly to avoid scorching, until the mixture is thick enough to coat a spoon. Remove from the heat and cool. Refrigerate for 2 to 3 hours before serving. Sprinkle with toasted almonds.

BIZCOCHUELO (Spongecake with Fruit and Cream)
Prepare the bizcocho (spongecake) on page 182. Serve the spongecake with fresh strawberries, a pitcher of Natilla, and freshly whipped cream. Absolutely divine!

SERVING SUGGESTION: Natilla is featured in a dessert common throughout Latin America: fruit with cream, or fruta en crema. To prepare, lightly poach your favorite fruit in water with or without a spice of your choice plus a touch of sugar or lemon juice, if needed. Serve warm or chilled with Natilla.

MAKES 6 SERVINGS (PORTION SIZE: ABOUT 1 CUP)

Arroz con Dulce

SWEET COCONUT RICE

For my mother, cooking was not a difficult task but rather a labor of love. It was from the kitchen that she nourished her family and friends, who had grown accustomed to her gifts of food. Each one of her eight children had a favorite dish, Arroz con Dulce being mine.

AL RODRIGUEZ

4 cups fresh coconut milk (1 cup thick and 3 cups thin) (see page 90)
1 large piece (3 inches) fresh gingerroot, peeled and sliced
30 whole cloves
3 cinnamon sticks, broken into pieces
1/4 teaspoon freshly grated nutmeg
1/4 teaspoon salt

2 cups short-grain rice
1 (12-ounce) can undiluted evaporated milk, plus additional as needed
3/4 cup granulated or packed brown sugar
3/4 cup raisins
Cinnamon sticks and grated nutmeg

1. *Making spiced coconut milk:* In a pot, combine the coconut milk, 2½ cups water, ginger, cloves, cinnamon, nutmeg and salt. Bring to a boil and vigorously simmer covered 20 minutes. Strain, discarding the spices, and return to pot.

2. *Soaking and cooking rice:* Meanwhile, rinse the rice and place in a bowl with cold water to cover for 20 minutes; drain. Add rice to coconut milk; bring to a boil. Reduce the heat and cook covered for 20 minutes over *very* low heat. Uncover and continue to cook, stirring occasionally, until the rice is soft but dry.

3. *Plumping raisins:* While rice is cooking, combine the evaporated milk, 1 cup water, sugar, and raisins in a small saucepan. Bring to a boil. Cover and set aside to plump the raisins.

4. *Finishing and serving:* Pour the raisin-milk mixture into the pot with rice; mix well. Continue cooking over very low heat until the rice absorbs the milk again. Garnish Arroz con Dulce with cinnamon and nutmeg. Serve at room temperature.

MAKES 6 SERVINGS (PORTION SIZE: 3/4 CUP)

Chocolate

FROTHY (EXTRA RICH) MEXICAN HOT CHOCOLATE

When I was about nine years old, I remember being up on a stool, hunched over a steaming pot of fragrant Mexican chocolate while rolling the molinillo (wooden beater) between the palms of my hands. As the foam sprang up from the bottom of the pot, my excitement grew. Upon my first sip of chocolate, I was amazed by the flavor. It was one of my first exposures to the food heritage that I have explored and grown to love as a fourth-generation Hispanic-American woman.

R.C. BOUBION

3 (3-ounce) tablets Mexican chocolate, broken into segments (see
Note)

5 cups whole or nonfat milk

1½ teaspoons almond or vanilla
extract

Pinch salt

2 eggs, beaten

1. *Simmering:* In a double boiler, combine the chocolate tablets and milk. Cook over medium heat, stirring occasionally, until the chocolate has melted. Mix in the almond extract and salt. Remove from the heat.

2. *Beating chocolate:* In a small bowl, whisk eggs together with ⅓ cup of the hot milk chocolate until blended. Using an electric mixer, beat the hot chocolate while slowly pouring in a steady stream of beaten egg mixture. Continue beating until frothy. Serve immediately.

NOTE: Mexican chocolate is a mixture of chocolate, sugar, and cinnamon, and can be found in specialty markets or the Latin American food section of supermarkets. For each tablet of chocolate, you can substitute 2 (1-ounce) squares unsweetened baking chocolate plus ¼ cup of sugar and ½ teaspoon of ground cinnamon.

SERVING SUGGESTION: On January 6, El Día de los Reyes Santos (Three Kings' Day), chocolate is served with a rosca de reyes, sweet bread ring.

MAKES 6 SERVINGS (PORTION SIZE: ABOUT ¾ CUP)

CORTADITO

EVERYDAY DRINK / CUBA

CUBAN ESPRESSO AND CREAM

In Miami you can stop at the window of any cafeteria (a small café) and order a Cortadito along with a sweet bread. No one bothers to carry the coffee to the car, as it is gone in two sips. It is a great way to begin the morning, wake up your afternoon, or jump-start your evening.

ENRIQUE MONASTERIO

Espresso-grind dark-roasted coffee   2 teaspoons granulated sugar
Milk

1. *Preparing espresso:* Fill the bottom of a free-standing pot with cold water up to the bottom of the screw. Fill the insert basket section of the pot with ground coffee. Do not compact the coffee. Screw the top half onto the bottom half and place over medium heat. As the water heats, the pressure pushes the water up through the grinds into the top half.

2. *Heating milk:* While espresso is brewing, heat milk in a separate saucepan over medium high heat. Set aside and keep warm.

3. *Grinding sugar into espuma (espresso "cream"):* Place 1 teaspoon of the sugar in a demitasse cup. When the coffee begins to rise to the upper half of the pot, take out 2 tablespoons of the rich foam and add it to the sugar. With the back of a teaspoon blend the sugar and espresso to form a smooth beige paste. Repeat process with remaining cup.

4. *Serving:* Pour the espresso halfway up demitasse cups. Stir until the sugar is dissolved. Top each cup with hot milk and serve.

MAKES 2 SERVINGS (PORTION SIZE: $1/3$ CUP)

To make this coffee, use a free-standing espresso pot with capacity to serve 2 to 4 demitasse cups. The key to Cuban coffee is to brew the espresso so that it is topped with a rich foam, referred to as espuma in Spanish or crema in Italian. A cortadito is espresso "cut" with hot milk.

PONCHE

CHRISTMAS PUNCH

A warm, floral-scented ponche poured into a jarrita (clay mug) signals the beginning of our posadas (Christmas party) on December 16th. What makes this punch unique are the ingredients: guayabas (guavas), jamaica (hibiscus flowers), caña (sugar cane), piloncillo (raw sugar cones), chabacanos secos (apricots), and rajitas de canela (cinnamon sticks). In Mexico, cooks have been known to add rose petals for a truly magical touch.

MARIA ELENA BENITES

8 (3-inch) cinnamon sticks
1 pound tamarindo (tamarind pods) (see Notes)
5 yellow apples
10 guavas
4 (5-inch) sugar cane pieces
1 pound tejocotes or 1 pound dried pears and apricots (see Notes)
1 cup dried prunes

¾ cup raisins
½ cup jamaica (hibiscus flowers), rinsed
1 cup granulated sugar
½ pound (2 to 3 ounces) piloncillo or brown sugar (see Notes)
2 cups rum
3 orange peel slices stuck with 15 cloves

1. *Cinnamon water:* In a large pot, bring 5 quarts water and the cinnamon sticks to a boil; lower the heat and cook over medium heat 20 minutes.

2. *Preparing ingredients:* Press the tamarindos in your palms to crack the pods, pull off the barklike shell, and remove and discard the veins. Make a crisscross cut into each of the apples and guavas; set aside. Carefully peel the sugar cane with a paring knife; cut into small strips. Stem 1 pound of tejocotes or combine the dried pears and apricots.

3. *Brewing and serving:* To the cinnamon water, add the tamarindo, apples, guavas, sugar cane, tejocotes (or pears and apricots), prunes, raisins, jamaica, sugar, and piloncillo. Bring to a boil, lower the heat, and simmer uncovered until the fruit is soft, about 1 hour. Before serving, add the rum and orange peel.

NOTES: Tejocotes are a very special fruit not generally found in specialty markets. Although no other fruit has the same flavor, fresh pears

200 • POSTRES Y BEBIDAS

combined with dried apricots are a good substitution. . . . Tamarind pods have a curved barklike shell that encloses a tart and sweet sticky pulp used to sweeten beverages or sauces. . . . Piloncillo is a processed dark brown sugar sold in cones. Both tamarind and piloncillo can be found in markets specializing in Latin ingredients.

MAKES 15 SERVINGS (PORTION SIZE: 1 CUP)

Coquito

CHRISTMAS / PUERTO RICO

COCONUT EGGNOG

I'll never forget my first parranda, the Puerto Rican tradition of a lively party held at Christmastime. I was recently married and we were invited to travel from house to house, celebrating the festivities with music, food, and dancing. It was at one of these homes where I had my first Coquito. Today, Christmas just isn't the same without it.

EVA JUDITH LOZANO

2 cinnamon sticks
½ teaspoon whole cloves (about 15)
3 tablespoons sugar
½ cup water
6 egg yolks
1 (14-ounce) can sweetened condensed milk

1 (12-ounce) can undiluted evaporated milk
1 (15-ounce) can coconut milk, cream of coconut, or condensed coconut milk
1 teaspoon vanilla extract
1 to 2 cups light or dark rum

1. *Preparing syrup:* In a small saucepan, cook the cinnamon, cloves, sugar, and water over medium high heat until reduced by half. Set aside and strain, reserving cinnamon.

2. *Mixing and storing coquito:* Beat the egg yolks in a bowl until creamy; add the cooled syrup, condensed milk, evaporated milk, coconut milk, and vanilla. Continue beating until combined. Add rum to taste. Using a funnel, pour the coquito into two 1-liter bottles. Place a cinnamon stick in each bottle. Refrigerate up to 1 week before serving.

MAKES ABOUT 2 QUARTS

CAFÉ TINTO (NEGRITO OR CAFEZINHO)

DEMITASSE COFFEE

Literally translated, Café Tinto is "an infusion of coffee," referring to the very strong black coffee served in a demitasse, a tiny coffee cup. In Brazil, it's called cafezinho; in Ecuador, negrito; in Colombia, tinto; and very often it's ordered as a demitasse.

2¼ cups boiling water   ⅓ cup coarse-ground coffee

STEEPING OR OPEN-POT BREWING METHOD

1. *Warming pot:* Warm the coffeepot by filling it with boiling water. Pour the water out and spoon coarse (medium) ground coffee into the warmed pot.

2. *Stirring and steeping the coffee:* Bring fresh-drawn cold water to a boil. Remove from the heat and let stand about 15 seconds before pouring into the pot. Stir the mixture once with a spoon. Place the lid on the pot and let it infuse (steep) for 3 minutes, or until most of the grounds have settled to the bottom of the pot.

3. *Straining and serving:* Pour the freshly brewed coffee into demitasse cups through a strainer. Serve immediately, very hot, with sugar.

NOTE: It is not uncommon to add a few grains of salt to the fresh-ground coffee, which is said to enhance its flavor. . . . To make the perfect demitasse coffee, use a ratio of 2 to 3 level tablespoons of freshly ground coffee per ¾ cup of water.

MAKES 3 DEMITASSE CUPS

SOURCES FOR LATIN AMERICAN INGREDIENTS

ARIZONA
Mr. Ranchito Mexican Food Products
601 N. 43rd Avenue
Phoenix, AZ 85009
602-272-3949

Offers Southwestern and Mexican food products.

CALIFORNIA
Liborio Market
864 South Vermont Ave. (near 9th)
Los Angeles, CA 90005
213-386-1458

One of the largest Latin American supermarkets in the area, carrying hard-to-find produce, meats, an exceptional variety of bacalao, harina Pan, a variety of flours, and seasoning blends.

Cotija Cheese Company
15130 Nelson Ave.
City of Industry, CA 91744
818-968-2284

Offers a diverse selection of nationally distributed Mexican-style cheeses, including queso cotija, pancia, fresco, enchilado, asadero, and others.

Monterrey Foods
3939 Cesar Chavez Blvd. (formerly Brooklyn Ave.)
Los Angeles, CA 90063
213-263-2143

A large selection of dried chiles, herbs, spices, corn husks, canned products, and cookware (molcajetes). Mail order catalog is available.

Marquez Brothers International
1670 Las Plumas Ave. #C
San Jose, CA 95133
408-272-2700

Specializing in Mexican-style cheeses, canned products, spices, and chiles for national distribution. Product listing available.

Mercado Latino
245 Baldwin Park Blvd.
City of Industry, CA 91746
800-432-7266
818-333-6862

Specializing in a large variety of Hispanic food products. Mail order catalogue available.

FLORIDA
Jamaica Groceries and Spices
9628 S.W. 160th Street
Colonial Shopping Center
Miami, FL 33157
306-252-1197

Specializing in Caribbean, Latin, and African food products.

Publix Supermarkets
13850 SW 8th Street
Miami, FL 33184
305-221-1924

A supermarket with over 500 locations specializing in Latin and Caribbean products.

GEORGIA
Dekalb Farmers' Market
3000 East Ponce de León
Decatur, GA 30034
404-377-6401

Offers a wide variety of local and international foods, including an extensive selection of produce, herbs, and spices.

ILLINOIS
La Preferida, Inc.
3400 West 35th Street
Chicago, IL 60632
800-621-5422
312-254-7200

A large selection of Latin American food products. Product listing available.

La Casa del Pueblo
1810 S. Blue Island Ave.
Chicago, IL 60608
312-421-4640

A neighborhood supermarket specializing in Mexican and Latin American produce, groceries, and meats.

NEW MEXICO
Bueno Foods
2001 4th Street SW
Albuquerque, NM 87102
505-243-2722
800-952-4453

Frozen chile purées, fresh and dried chiles, pozole, and blue corn products. Mail order catalogue is available.

Stuart Hutson
Chile Gourmet Catalogue
Rancho Melissa, Inc.
PO Box 39
Mesilla, NM 88046
505-525-2266

An outstanding selection of chiles and other Hispanic ingredients. Mail order catalogue is available.

NEW YORK
Stop One Supermarket
210 W. 94th Street
New York, NY 10025
212-864-9456

Specializing in Latin American products and hard-to-find ingredients.

Latin American Products
c/o Mi Princesita Hispana
142 W. 46th Street
New York, NY 10036
212-501-8676

Caribbean foods, dried beans, spices, and herbs.

TEXAS
Pendery's
1221 Manufacturing Street
Dallas, TX 75207
800-533-1870

Southwestern and Mexican food products. Mail order catalogue is available.

Taxco Produce
1801 S. Good Latimer Expressway
Dallas, TX 75226
214-421-7191
800-229-7191

A distributor of Hispanic food products and produce. Product listing available.

WASHINGTON
El Mercado Latino
1514 Pike Place
Seattle, WA 98101
206-623-3240

Offers a wide variety of Latin American products, grocery items, fresh produce, spices, seasonings, masa, tortillas, and chiles.

INDEX